CHRISTINE DE PIZAN
AND THE
FIGHT FOR FRANCE

CHRISTINE DE PIZAN
AND THE
FIGHT FOR FRANCE

Tracy Adams

The Pennsylvania State University Press
University Park, Pennsylvania

Library of Congress Cataloging-in-Publication Data

Adams, Tracy, 1959– , author.
Christine de Pizan and the fight for France / Tracy Adams.
p.   cm
Summary: "Evaluates Christine de Pizan's literary
engagement with fifteenth-century French politics. Locates
the writer's works within a detailed narrative of the
complex history of the dispute between the Burgundians
and the Armagnacs, the two largest political factions"—
Provided by publisher.
Includes bibliographical references and index.
ISBN 978-0-271-05071-3 (cloth : alk. paper)
1. Christine, de Pisan, approximately 1364–approximately
1431—Political and social views.
2. Christine, de Pisan, approximately 1364–approximately
1431—Criticism and interpretation.
3. Politics and literature—France—History—To 1500.
4. Political poetry, French—History and criticism.
5. France—History—Charles VI, 1380–1422.
I. Title.

PQ1575.Z5A34   2014
841'.2—dc23
2014017173

The Pennsylvania State University Press is a member of the
Association of American University Presses.

It is the policy of The Pennsylvania State University Press
to use acid-free paper. Publications on uncoated stock
satisfy the minimum requirements of American National
Standard for Information Sciences—Permanence of Paper
for Printed Library Material, ANSI Z39.48–1992.

This book is printed on paper that contains
30% post-consumer waste.

Frontispiece: Miniature from British Library,
Harley MS 4431, fol. 259v.

FOR HELENA OLIVER (1965–2013)

A woman of uncommon valor

Contents

Acknowledgments

This monograph came into being during my year as a Eurias Senior Fellow at the Netherlands Institute for Advanced Studies, 2011–12. My heartfelt thanks to the Eurias Fellowship Program and to everyone at NIAS, a place of perfect tranquillity and stimulating intellectual exchange, not to mention spectacular cuisine, for making that year possible. In addition to the warm, competent staff and my colleagues there, I would like to acknowledge Rector Aafke Hulk and research planning and communication director Jos Hooghuis for their friendship and encouragement. Next, I would like to thank my colleagues and friends in the International Christine de Pizan Society. As all scholars of Christine de Pizan know, research on the poet is possible because of the codicological and editing work carried out by the members of the Christine community. Thanks to all of you.

Special thanks to James Laidlaw, Kerryn Olsen, Glenn Rechtschaffen, and Christine Adams, who read all or parts of this study, and to Julia Sims Holderness for the many sparkling insights on Christine that she has shared with me over the years. I am grateful as always to Steve Nichols for his continued willingness to read and advise. Thanks, too, to Jeff Richards for his scholarly generosity, and to Gilles Lecuppre for patiently responding to my questions about fourteenth- and fifteenth-century France (any mistakes in this study, of course, are my own). I am grateful to Ellie Goodman at Penn State Press for taking on this project and helping me to realize it, and to the two anonymous readers for their careful readings and insights. I owe a large debt to copyeditor Suzanne Wolk for her painstaking work in preparing this study for publication. Many thanks to the people and the institutions that allowed me to present and receive feedback on this study: Peggy McCracken at the University of Michigan, Virginie Greene at Harvard University, and Cynthia Brown at the University of California, Santa Barbara. Thanks to the University of Auckland for granting me research leave in 2011–12, during which I completed the first draft of this monograph, and to our interlibrary loan staff, and, especially, our subject librarian, Mark Hangartner.

Thanks to my "family" in Paris, Tanguy, René, Nadine, Chérine, and Jean-Jacques, for giving me a home away from home, and to Sylvie for teaching me French and many other things. Endless gratitude to Glenn, Danny, and Elf for their patience with the long hours that I put into revising once I returned from NIAS.

Finally, in January 2012, while working on this study, I had the privilege of meeting, electronically, a woman whose spirit and courage in the face of the illness that ultimately took her from her family and many friends will humble and inspire me for the rest of my life. Although I would not presume to call her my friend, in deference to those who truly enjoyed that right, in the beautiful words that she wrote to me I continue to feel her presence. I believe, like Christine de Pizan, that through words we can cultivate friendships across time and space. This is for you, Helena. I had hoped to hand it to you in person, but I will do that in a better place.

In using Jean of Burgundy rather than John of Burgundy, my goal was to avoid inconsistency when juxtaposing the latter with such examples as Jean Gerson and Jean de Montaigu, never rendered John. Rather than refer to individuals by their territories or ancestral homes, I use first names throughout (e.g., Jean, Louis, and Christine rather than Burgundy, Orleans, or de Pizan). I have used "of" rather than "de" when the name refers to a territory. Although "Christine de Pizan" gives pause, I have used the name by which she is internationally known. To avoid confusion, I refer to Louis of Orleans as such even before he becomes the Duke of Orleans in 1392, and I use "Armagnac" to refer to Orleanists after 1410.

Where the translations are not mine, I have indicated the sources.

The bibliography contains only manuscripts that I have consulted personally, whether in person or online. I have not included the URLs for those available online because this changes so rapidly that the list would be outdated before this book is in print. In citing Christine's works, I use the titles used by the editors and translators of her published works.

The feud between the Orleanists, or Armagnacs, and Burgundians, that "sickness that so tears through the land" brought on by mad King Charles VI's inability to reign, is a central theme in Christine de Pizan's corpus.[1] An observer of the strife, Christine laments the conflict's devastating material effects on her society throughout her career.

And yet her literary engagement with the feud, her use of "literature as a potent social mediator"[2] to influence the course of the conflict, has received little attention. Although scholars acknowledge Christine de Pizan as one of a group of fifteenth-century political writers to treat "immediate reality and, consequently, what one can call contemporary history,"[3] attention to date has focused more on what she said about women, authorship, and authority, and, in the abstract, kingship, peace, and warfare, than on how she sought to influence her immediate political situation. Scholars who have considered her engagement with contemporary politics have relied heavily on superseded histories, creating a confused narrative of her political loyalties and goals.[4] The poet is depicted as politically neutral ("Christine de Pisan hated factions and had no sympathy for partisan politics") and/or fickle, switching sides from the Orleanists to the Burgundians and back again.[5] No one disputes that by the second decade of the fifteenth century she was an ardent Armagnac, as the Orleanists were called after 1410, fleeing Paris along with fellow Armagnacs fortunate enough to escape the Burgundian massacre of 1418, and celebrating the triumph of the Armagnac leader King Charles VII in the 1429 *Ditié de Jehanne d'Arc*.[6] But many scholars place her in the Burgundian camp before this, after a still earlier flirtation with the Orleanists. This narrative has her soliciting the patronage of the brother of the mad king, Louis, Duke of Orleans, regent during the king's episodes of insanity, but, irritated by a slight (Louis is supposed to have refused to find a place for her son in his household) and disillusioned with his profligacy, she abandons him to become a discreet propagandist for the king's uncle, Philip of Burgundy.[7] Although some believe that she was less enthusiastic about Philip's successor, the notion that after Jean sans Peur (the Fearless) succeeded his father as Duke of Burgundy in 1404, Christine remained in her "secure seat in the Burgundian camp" as a "paid Burgundian propagandist" continues to hold force.[8] The most widely read biography of the poet in English reports the presumed shifts of allegiance without comment, slipping in the space of one paragraph from "Christine had enjoyed the patronage of two dukes of Burgundy," to "her son was now one of the dauphin's [the future Charles VII's] secretaries," to Christine's "family was fortunate to escape [the Burgundian massacre] with their lives."[9]

The incoherence results from a narrative of political activity at Charles VI's court developed by historians influenced by the ideals of the French Revolution, a narrative itself derived from Burgundian propaganda circulated after Jean of Burgundy's assassination of the Duke of Orleans in 1407.[10] Republicans like Louise de Kéralio uncritically adopted Burgundian images of the king's brother and the queen as greedy wastrels, and that of the dukes of Burgundy as men of the people. In her 1791 diatribe on the queens of France, Kéralio paints Queen Isabeau as an early Marie Antoinette and Louis as the Count of Artois.[11] This narrative passed into the works of nineteenth-century historians: Michelet, Guizot, Martin, Coville, and Thibault reinforced the pair's negative reputation. True, monarchist historians viewed Louis positively (although they were less favorable toward Isabeau), but they were few in number compared to their Republican counterparts.[12]

The 1838 essay by Raimond Thomassy, an early scholar of Christine's political thought, manifests these Burgundian biases. Thomassy writes of Louis of Orleans that, "as brother of the king, he claimed to be invested with principal authority to govern during the illness of Charles VI," as if the duke had no legitimate claim to regency. Moreover, Thomassy asserts that Louis "destroyed the people with exactions, dilapidated without shame the public treasury," without mentioning that the taxes were for the war with England or that such complaints were routinely leveled for political reasons against anyone possessing the right to tax.[13] By contrast, Thomassy describes Philip as the "heir in

wisdom and determination of Charles V." As for Isabeau of Bavaria, the odi-
ous queen "brought shame and infamy to sit on the throne of France and
betrayed at the same time her feminine, maternal, and wifely duties."[14] Nor is
it widely understood that the assumption that the queen suffered from a bad
reputation during her lifetime is based on four unflattering comments in the
chronicle of Michel Pintoin, the Burgundian-biased monk of Saint Denis, all
from the same year in which Jean of Burgundy first tried to seize control of
the mad king.[15] And it is rarely acknowledged that evidence for the unpopu-
larity of Louis of Orleans comes primarily from the same source, along with
another anti-Orleanist chronicle, that of Pierre Cochon, and the justification
of Louis's assassination pronounced by Jean Petit on behalf of Jean of Burgundy. Even recent Christine scholarship continues to show the influence of
the Burgundian narrative, drawing an equivalency between Louis's regency
claim and the attempts of the dukes of Burgundy to seize control of the government, seeing both as the "usurpation of power by the king's brother, uncles
and nephews."[16] About Christine's view of the Duke of Orleans, we read that
it is "evident that she wanted [him] in particular to take heed" of her writings
on prudence.[17] Philip of Burgundy, by contrast, was "an effective diplomat as
well as a sound military adviser," and, more important, functioned as "a mod-
erating force in the polemical atmosphere of the court."[18] Isabeau, Charles
VI's "beautiful, sluttish wife," "encouraged" him "in his taste for pleasure."[19]
King Charles VI is imagined to have been reduced to rags while his family
members pillaged the treasury to support their own luxurious lifestyles; gossip circulated about "the relations between the queen and the duke of Orleans,
a liaison that lasted until the duke's assassination in a Paris street near the
queen's residence in November 1407."[20]

This study rereads Christine's major works from a perspective informed by
recent historical scholarship on the Armagnac-Burgundian feud. Because the
views of Burgundian chroniclers represent just one of several contemporary
feud narratives, I widen the set of documents generally relied on to reconstruct
Christine's historico-political context. My argument, laid out in the following
chapters, is that when Christine's works are reread within this broader context—that is, when the Burgundian images of Louis, Isabeau, and Philip are
recognized as propaganda and supplemented with other sources—it becomes
clear that the poet's many narrative voices consistently support the Orleanists.
She is of necessity discreet, but she does indeed "challenge the particular interests of the princes," at least the Burgundian princes.[21] Such a claim requires
untangling two frequently confounded perspectives on the poet's political

interactions: first, her beliefs about regency, which follow from her view of kingship, and second, her interactions and personal friendships with noble patrons. Flattery of Philip of Burgundy has often been assumed to be tantamount to promoting his regency claim. As I hope to show, however, Christine's conception of regency was motivated by principles that remained steadfast throughout her career.

Furthermore, I hope to show that Christine intended her interventions in the conflict to produce effects. Studies by scholars like Larry Scanlon and Alan Cottrell on *auctoritas* and *potestas* offer useful terms for conceptualizing Christine's method. Two of Charles VI's relatives, both of them powerful, claimed regency during the king's periods of madness. The question was which one possessed the authority necessary to realize his claim. Had clear laws existed for dealing with the emergency of Charles VI's madness, the regent would have possessed both power and the authority necessary to govern.[22] But not only did no widely accepted regency plan exist; the very notion of kingship was still sufficiently vague to allow both Philip and Louis plausibly to press their claims. To paraphrase Scanlon, for Christine and contemporary political writers, kingship (and by extension regency) was not a fully formed institution but rather a "dynamic political structure" attempting to define itself ideologically.[23] In rallying support behind Louis, I argue, Christine participated in fixing the definition of kingship. As the situation between the dukes worsened, Christine sought for a time to augment the queen's authority, promoting Isabeau as the face of the regency while continuing to create authority for Louis as its force. Thus Christine also profoundly affected female regency as it developed in France from the fifteenth through the early seventeenth century. After Louis's assassination, she continued to legitimize the Orleanists. She was always cautious: the Burgundians were not only important patrons but, particularly after Jean's seizure of power in late 1409, extremely dangerous enemies. Only when Jean was temporarily disgraced and fled Paris after the Cabochian revolt did Christine openly throw her influence behind the dauphin, Louis of Guyenne.

In each of the six chapters of this study, I first summarize what was happening between the Orleanists and Burgundians and then trace Christine's engagement with the events in her texts. The historico-political sections of the chapters are based on contemporary chronicles and documents, many easily accessible today online, along with the excellent studies of the period that have appeared since the 1980s.[24] As for the relationship between the historical material and Christine's works, it is sometimes straightforward. The poet often refers directly to the immediate situation. She has a clear notion of her different publics, appealing to them variously through courtly poetry, relatively simple verse allegory, complex, obscure prose allegory, and prose treatises. However, it is equally instructive, I argue, to trace the "political unconscious" of her writings. To fully grasp the political work that Christine carries out, that is, we must examine the competing ideologies that animate her writings and consider how she resolves, or fails to resolve, their internal contradictions.

In chapter 1, I make the case for reexamining Christine's political attitudes. Historians disagree over the extent to which the dukes of Orleans and Burgundy represented discordant visions of monarchy. I do not enter this debate, arguing rather that whatever the dukes and their satellites may have believed, Christine herself promoted the Valois monarch as a single figure aided by a diverse group of counselors, a system that she believed was threatened by the Burgundians. For her, Charles V had been the guarantor of an ideally ordered society, protecting the throne against challenges from Charles of Navarre and Edward III of England while consolidating power in ongoing negotiations with the great lords of the kingdom. For counsel, he had relied on a close group of minor or even nonnoble advisors, and he had kept his brothers, the dukes of Anjou, Berry, and Burgundy, under control by assigning them appanages over which he retained ultimate control, as Françoise Autrand has shown. Embedded in this experience, Christine would have seen Louis of Orleans—who as son of the previous king and brother of the present outranked his uncle—as the only possible regent during the absences of Charles VI. Philip demanded rule by a council headed by himself, a form of kingship with a long history, associated by the Burgundians with rule by the three estates. I argue that Christine rejected this vision.

This discussion of Charles V's conception of kingship and Christine's reaction to it lays the groundwork for the second chapter. Although Charles V left a blueprint for regency when he died in 1380, leaving a minor son on the throne, Philip of Burgundy seized power. In 1392, after Charles VI's first episode of madness, Philip struck again. This time, the adult Louis resisted. Many historians believe that the dukes' quarrel did not become serious until about 1398; I argue that although it did not become a feud until about 1400, the quarrel arose almost immediately after the king's initial frenzy, evidenced by Philip's accusations that the Duke and Duchess of Orleans were bewitching the king. The conviction that the king was divinely ordained, coupled with the fiction that he was in control when he appeared lucid, maintained through a series of royal ordinances that treated his mental illness as temporary "absences," prevented his deposition and the installation of a permanent regent. This is the setting for Christine's first interventions, lyric poetry mourning the great absence at the center of things. Like Guillaume de Machaut and Jean Froissart, Christine encodes the relationship between self-mastery and effective government in love poetry, containing her poetic dramas of amorous intrigue within a framework of Boethian consolation. There is no easy solution to the disorder at court, as her indecisive love debates suggest. Still, virtue, acceptance of hierarchies, and unstinting love—in other words, Boethian resignation—are the best solution.

Chapter 3 picks up the conflict between the dukes as it worsens after a narrowly missed showdown in October 1401. As the dukes fought to control policy regarding the Great Western Schism and the war with the English, royal ordinances designated the queen, first, mediator between the dukes, and then effective although unofficial regent. During this period, Christine developed a wide set of images and methods for guiding her readers' understanding of the quarrel. In the *Epistre d'Othea a Hector*, dedicated to Louis, she develops his *auctoritas* by declaring his position in the kingdom second after the king alone, as well as her own, by showcasing her erudition and prudence for the first time. Christine solicits another readership for her work with her participation in the debate over the literary merits of the *Roman de la rose*. Attacking Jean de Meun through an argument made earlier by members of the French chanceries defending their Latin against Italian attack, she bolsters her reputation among some members of the chancery circles. At the same time, she unites courtiers eager to soothe tensions between the dukes around the common ideal of honoring women, which she concretizes by presenting the queen with a copy of the debate. In her rhymed allegories, Christine ventures into new territory by situating the ducal conflict historically, assigning blame by showing similarities to earlier political struggles. In the *Chemin de longue étude*, she promotes Louis as the only remedy for the chaos into which the kingdom has descended. With the Cumaean Sibyl as her guide, she draws on the Second Charlemagne prophecy, which predicted that Charles VI would become Holy Roman Emperor, and promotes Louis as king of the world in the mad king's place. Although in her courtly lyrics she had figured the king's malady as the work of perverse Fortune, she mourns the absence at the center of things yet more profoundly in the pessimistic *Livre de la mutacion de fortune*. The narrator's gender transformation in response to the loss of her ship's captain echoes the position of Isabeau.

The conflict took a deadly turn when Jean of Burgundy succeeded his father. Chapter 4 begins with the succession of the new Duke of Burgundy in 1404. Although popular with some Parisians and, for a time, the university, he made demands that, to Christine's mind, amounted to attempts at usurpation: a cousin of the king, he was not equal in rank to his father, let alone to Louis. He attempted to gain authority by discrediting his cousin, continuing his father's strategy of demanding money from the royal treasury even as he publicly denounced mismanagement and called for reform of the realm. Once again, the Orleanist-Burgundian strife narrowly missed breaking into open war in 1405. It is characteristic of Christine's responses to Jean's attempts to control the government that she begins to write primarily in prose rather than verse, completing the transformation into female cleric that she had begun with the *Roman de la rose* debate. Although commissioned by Philip of Burgundy, her biography of Charles V, the *Livre des fais et bonnes meurs du sage roy Charles V*, unmistakably critiques Burgundian positions. But her fear that the Burgundians were winning the battle with the Parisians for control of the discourse on political authority drives the rest of her work during this period. In the *Cité des dames*, Christine positions Isabeau as the face of the regency after the model of the mediating Virgin, a solution that complements royal ordinances naming the queen mediator between the quarreling dukes. The *Epistre a la reine* was followed quickly by a royal ordinance authorizing Isabeau to mediate between the dukes to end the standoff of 1405, suggesting how closely Christine followed the dukes' political struggle. The *Livre des trois vertus*, generally viewed as moralistic, in fact discusses "worldly prudence" and other practical qualities the queen needed to maintain peace among unruly men. The letter of Dame Sebille de la Tour in the *Trois vertus* presciently cautions princesses on the dangers of jealous gossip, offering a bridge into the *Livre du duc des vrais amans*, which reproduces the letter. The *Duc des vrais amans*, mixing verse and prose, uses a sad love story to recount allegorically the dangers faced by the now allied queen and Louis, both harassed by the Burgundian propaganda machine. Sebille in this context foretells the violence that is about to strike.

Chapter 5 turns to a yet more advanced state in the hostility between the dukes. A joint campaign to oust the English from France failed to build solidarity between them, and Jean continued to gather support for himself. Christine backs Louis and opposes Jean in a trio of works. In the *Livre de prodomie de l'homme selon la diffinicion de Monseigneur d'Orleans*, Christine warns her readers about the danger of the slander propagated by Louis's enemies. With the strange *Livre de l'advision Cristine*, she recounts how Charles VI and Louis were persecuted by their uncle, and warns against the coming disaster through the bloodied figure of France, Libera. As in the *Mutacion de fortune*, in the *Advision* the narrator's autobiography serves as a lens through which to focus the conflict. Because Christine, like Boethius, is consoled by philosophy, her vision unclouded by false opinion, she is in a position to act as the conscience of the kingdom. Finally, I suggest that the *Livre du corps de policie* makes a very precise argument against Jean of Burgundy in its unique configuration of the third part of the body politic. Christine's inclusion of the university in the group and her division of merchants into two separate categories, a repartition that reflects the contemporary distinction between highly placed merchants and powerful butchers, suggests that if the university made common cause with the ruling burghers and well-placed merchants, they could subdue their more restless fellow Parisians, whom the Duke of Burgundy would incite in 1413 in the Cabochian revolt.

On November 23, 1407, Jean had Louis assassinated, the incident with which chapter 6 begins. After initially fleeing, Jean returned to Paris in March 1408 with the theologian Jean Petit, who proclaimed a justification for the murder. Jean sans Peur became master of Paris. But the feud did not end. After a lapse of a few years, Louis's heir, Charles of Orleans, vowed to avenge his father's murder, and the conflict reached new levels. Disasters accumulated: the Cabochian revolt; the Battle of Agincourt; the death of the dauphin Louis and that of his successor, leaving the dauphin Charles, raised in the Armagnac House of Anjou. I follow Christine's engagement in four texts as she continues to promote peace but begins to support violence where justified.[25] The *Lamentacions sur les maux de la guerre civile* backs the peace efforts of the autumn of 1410, lending authority to the Duke of Berry and the queen by presenting them as figures capable of brokering an accord. And yet the work also seems to urge the queen and the Duke of Berry to team up against Jean of Burgundy, should peace remain elusive. The *Livre des fais d'armes et de chevalerie* is interesting for its promotion of the Armagnac cause in its discussion of the just war. The *Livre de paix* is filled with optimism, as Christine presents the dauphin as the image of his grandfather, Charles V. True, the introduction to the work strikes an ominous chord, revealing that the peace that the dauphin has just mediated has been disrupted and that the Cabochian revolt has intervened. But peace returned, and Christine takes up where she left off, castigating Jean, who had been forced from Paris by the Armagnacs. Her optimism does not last, however, as the *Epistre de la prison de vie humaine*, composed in the aftermath of Agincourt, in early 1418, makes clear.

The epilogue begins with Christine's near silence between the Burgundian massacre of 1418 and the appearance of Joan of Arc in 1429. The Duke of Burgundy was himself slain by the dauphin Charles's men at a moment when peace between the Armagnacs and Burgundians seemed possible. Teaming up with the English, the Burgundians facilitated the occupation of France and the Treaty of Troyes, which eventually placed the English kings Henry V and VI on the throne. The *Heures de contemplation sur la passion de notre Seigneur* of 1420 expresses Christine's resigned sorrow, while the *Ditié de Jehanne d'Arc*, a triumphant and prophetic work championing the warrior-maid as the savior of Charles VII and the French, communicates her renewed joy at the reascendance of the Armagnacs and her heightened sense that peace might be achievable only through violence. One of the goals of Christine's political intervention, to avoid bloodshed, has been dashed. Still, two others, to keep the monarchy in the hands of the Valois and to create a place for women in politics, would be realized. The Valois line continued until 1594; between 1483 and 1651, France saw five female regencies.

No single critical approach to Christine's corpus is adequate, and I do not pretend that the one that I offer here does anything but supplement the many existing studies of the poet's body of work. As Andrea Tarnowski has written so eloquently, for Christine, "the individual life, or moment, only means insofar as it represents. If the twentieth century called the literary genre of allegory 'intolerable,' it is because we no longer require a simultaneity of levels of meaning." In this way, Tarnowksi concludes, "we perceive as an aesthetic mistake what for Christine was a moral necessity."[26] My study deals with just one of many levels of meaning present in Christine's works. Still, it is a significant level, and in charting it the study fills a gap and focuses attention on features previously neglected. Two recent studies in French offer important historical information about the poet, but their readings of her works are summaries of the contents rather than analyses relating her literature to her political environment.[27] Biographies of the poet in English, although offering much of interest, reproduce the caricature of Charles VI's court that I have described above, treating the feud in the tones of farce: "the unscrupulous Louis and the questionable Isabeau had been garnering ill repute for massive debauchery and financial greed, both individually and, supposedly, as a couple."[28] A number of excellent studies document the sources for Christine's political ideas, but how she used her sources to make sense of the feud has not been explored.[29] I hope that the reexamination of the Armagnac-Burgundian conflict offered here, along with the reconsideration of the relationship between Christine and Louis of Orleans and, especially, Isabeau of Bavaria, opens new directions for study.

As with my previous work, this study seeks to rehistoricize by reexamining material long controlled by a particular narrative. All scholars of early periods confront the "text-context conundrum," that is, the problem of how to create the social context against which to measure our interpretation of a given piece of writing.[30] The problem is that the writings we want to check are often major sources for re-creating the social context, which means that the process easily becomes tautological. In the case of Christine, whose autobiographical details are known almost exclusively through her own writings, the problem is particularly acute. Still, I hope to show here that we can achieve a fuller and more accurate picture than has been the case when we begin not with Christine's own writings but with documents that reflect the principal arguments of the warring factions. When we read Christine's writings as part of a set of competing feud narratives, her arguments take on a new coherence. As with my previous work, the point is not to whitewash figures previously held to be debauched, ambitious, and greedy. It is still less to suggest that the historical Christine was never critical of Orleanists. But whatever she may have thought of Louis, she never ceased supporting his regency, certainly not in favor of a candidate whose claim she held to be illegitimate. Literary scholars deal with probabilities, not truths. However, not all interpretations of a given work of literature are equally probable, and I believe that my readings of Christine's writings represent more closely what she believed than those offered by the nineteenth-century literary historians. In examining Christine's major works, I see a steadfast loyalty to the Orleanists. But this study is intended to suggest perspectives for further study, and if it provokes debate about Christine's attitudes toward the Armagnac-Burgundian conflict, it will have accomplished its purpose.

1

CHRISTINE AND THE ARMAGNAC-BURGUNDIAN FEUD
Regency and Kingship

The sun had not yet risen on May 29, 1418, when Perrinet Leclerc unlocked the Porte Saint Germain with keys pilfered from his father's bedside.[1] Waiting outside was the Burgundian Jean de Villiers Seigneur de L'Isle-Adam, accompanied by a group of several hundred mounted men armed for battle. They burst through the gate, heading toward Châtelet. When the last had entered, Leclerc relocked the gate and tossed the keys over the wall to prevent the escape of the Armagnacs, who would soon be trying to flee. On reaching Châtelet, the Burgundians were greeted by crowds eager to avenge four years of Armagnac oppression. Hastily convoking, they decided to seize Armagnac leaders in their hotels. The group then continued through the streets shouting, "La paix, la paix, Bourgogne!" and "Vive Bourgogne!" as yet more supporters poured from their houses to join the fray.[2] One contingent rode to the Hotel Saint Pol, just inside the city wall on the north bank of the Seine, to lay hold of the mad king, who cheerfully agreed to everything they demanded. Another made for the hotel of Bernard Count of Armagnac, near the Louvre, but Bernard, having been tipped off, was hiding in a nearby home, disguised as a mendicant. Still another galloped toward the Palais des Tournelles, north of the Hotel Saint Pol, in search of the fifteen-year-old dauphin Charles. However, the Armagnac *prévôt* of Paris, Tanguy du Chastel, alerted by the commotion in the streets, had hurried to rouse the sleeping dauphin. Tanguy used his own robe to clothe the young man and spirited him first to the Bastille and then to Melun.[3]

Juvénal des Ursins writes of the massacre, "to describe the murders, pillaging, stealing and tyranny carried out in Paris would be a thing too long and pitiful to recite."[4] The Burgundians knew that their opponents would seek revenge. On June 1, Tanguy du Chastel led a small force of Armagnacs back into the city by way of the Porte Saint Antoine. The Burgundians repelled them and then rampaged, hacking Armagnacs to pieces wherever they found them. Burgundians unable to join in the butchery—children, the unarmed—cursed their prostrate enemies. On June 12, crowds broke into prisons, seizing, among others, the Count of Armagnac, denounced by the man in whose house he had been hiding.[5] The crowds murdered the count and his friends along with other prisoners, stripping the bodies and exposing them for public display.

The frenzy continued into the following months. The arrival in Paris on July 14 of Jean sans Peur and Queen Isabeau, whom Jean had released from Armagnac imprisonment the preceding November, did not halt the violence. A group led by Capeluche, the executioner of Paris, massacred another set of prisoners on August 21. Jean regained control of the situation only after persuading several thousand rebels to leave the city to fight the Armagnacs in Montlhéry. He then had the city gates barred while he rounded up and executed the instigators of the second prison massacre. Before order was restored, the slaughtered would include, in addition to the Armagnac leaders, the humanists Jean de Montreuil, Gontier Col, and possibly Laurent de Premierfait. The theologian Jean Gerson was fortunate enough to be in Germany at the time, having stayed on after the Council of Constance. Although the Armagnac-Burgundian feud had been under way for nearly two decades at the time of the Paris massacre, according to contemporary chroniclers, this episode surpassed all others in violence.[6]

I open with this description of violence because the Orleanist-Burgundian feud is the context for Christine de Pizan's political writing. Recognizing this context has important implications for how we read her corpus. In her study of Joan of Arc, Colette Beaune notes the reluctance of modern historians to recognize the maid as an Armagnac, although she surely was.[7] A similar hesitation marks Christine scholarship. The first step in the case that I make through an accumulation of evidence in the course of this study—that Christine, like Joan of Arc, must be seen as an Orleanist or Armagnac sympathizer—is the observation that members of feuding societies tend to be partisan rather than impartial. This point itself, however, requires justification: was the conflict that so preoccupied Christine a feud?[8] The phenomenon described by scholars of feuding is compatible with descriptions of the Orleanist-Burgundian conflict in its early days: provocation, response, provocation. Bloodshed follows a long escalation of hostilities (as we see in the assassination of Louis of Orleans and, later, Jean sans Peur). Scholars commonly distinguish feuding, "armed combat *within* political communities," from warfare, "armed combat *between* political communities."[9] A feud displays "clear rules (about who retaliates, when, how, and against whom), governed by norms that limit the class of possible expiators (women and children are usually excluded) and the appropriateness of responses."[10] True, the massacre of 1418 was thought to exceed these limits. However, even it was not spontaneous but tactical, a response to a particularly grievous long-term set of injuries. Michael Sizer has shown that the Burgundians targeted institutions and persons under whom they had suffered massively during Armagnac rule, denuding the bodies of their victims to protest social distinctions, lining up behind Capeluche to reclaim the right to mete out justice, and massacring prisoners because the prisons were insecure, which meant that the Armagnacs held in them posed a genuine threat.[11] Moreover, the rampages responded to a specific event: the Count of Armagnac's rejection of a treaty negotiated between the king's ambassadors and the Duke of Burgundy in mid-May in La Tombe, north of Paris.[12] When ambassadors arrived in Paris with news of peace, the Parisians had danced in the streets, anticipating a life free from the threat of war and Armagnac oppression. But when the Count of Armagnac rejected the treaty, the Burgundian Parisians began to plan their revolt. Although the shouts of "La paix, la paix, Bourgogne" from people in the midst of committing horrific acts may seem "grimly ironic," Sizer explains, the Burgundian Parisians were indeed seeking peace. It was just that they believed "that the only end to the war was through extermination of the enemy infecting the body politic."[13]

To return to historians' reluctance to see Christine as partisan, feuds polarize populations, although the process can be slowed to some extent by intimate interactions among the members.[14] This was true for the Orleanists and the Burgundians, who lived in close proximity. Still, Emily Hutchison has shown in her study of Orleanist and Burgundian emblems that by 1411 everyone had been forced to choose a side: "The symbols used, the violence faced and the implications of being called an 'Armagnac' or a 'Burgundian' forced ordinary people of the realm to join one faction or the other."[15] As to why nonpartisanship would have been difficult even earlier than 1411, the bone of contention was regency—that is, who would govern for the mad king—and the Orleanists and Burgundians represented the only choices available. Some historians have hypothesized the existence of a neutral "royalist" party. But there was no third claimant for regency apart from a period of a few years, when, as R. C. Famiglietti has shown, the dauphin Louis of Guyenne worked to create his own faction.[16] Indeed, Christine threw her weight behind the dauphin when he began to move in this direction. But without a third regency candidate, a neutral royalist party would have been meaningless.[17] Timur R. Pollack-Lagushenko has shown that the Orleanist and Burgundian factions were nothing like modern parties with stable membership based on a common ideology.[18] Rather, they were groups associated with a leader from whom they expected reciprocation. At different times, a given baron, occupied with his own business, might not be actively engaged in the conflict. Also, even important leaders—the king himself, the queen, the Duke of Berry, the dauphin, the Duke of Anjou, and even Jean of Burgundy's brothers—switched sides, joining up with a faction when they needed the support of one of the leaders and remaining involved until they had achieved what they wanted.[19] This is not the same as neutrality, a principled refusal to support either faction.

True, Christine was different from powerful barons in that she had neither physical force to contribute to the struggle nor personal quarrels to settle. She worked, like other contemporary court writers, to give a form to kingship based on abstract principles in addition to personal devotion.[20] It has been suggested that because writers attached to the houses of Orleans and Burgundy manifest the same fundamental preoccupations—financial reform, for example—their writings cannot be viewed as partisan.[21] But one's conception of kingship is closely linked to one's notion of regency, and in these areas political writings do differ. Like the Burgundians and the university, Christine might have called for rule of the kingdom by a council representing the three estates.[22] She did not do this.

In the rest of this chapter, I set the stage for the reexamination of Christine's work that I present in the chapters that follow. I first consider the different visions of kingship that Christine's society offered her, including Charles V's. I then review her comments in the autobiographical sections of her work on Philip of Burgundy's betrayal of Charles V's regency ordinances, concluding that these justify reexamining her corpus.

Kingship and Regency in Late Medieval France

Christine's family ties would have inclined her toward the House of Orleans from the feud's beginnings. As we will see, her husband, Étienne de Castel, moved in chancery circles, Louis's ambit. But equally important to the poet would have been Charles V's vision of kingship, transmitted to her by her father, Thomas de Pizan, an advisor to the king, and reinforced by public readings of open letters and royal ordinances, in conversations held within the complex of buildings that formed the Hotel Saint Pol, and in manuscripts that she read or heard read, including the *Grandes chroniques de France*, an important source for her.[23]

Charles V's regency ordinances betray two interests central to his vision of kingship that Christine will echo: maintaining rank and taking counsel from a group of devoted men of somewhat diverse social backgrounds. As for rank, the earliest of the regency ordinances, dated August 1374, stipulates that the king will be crowned at age fourteen. A set of ordinances dated October of the same year foresee and attempt to prevent a power struggle among the king's brothers should the succeeding king be younger than fourteen. One ordinance notes tellingly that the task of the king is to administer the public good wisely, especially regarding those things from which the greatest danger might arise in the future. It then awards the king's eldest brother, Louis of Anjou, *gouvernement* of the realm during a minority reign. Another ordinance of the same day draws attention to the king's direct line, mentioning his second son, Louis, by name and specifying that if young Charles dies, Louis will succeed him.[24] These regency ordinances thus emphasize rank, with the king's eldest brother leading the younger brothers, but stressing, too, that the king's two sons both precede all his brothers. Françoise Autrand describes Charles V's assiduous maintenance of order, a reaction against his father, King Jean, who had allowed "poor" relations to serve as counselors.[25] Bernard Guenée, too, notes that the interest in rank intensified during the reign of Charles V, so that under Charles VI some seventy "cousins" were minutely arranged on the basis of how closely they were related to the reigning king.[26]

The importance of rank runs through the continuation of the *Grandes chroniques* devoted to the reign of Charles V.[27] Promoting the king against challengers like Charles of Navarre and defending the French position in the war against England, the chronicle records the precedence followed during royal entries and dinners, an attention that Christine will echo in the *Livre des fais et bonnes meurs du sage roy Charles V.*[28] As for its treatment of Charles V's regency ordinances, the *Grandes chroniques* reports that the ordinances, proclaimed before the Parlement de Paris with great numbers of notable lords attending, fixed the age of succession at fourteen.[29]

Christine surely observed that just after Charles V's death, Philip of Burgundy, the youngest brother of the dead king, demanded that Louis of Anjou be denied regency, that the eleven-year-old king be crowned immediately, and that a council headed by Philip himself rule for the young king.[30] Regency by a council was not unprecedented. However, violation of a royal ordinance so publicly recognized required justification. The *Grandes chroniques* mentions in its final pages that because the uncles disagreed about the ordinances, it was advised that it would be expedient for the king to be crowned immediately.[31] Pintoin's chronicle supplies more detail, relating that Louis of Anjou's spokesman argued before the Parlement that, following the custom of France enshrined in Charles V's royal ordinance of 1374, the young king should ascend at fourteen and that until then Louis would not be done out of the regency.[32] Philip's spokesman, Pierre d'Orgemont, chancellor of Charles V, countered that the late king had changed his mind about regency just before his death, deciding that he could best guarantee the peaceful succession of power by having his son crowned co-ruler with him before he died (a habit of the Capetians through Philip Augustus) rather than having him ascend at fourteen. Charles V had revealed this decision secretly to a small group, including Pierre.[33] But the king fell terminally ill before he could carry out the plan, and, according to Pierre, simultaneously realized that associating his son as king would violate the ordinance that he had recently passed setting the age of succession at fourteen, that is, the ordinance on which Louis of Anjou based his case. Thus Charles V had asked that this regency ordinance be invalidated and that his son be crowned immediately upon his death and placed in the care of Philip and Duke Louis of Bourbon, brother of the deceased queen. Pierre does not explain why Charles V considered this new regency arrangement more likely to result in a peaceful succession.

The story that Charles V planned to associate his son with him on the throne before his premature death may or may not be true, as Yann Potin has demonstrated. On the one hand, although Pierre was in a position to know, he would have had a motive to lie for Philip—the hope of retaining his office. As it turned out, Pierre was dismissed the day after his appearance before the Parlement, but undoubtedly he had hoped for better.[34] Further casting doubt on Pierre's story of deathbed revision is the treatment of Bureau de La Rivière,

Charles V's *chambellan* and closest advisor, in whose arms the king had died and whom he had assigned to supervise his brothers after his death. This leads to the second interest manifested in the royal ordinances, the importance of counselors. Although an ordinance awards Louis of Anjou *gouvernement*, it places him under the surveillance of Bureau de La Rivière. After laying out the sources of income with which Louis will govern the kingdom, the ordinance states that he will turn all that remains over to Bureau de La Rivière. Another ordinance, noted above, awards *tutelle*, or guardianship, of the dauphin to the queen, Jeanne of Bourbon, assisted by Philip and Louis of Bourbon (the king's middle brother, Jean of Berry, for reasons unknown, receives no position at all). Again, Charles V places all the guardians under the watch of Bureau de La Rivière, "who completely understands [Charles V's] will and intention regarding the children mentioned above." He gives the *chambellan* veto power over all decisions made by the guardians, commanding that they "do nothing without [Bureau de La Rivière's] counsel and deliberation."[35] He further lists the members who will serve on the grand council to advise these guardians. The list includes his advisors, known collectively as the "marmousets."[36]

It cannot be a coincidence that the king's *chambellan*, along with two other men identified by John Bell Henneman as Charles V's closest advisors, Jean Le Mercier and Jean de Montaigu, both ennobled commoners, vanished after the king's death, to reappear, along with the larger group of marmousets, only when Charles VI asserted power in 1388.[37] A fourth, Olivier de Clisson, remained and was named *connétable*, backed by Louis of Anjou, as Françoise Lehoux explains.[38]

On the other hand, with Louis of Anjou set to inherit the provençal and Italian holdings of Jeanne of Naples as of 1379, Charles V may indeed have intended to head off problems that would have arisen from this diversion of attention by consecrating care of the kingdom and the dauphin to Philip in the form of *tutelle*.[39] As we will see, whether *tutelle* or *gouvernement* of the realm was more significant varied: possession of the dauphin often carried more weight than administration of the realm. Whatever the truth, even as Pierre elaborated on the king's last wishes, Philip's troops swarmed around Paris, and the barons of the realm, apparently fearing violence, opted that Louis of Anjou be stripped of regency. Although unhappy, Louis consented for the good of his nephew.[40] On November 30, 1380, the uncles installed what Lehoux calls a "polyarchy," or ruling council, to govern.[41]

As noted above, Charles VI asserted his rule in 1388. But Philip seized power again with the onset of Charles VI's madness in 1392, sending the marmousets fleeing once more.[42] During a long lucid period in 1393, Charles VI attempted to dislodge his uncle with an ordinance granting *administracion* of the kingdom to his brother, who preceded his uncles, as Guenée explains, who could boast that they were son, brother, and uncle of *kings* of France, but only uncles of the *reigning* king.[43] In another ordinance, Charles VI awarded guardianship to the queen, assisted by the princes of the blood, including Philip and Jean of Berry. The result was conflict. Over the years, Philip protested Louis's preeminence in the government, citing the duke's youth. The chronicle of Juvénal des Ursins reports that in 1401 Philip (along with several notable people) was still complaining that it was neither reasonable nor honorable that Louis should be governing, given his age—he was thirty years old at the time.[44]

The Burgundian power grabs, part of the long history of factionalism and reform in France, were nourished by nostalgia for a golden past of seigneurial liberties.[45] The gist of Philip's claim can be gleaned from later accounts of Burgundian activity. Pierre Cochon's chronicle, for example, associates Jean of Burgundy's regency claim with an ancient principle of governance through the three estates.[46] University representatives speaking before the king in 1410 also proposed government by the three estates. The king of Navarre, speaking for the Duke of Burgundy, evinced eagerness to adopt such a rule.[47]

Because I am arguing that Christine's vision of kingship and regency follows Charles V's rather than the Burgundians', it will be useful to consider how the king formed his view. During his reign, Charles V successfully negotiated multiple baronial threats, increasing the prestige of the monarchy by regaining most of the territory lost to the English during the first two Valois reigns and keeping his brothers under control. However, his hold on his own throne and, during his regency, the throne of his imprisoned father, King Jean, was often tenuous. Indeed, when King Jean died in 1364, it was not a given that his son would succeed him.[48] The dauphin's doubt as to his succession is betrayed by his interest in astrology, apparent from 1358 on. One astrological guide written for him in 1361 purported to answer such questions as "whether a kingdom will have a certain man as its leader" and "whether a man will have a kingdom."[49]

What Raymond Cazelles referred to as the "crisis of royalty," brought on by a succession crisis that extended from roughly 1314 to 1364, created in Charles V a lifelong mistrust of ambitious barons, including his own relatives.[50] The principal threat throughout his regency and kingship came from "barons from the west," as they have been designated by Graeme Small and others, strong princes whose territories lay within or adjacent to the French kingdom but who did not recognize the king of France as their superior. Most dangerous was King Edward III of England, who demanded sovereignty over his French territories, and, for many years, Edward III's sometime ally Charles Le Mauvais, or the Bad, king of Navarre (1332–1387), a pretender to the French throne who controlled large areas of Normandy as well as his own kingdom.

The basis for Edward III's challenge was the transfer of Eleanor of Aquitaine's French territories to the English Crown. But, more immediately, the challenges of both Edward III and Charles of Navarre reached back to Philip IV (1268–1314), great-uncle of the wise king. When Philip IV's first son, Louis X, died in 1316, leaving a four-year-old daughter, Jeanne, his second son, Philip V, assumed regency, initially promising to consider succession when little Jeanne came of age. The promise was forgotten when Philip later negotiated his niece's renunciation of the throne with her maternal relatives, the dukes of Burgundy. Philip then became King Philip V, basing his claim on feudal law.[51] He construed the kingdom as a sort of fief, and feudal law concerning female succession varied, though male preference prevailed. In some cases, only males could inherit; in others, a woman might inherit in the absence of a male heir. However, as Ralph Giesey observes, "political and patriotic pressures ultimately tipped the balance in favor of one and not another rule."[52] The idea that women could not succeed to the throne solved a pressing problem by delaying the succession of an heir who was only a child, and it avoided the succession threat of the heir's maternal relatives who were hostile to the royal family.[53] The same idea was marshalled to solve the next problem of succession, which arose when Philip V died in 1322, leaving only daughters. His brother Charles IV succeeded without challenge.[54]

But when Charles IV also died without a male heir, Edward III of England, grandson of Philip IV of France, challenged the 1328 succession of Philip VI of Valois. Although Edward III accepted that women could not rule France, he argued that the right to succession could pass through a woman, in this case his mother Isabella, daughter of Philip IV. So viewed, Edward III's claim was stronger than that of the French claimant, Philip VI, son of Philip IV's brother, Charles of Valois. An English king on the French throne was unacceptable to Philip VI's followers, and thus it was decided that succession could not pass through a woman. It seems in any case that Edward III was more interested in forcing the Valois to cede him sovereignty over his territories in France than in assuming the French throne, and that he used the challenge to the throne as a bargaining chip.

As for Charles of Navarre, his claim through his mother, Jeanne, whose father, Louis X, had been Philip IV's first son, was still greater, if one assumed that succession passed through women. For decades, the king of Navarre menaced Valois kings Jean and Charles V, drawing support from power bases in Normandy, Champagne, and Brie, although his precise goal is not as clear as that of Edward III.[55] King Jean married his daughter to the aggressive young man in 1352 in an attempt to manage him, but then failed to pay the dowry and ceded Angoulême to his new *connétable*, Charles of Spain, without compensating Charles of Navarre for his rights there. Thus in 1354 Charles of Navarre had the *connétable* murdered, an affront that the king accepted for fear of an alliance between his son-in-law and the English.[56] In late 1355, Charles of Navarre seems to have won over the dauphin Charles, persuading him to take part in a mysterious visit to the Holy Roman Emperor, Charles IV, uncle of the dauphin. King Jean foiled the visit. Although historians dispute the significance of the incident, some believe that the two Charleses were hatching a plot to replace King Jean with the dauphin.[57] The king reconciled with the dauphin, making him Duke of Normandy, but remained suspicious: on April 5, 1356, in a fury, the king had Charles of Navarre arrested in the dauphin's castle at Rouen and thrown in prison.[58] But this was not the end of Charles of Navarre. In September 1356, King Jean was taken prisoner when the English defeated the French at the Battle of Poitiers. The dauphin summoned the Estates General to gain consent for taxes to raise the exorbitant ransom demanded by the English. The consequent loss of prestige, coupled with the new taxes, led to popular revolts in 1357–58; Charles of Navarre, liberated in November, eventually joined up with the *prévôt* of the merchants of Paris, Étienne Marcel, to take possession of Paris throughout part of 1358. The 1358 peasant uprising known as the Jacquerie, instigated by Marcel, shook the area around Paris, but the dauphin regained control.[59] As Autrand observes, the dauphin's power was contested by well-established members of King Jean's administration, like Jean de Craon, who proposed "purging" his counselors because the dauphin "has a great and heavy duty to govern given the present state of France, and he is very young," meaning that he needed to be strictly guided.[60] Charles of Navarre continued to agitate, rebelling again in 1364, just before the death of King Jean. As Charles V made his way to his coronation in Rheims, he received word that the royal army under Breton Bertrand du Guesclin had decisively beaten the Navarrese at the Battle of Cocherel.[61]

The new king embarked on the "gradual re-establishment of royal power which was the salient characteristic" of his reign.[62] Charles of Navarre, losing noble support, was less of a threat after 1364; many Breton lords, including Olivier de Clisson, joined Charles V, increasing the king's influence in Brittany. Although the Treaty of Brétigny of 1360 had brought the return of King Jean and peace, it also had included a significant transfer of lands to the English. Charles V gained most of them back over the course of the decade, aided by the gradual installation of regular taxation for war, a development that made possible a "major French revival" under Charles V, as Henneman writes.[63] Regular taxation came to be accepted because of the need for protection against mercenary companies, who, unemployed during lulls in the war, pillaged the countryside. Controlling fortresses throughout the south, they terrorized the surrounding areas. Also, borders of English territories in southern France could not be defended easily, allowing the French to wage a long war of attrition. Furthermore, when taxed by Edward the Black Prince, the English leader in Aquitaine, to support his allies in the War of the Castilian Succession, the Gascons refused and appealed to Charles V for support. Charles V enlisted the legal advice of a series of prominent jurists from Bologna, Montpellier, Orleans, and Toulouse, who assured him of his right to intervene.[64] After summoning the Black Prince and receiving no response, Charles V declared war, the final result of which was the Black Prince's return to England. In the north, French troops under Guesclin, then *connétable*, successfully held off English offensives.

Relative prosperity returned to France. But with the English under control, Charles V also needed to manage his brothers, which he accomplished by granting them appanages and lieutenancies, in return for which they served his interests.[65] Tensions threatened while Charles V surrounded himself with devoted and competent counselors, his marmousets. The royal brothers resented this. But the charismatic king intimidated them when necessary, ceding none of his royal authority.[66] In this newly peaceful environment, the king devoted time and resources to cultivating a court where intellectual exchange took place and where he could construct and embody his ideal of kingship. Among the more than eleven hundred volumes that he left at his death were many "mirrors for princes," confirmation of his commitment to justifying himself within a legal framework.[67] Further witness to Charles V's reflection on kingship is the care that he took to explain his understanding of the role of the monarch in the introductions to his royal ordinances. Typical of this approach, he begins an ordinance on care for lepers by avowing that he wishes with all his heart to care for the public good and the good government of his people.[68]

Still, the theories of kingship laid out in writing would have been accessible to a fraction of his subjects, most grasping kingship only as it was embodied in a specific human being. As Philippe Contamine has emphasized, the Valois made this relationship felt by means of "a political imagery, ephemeral or lasting, public or private, which was above all . . . an imagery of established powers: coins, medals, seals, frescoes, stained glass windows, sculptures [especially funerary], painted ceilings, paintings on wood or, even more, manuscript miniatures."[69] Charles V consciously cultivated his image not only in manuscript illuminations and sculpture but in joyous entries into the towns of his kingdom calculated to magnify his majesty.[70] He also cultivated the religious dimension of his kingship, modeling his coronation ceremony on bishops' ordinations and touching his subjects to cure their scrofula.[71] Most interesting for our purposes, he took care to promote visually the principles of succession laid out in his regency ordinances. In the illuminations of the *Grandes chroniques*, his heir, Charles, is nearly always depicted with his brother, Louis, emphasizing the importance of rank.[72] This emphasis is also made explicit in a set of dynastic sculptures decorating a pillar supporting the north tower of the cathedral at Amiens, commissioned by the king's counselor and president of the Cour des aides, Jean de La Grange (1325–1402), bishop of Amiens from 1373. François Salet has described the ensemble of sculptures as a transcription in stone of the ordinances of 1374—in other words, of the fundamental principles of Charles V's conception of the monarchy. The sculptures are arranged in three registers. Adorning the highest level of the ensemble are the figures of the Virgin and child and the patron saints of Amiens, Saint John the Baptist and Saint Firmin. The middle register is inhabited by Charles V, the dauphin Charles, and his younger brother, Louis. The occupants of the bottom register are the king's advisors: Bureau de La Rivière, Jean de Vienne, and Jean de La Grange himself. The king's brothers do not appear in the schema. On the contrary, the sculptures illustrate the line of succession: after Charles V, the dauphin, and, should something befall the dauphin, the younger son, all of them supported by the king's advisors. Of course, history proved the sculptures a "costly and useless act of patronage," writes Salet, for "everyone knows the fate of the ordinances when Charles V died, too early, certainly, in 1380."[73]

Christine as Political Observer

Charles V's final regency plans remain somewhat unclear, as noted above. However, if the wise king did indeed decide to appoint Philip head of a regency council, as Pierre d'Orgemont claims, this information, as we have seen, was contested. As for Christine's perspective, I argue in what follows that she believed that Charles V had left regency of the kingdom to Louis of Anjou and that Philip of Burgundy was a usurper.

Most of what we know about Christine's life comes from her autobiographical writings in the *Livre de la mutacion de fortune*, the *Advision*, and, to a lesser degree, the *Chemin de longue étude*. Other works, including her poetry and the *Fais et bonnes meurs*, add important details. In this section I refer to these works for autobiographical information on the poet's feelings toward royal power and the Burgundians. Christine suggests that her earliest memories were of Charles V and the French royal court. She recounts in the *Advision* that Charles V invited her father to Paris to serve as his astrologer and physician, a great honor to the "da Pizzano 'dynasty' of notaries," a noble family that had resided in Bologna from at least 1269. Christine's paternal grandfather, Benvenuto, and her father, Thomas, were both doctors in the Faculty of Medicine in Bologna. Her maternal grandfather, Thomas di Mondino, also received a doctorate of medicine at Bologna, where he must have met Thomas da Pizzano before moving to Venice. Sometime before 1357, Thomas too moved to Venice and married Thomas di Mondino's daughter. The couple eventually returned to Bologna and had three children, two boys, Paulus and Aghinulfus, and Christine, born in about 1365.[74]

Thomas accepted Charles V's offer. Initially, he went alone, planning to spend only one year in France, but Charles V requested that he summon his family from Bologna. After delaying for three more years, Thomas complied. When the family arrived, writes Christine, "the very good and wise king" received them "with joy."[75] The relationship between Thomas and the king grew still closer over the years, as Suzanne Solente has verified by tracking Thomas's changing appellations. In 1372 he is referred to as "our astronomer"; later that year he is "our beloved and faithful physician" (nostre amé et feal phisicien), and, in 1380, "our beloved and faithful counselor and physician" (nostre amé et feal conseillier et phisicien).[76] Moreover, Autrand suggests that Thomas served Charles V in diplomatic missions.[77] Thomas was well compensated for his services. Christine claims that he received one hundred francs a month, plus that much again in books and gifts. In addition to his salary, the king promised to provide for Thomas's future with a pension of five hundred livres.[78]

Charles V, gift giver, is inextricably associated in the poet's writings with harmony, wealth, and joy. The order embodied in the king extended into his kingdom, even into Christine's own life. As long as the king remained at the summit of the social hierarchy, prosperity was assured. Embracing her own place in the hierarchy, Christine benefited from the good that flowed from Charles V's kingship. Although she gently mourns Thomas's inability to manage his money, she fully accepts her father's authority and celebrates his positive qualities.[79] She also describes her marriage to Étienne de Castel, of a noble Picard family, as a happy result of the hierarchical system of reciprocal obligation. Étienne seems to have been a particularly apt choice, probably the son of another close associate of Charles V. Gilles Malet, who created the first inventory of the holdings of the king's library in 1373 (a second was done in 1380), was the executor of the will of an Étienne de Castel, "armurier, valet de chambre et brodeur" of Charles V.[80] In any case, Thomas selected the younger Étienne for his erudition, although a man so esteemed by the king could choose his son-in-law from a large pool of eligible candidates, as Christine explains.[81] As a notary for the king, Étienne would have moved in circles associated with early Parisian humanists like Jean de Montreuil, Pierre and Gontier Col, and others with connections to Louis of Orleans.[82]

In 1380, the king offered Thomas accommodation in the Tour Barbeau, the equivalent of a few city blocks from the Hotel Saint Pol, just off the Seine, and in the house next to the Tour.[83] Although we do not know where Thomas had lodged his family earlier, it is likely that they resided near the Hotel Saint Pol. The complex, bursting with human and animal life, housing roaming lions and other exotic animals, was the space Christine would have associated with the king. In addition, Christine would have been aware of the intellectual activity of which he was the center. She may have known Charles V's library, the volumes of which resided in the various royal residences, with a special collection of precious volumes imparting the history of the Valois stored in the hold at Vincennes. The principal library, covering three floors of the Falconry Tower in the northwest corner of the Louvre, held a large collection.

The golden period that was the first fifteen years of Christine's life ended with the king's death. Philip and Louis of Bourbon, aided by Jean of Berry, took control of the government in the name of the young Charles VI, as we have seen. With their assumption of power, numerous courtiers lost their jobs. Christine observes in the *Advision* that when powerful men die, "the shake-ups and changes in their courts and territories are great."[84] Among the victims were the marmousets. Christine makes clear her affection for the marmousets in the *Fais et bonnes meurs*, singling out Jean de Montaigu for praise. She also describes Bureau de La Rivière as "wise, prudent, eloquent, a man with beautiful ways," and notes that "many others of diverse status were graced by the king for their virtues of chivalry, wisdom, loyalty, intelligence or excellent service."[85]

The marmousets were not the only courtiers to lose their jobs. Thomas's prosperity ended with Charles V's death. In the *Advision*, Christine writes that her father's large pensions dried up, although the *princes gouverneurs* retained him "for wages sadly decreased and irregularly paid." Thomas subsequently "fell from power and into illness."[86] The family must have hoped for better: just months before Charles V's death, the Duke of Burgundy had awarded Thomas a hundred livres tournois "to recognize his services and strengthen bonds with him in the future."[87] Thomas was not completely neglected: in return for the "good and agreeable services" rendered to Charles VI and his father before him, on May 23, 1384, the new king awarded him two hundred francs in gold to help him to "maintain his estate."[88] But Philip seems to have shown no more interest.

With Charles V gone, the interest at court in astrologers, always controversial, seems to have diminished. Thomas in any case was a controversial figure. Philippe de Mézières ridicules him in book 2, chapter 67 of the *Songe du vieil pelerin*. Lynn Thorndike relates that Thomas had had both good and bad moments in his capacity as an astrological and medical advisor.[89] As for his successes, at one point he had soil collected from the "centre and four quarters of France," placing five lead statues of naked men marked with astrological signs and the names of the king of England face first on the spots from which the soil had been collected, on an astrologically auspicious date. The ritual was completed with a spell intoning that as long as the statues lasted, the English army would be defeated and chased from France.[90] The spell seems to have done the trick. On the negative side, Thomas may have been accused of trying to poison the young king and the dukes of Burgundy and Berry. In a long letter of 1385 to the alchemist Bernard de Trèves, Thomas explains that he had prepared a medicine for the royals made of gold and mercury, designed to cure sickness and expel poison.[91] However, something had gone amiss; the gift had been confiscated, possibly without the knowledge of the princes, and subjected to an examination that failed to grasp its importance. Thomas requests that Bernard intervene with the princes on his behalf.[92] But the bulk of the letter is an alchemical "traité sur la pierre philos-ophale," possibly included to boost Thomas's credibility in light of the medi-cal catastrophe. Bernard appears not to have delivered the help that Thomas solicited, for his long response, covering nearly thirty folios in the same man-uscript, makes no mention of the request. Worse, he essentially refutes the efficacy of the method that Thomas outlines in his treatise.[93] Christine men-tions Bernard with scorn in the *Advision*.[94] It is understandable that the Duke of Burgundy might have lost interest in a doctor he believed had tried to poison him, but this lack of appreciation for her father was another thing for Christine to hold against Philip.

Besides the early animosity that Christine betrays toward Philip as one of the *princes gouverneurs*, in concluding this case for a reexamination of Chris-tine's political views, it is also important to address the most tenacious argu-ment in favor of the poet's devotion to Philip: that after initially courting Louis of Orleans as a protector, the disillusioned Christine transferred her loyalty from Louis to Philip. The story entered Christine scholarship in large part through the 1927 biography and survey of her work by Marie-Josèphe Pinet.[95] After Henry IV's overthrow of Richard II, Christine's son, Jean de Castel, who in 1399 had been taken into the household of the Earl of Salis-bury, was held in England by the new king, Henry IV, who requested that Christine join her son at the royal court.[96] Deeming Henry IV a usurper, Christine pretended that she would return to England with her son if he first were allowed to come to France for her. The ruse worked, and Jean, then about sixteen, was allowed to return in 1401 or 1402. However, this meant that he needed a new protector. Pinet's case that Christine solicited the Duke of Orleans for a paid position for Jean at his court is based on (1) *balade* 20 of the *Autres balades*, which she reads as Christine's initial request; (2) an auto-biographical passage in the *Advision* (ca. 1405) in which the poet complains that although she had asked a great lord to retain her son, the young man was given only a unpaid position at his court; and (3) a further passage in the *Advision* where she notes that her son was in the household of the Duke of Burgundy.[97] Pinet concludes that the lord who failed to come to her aid was Louis and that Christine therefore turned to Philip.

A break with Louis is not borne out in any of Christine's subsequent works. It is necessary, then, to revisit Pinet's interpretation. Here, it becomes clear that the assumption that *balade* 20 represents a request is not certain. It might be read as such, but within a gift-giving society it might equally well be read as a countergift, or thank-you present, for a service rendered, with the poet offering her son's service in return for an unspecified favor.[98] The *Advision* suggests what this might have been. Immediately following the story, which Pinet cites, of the lord who had failed to offer her son a wage, Christine describes receiving an invitation to live and write at the court of Giangaleazzo Visconti, Duke of Milan, father-in-law of Louis, adding that she, Christine, never sent her volumes to princes herself but that others did so on her behalf.[99] Who would have sent her work to Giangaleazzo? In August 1401, the king, then lucid, sent the Maréchal de Boucicaut and Guillaume de Tignonville, *chambellan* and counselor of the Duke of Orleans, appointed *prévôt* of Paris the month before, as ambassadors to Giangaleazzo in Milan. They were to offer a royal princess for the Duke of Milan's son in return for a promise to subtract obedience from the Roman pope.[100] Louis, Giangaleazzo's son-in-law and chief ally in Paris, was behind any French embassy to Milan. Thus it might have been during this trip to Milan that Christine's work was made known to Giangaleazzo, resulting in an offer of patronage for her and a position for her son. This seems likely, because she presents a trio of writings, beginning in February 1402, to the queen, Tignonville, and Louis. Just after presenting the documents related to the quarrel over the *Roman de la rose* to the queen, Christine offered Tignonville the gift of a copy of the dossier, and, on February 14, 1402, she dedicated the *Dit de la rose* to Louis. A place in the Duke of Milan's household for the young Jean would have been a boon, an apprenticeship in Italian-style Latin and culture to prepare him for a position in the French Royal Chancery or that of Louis of Orleans.[101] Such an education would have been necessary: the Royal Chancery was an "essential administrative organ," engaged not only with the redaction of official documents but also with diplomatic missions.[102] Many of its members had university degrees, and, beyond French and Latin, they were required to know "customary and Roman law, in addition to the royal ordinances and the jurisprudence relevant to the kingdom."[103] Louis's standards, too, were high, his court attracting, in different capacities, the most prominent humanists of the time: Jean de Montreuil, Gontier Col, Ambrogio Migli, Jacques de Nouvion, Guillaume Fillastre, Jean Lebègue, Pierre l'Orfèvre.[104] Gilbert Ouy cites a letter from Ambrogio Migli, who began his long career with the House of Orleans as a secretary for Louis while the duke was in Italy. Migli's job was "to take care to the extent possible that Louis speak ornately, effectively, and honestly in his letters."[105]

In this context, *balade* 20 could be a response to Louis's securing positions for Christine and her son at the court of Giangaleazzo. Christine describes herself requesting Louis's help in the *Fais et bonnes meurs* and being granted what she asked.[106] Waiting more than an hour for her turn to speak to the duke, she watched his face with great pleasure as he listened to those asking his aid and then set their affairs in order. Unfortunately, Giangaleazzo died in September 1402, before Christine could depart for Italy; in the *Mutacion de fortune,* she describes being hit with a serious illness, and this too may have prevented her departure even before the news of Giangaleazzo's death.[107]

The final question is what Jean de Castel was doing in the household of the Duke of Burgundy around the time that Christine was writing the *Advision.* The chronology is hazy, but after Giangaleazzo's death, Louis was away from Paris for long periods of time; indeed, he was absent from Paris when the Lord of Milan died.[108] Given the dukes' rivalry, Eric Hicks's hypothesis seems plausible: "The courtly poetess of the *Dit de la Rose* would be a handsome acquisition for the duke's collections."[109] Philip may have offered aid along with a commission to write the *Fais et bonnes meurs,* and Christine, needing to support her son, would have had no reason to refuse.

Conclusion

Christine's autobiographical writings betray an early resentment of the Duke of Burgundy originating in her father's ill treatment by the *princes gouverneurs* after the death of Charles V. This personal response, coupled with her strongly positive view of Charles V, who successfully put down attempts to overthrow him and whose regency ordinances Philip ignored, justifies revisiting the assumption that Christine ever supported the Burgundians. She does not overtly criticize them, which would have been politically suicidal early in her career and literally suicidal under Jean. Some of her references to Philip suggest a positive attitude. She offers him a manuscript of the *Mutacion de fortune*; she reports with pride that he asked her to compose a biography of his brother, King Charles V; she writes sadly of his death; and she notes that he took her son into his household. And yet the fact that a politically engaged poet dependent on selling her work to a wealthy clientele would write of the Duke of Burgundy in flattering terms requires no explanation. She praises other contemporaries and princes of the blood in terms at least as flattering as those she uses to describe Philip.

Autrand has seen behind the Orleanist-Burgundian conflict a centralizing movement toward statism on the part of the Armagnacs, countered by the

Burgundians' more traditional view. Claude Gauvard makes a similar point in showing how attitudes toward royal pardons conform to two distinct visions of the state: the Armagnacs insisting that people of all levels must be subject to one justice, and the Burgundians guarding the "liberties" accorded to different social groups.[110] As I have noted, Charles V visualized his kingship as one of a strong single figure surrounded by devoted counselors, whereas the Burgundians favored rule by the three estates. It is not clear to what degree Christine saw the conflict in terms of a clash between definitions of government. However, her loyalty to Charles V was unshakeable, and we have seen her avowed affection for the most important marmousets, Bureau de La Rivière and Jean de Montaigu, who were persecuted by the Burgundians. Throughout her corpus she expresses her belief in the importance of the king's council as a set of trusted advisors of diverse social backgrounds. This tradition was continued by Charles VI and Louis, who summoned the marmousets back to power in 1388, not by Philip and his polyarchy.

I have tried to show in this chapter that, a priori, Christine seems more likely to have supported the Orleanist than the Burgundian faction. Her reverence for Charles V and her early reproaches of Philip do not absolutely preclude the possibility that she backed that duke's claim to regency. However, the question remains to be investigated.

2

THE BEGINNINGS OF THE FEUD AND CHRISTINE'S
POLITICAL POETRY, 1393–1401

The dukes' rivalry is mentioned explicitly for the first time in 1401. Pintoin describes the dukes as barely able to conceal their animosity for each other. Their competition was aggravated by courtiers, he continues, who themselves were locked into "the constant excessively jealous and stubborn struggle for superiority . . . ceaselessly attempted through spouting flattery to ignite into a giant fire the sparks of hatred hiding under the embers of dissimulation, with the object of provoking the dukes to shows of public enmities."[1] The word "enmities" (inimicicias) is a legal term denoting a state of hatred between two parties.[2] To have reached such a state, the rivalry may have existed for some time. Historians disagree on when the conflict between uncle and nephew began: some, like Jarry, date it to the first years of the 1390s, and others trace it to 1398 or even 1401, when the dukes nearly came to arms in Paris.[3] I make the case in this chapter that although the feud—that is, the public exchange of insults leading to violence—may have begun only in 1400 or so, the bad blood began immediately after Charles VI's illness, when Philip of Burgundy seized control of the government for the second time.

Philip put an enduring positive slant on his two seizures of power. Through public discourse and open letters, he presented himself as a reformer, while discrediting Louis (later, Jean of Burgundy would include the queen in the attacks) as a spendthrift and imposer of massive taxes.[4] In the first section below, I attempt to correct for the Burgundian bias in retracing the opening years of the feud.

The Early Days

To create a larger context for this discussion of the first years of the feud, I begin by examining some of the troubles that appeared around the time of Charles V's death. Charles V left the Valois kingship a significantly more prestigious institution than the one he had inherited. Still, at the moment of his death, a number of problems, old and new, were emerging. The Western Schism, dividing Christendom between Roman and Avignon popes, had been accepted and possibly encouraged by Charles V.[5] Pope Gregory XI, the seventh and last of the nonschismatic Avignon popes, died in 1378 in Rome, where he had returned shortly before his death. Pope Urban VI was elected in Rome as his successor. Several months later, however, a group of French cardinals declared the election void, claiming coercion. Returning to Avignon, they elected Clement VII, beginning the Great Schism.

In addition, despite the relative peace of the end of Charles V's sixteen-year reign, when Charles died in 1380, revolts against heavy taxation began to agitate the kingdom, continuing several years into Philip's regency. Uprisings in the Languedoc, starting in 1379, against the taxes for war with the English had been followed by slightly less violent rebellion in Auvergne. Like many of his ancestors, the dying Charles V repented of having taxed his subjects and abolished the *fouage*, source of 30 to 40 percent of the kingdom's tax revenues.[6] An anonymous chronicler comments that the king's many activities had "greatly burdened the people."[7] Although Charles V soothed his own conscience and temporarily cheered his subjects, his decision created a dramatic shortfall for his successors.[8] This worsened when, under pressure from the Parisians, twelve-year-old King Charles VI promised to eliminate all taxes.[9] In a panic, the royal uncles convened the Estates General to request funds under a different guise.[10] On February 17, 1381, the Estates General decided on a new *fouage*. However, by early 1382, when it became clear that the revenues collected for the *fouage* were inadequate, the uncles attempted to go around the Estates General to impose a sales tax.[11] Insurgency followed in Paris, the north, and into Flanders.[12] In the end, the uncles crushed the Parisian rebels and suppressed the other revolts, defeating the Flemish in the Battle of Roosebeke on November 27, 1382.

Also pertinent to the coming conflict between Philip and Louis of Orleans, Philip had a history of causing discord. At the young king's coronation, a fight nearly broke out between him and Louis of Anjou over who should sit beside the king. Philip's *audacia* prevailed over respect for age ("verecundiam etatis").[13] Jean of Berry offers further evidence of Philip's propensity for conflict in a letter to the Count of Armagnac of February 18, 1381, explaining his delay in Paris: "As you will have heard, there is much dissension between my brothers of Anjou and Burgundy, which only I can appease."[14] This conflict was resolved by Louis of Anjou's departure in the winter of 1382 to conquer the kingdom of Naples, although he created a new problem in attempting to raise a hundred thousand francs in taxes to finance the expedition.[15] Louis had been adopted as heir by Jeanne, queen of Naples, but, his succession contested by Charles Durazzo, he was obliged to lead an army to defend the queen, who was assassinated in any case before he even reached Naples. The Duke of Anjou died on September 20, 1384, having failed utterly in his attempt to claim the throne of Naples.[16] Back in Paris, although the dukes of Burgundy and Berry seemed in general a compatible duo, their relationship, too, showed signs of strife. In 1382 the king of Castile received a report that King Charles VI had been ready to travel to the Languedoc but had waited because of "discord" between the dukes of Burgundy and Berry. Louis of Anjou, already on the way to Italy, was recalled to Paris. Jean of Berry's rule over the Languedoc created further tensions between him and Philip.[17]

Still, Philip and Jean of Berry went on to govern until November 1388, when the twenty-year-old Charles VI decided that he would rule on his own from that point on.[18] Announced during the French army's return home from a military expedition to subdue William of Guelders, an old enemy of Philip's and rival for the duchy of Brabant, the assertion of power seems to have been long in the making. In June 1387, Olivier de Clisson, greatly loved by Charles VI, had been taken prisoner by the Duke of Brittany, ally of the royal uncles. The uncles' implication in the incident so enraged the king that he turned against them.[19] Charles VI's independence was declared in Rheims by the cardinal of Laon, a former marmouset, during a meeting of the Royal Council.[20] Once in power, Charles VI recalled the marmousets to positions of financial influence. These new advisors tried to implement numerous reforms, although many contemporaries did not appreciate their efforts, especially the university, whose traditional privileges the marmousets often ignored, and those who continued to bear the burden of taxes.[21] Philip bitterly resented the marmousets for their potential to restrict his access to royal funds. As for Jean of Berry, between September 1388 and February 1389, the marmousets scrutinized his administration of the Languedoc. They removed him from his post, suspended his officers, and burned his secretary at the stake for heresy and sodomy.[22]

Charles VI presented his emancipation from his uncles as a new beginning for the kingdom, with the queen and his brother as support. A truce with the English signed at Leulinghem on June 20, 1389, was celebrated with the queen's coronation in August.[23] The first queen of France to be crowned in a ceremony separate from the king's, Isabeau was honored with an entry and coronation, replete with Virgin imagery, emphasizing her capacity to unify. Accompanying Isabeau was Valentina Visconti, Louis's new wife, who had arrived in Paris just five days earlier.[24] The date of the entry, the octave Sunday of the Assumption of the Blessed Virgin, created the first of many parallels between Isabeau and Mary.[25] As her cortège meandered from Saint Denis and into Paris and finally to Notre Dame for the coronation, the queen was regaled with reenactments from the life of the Virgin.[26] At the Porte Saint Denis, the intersection of the present-day rue Saint Denis and boulevard Saint Denis, she was crowned by two angels proclaiming her the queen of paradise, a theatricalization of the sacred nature of her coronation. Above the gate the Virgin with child was visible, a reference to the queen's own pregnancy, then in its sixth month. Other pageants along the way represented the kingdom "transformed into paradise by the peace and harmony that the queen's advent had brought to France."[27]

The king also enhanced the role of his brother. Just after the coronation, as noted above, the Duke of Berry was removed from his lieutenancy of the Languedoc, and on September 2 the king, accompanied by Louis, set off on a five-month journey to inspect the territory. During his travels he helped to achieve one of the "happiest results of the royal voyage," peace between the houses of Armagnac and Foix, whose rivalry had weighed heavily on the Languedoc.[28] On a lighter note, the trip was the occasion of the poetic debate that resulted in the *Cent ballades* of Jean le Seneschal, a first association of Louis with courtly poetry.[29] In this collection, Louis is credited with a poem extolling *loyauté* in love, while the Duke of Berry's poem expresses relief that he has managed to avoid love and promotes artful lying—saying one thing while doing another. Before the trip, the king had already made Louis his closest advisor, inviting him to sit on the Royal Council, and he would later award his brother personal governance over his appanage, the duchy of Orleans.[30] Charles VI further facilitated Louis's rise through marriage to Valentina Visconti. Besides reinforcing Louis's financial situation, the marriage brought him the county of Asti, which soon resurrected the possibility of a kingdom in Italy, a possibility that had evaporated with the death of Louis of Anjou.[31] In the case of Louis of Orleans, the kingdom, which would be called Adria, was to be created of papal fiefs in central Italy.[32]

These efforts to realize the kingdom of Adria are the first sign of an attempt to amass territories for Louis commensurate with those of Philip of Burgundy. As we saw in chapter 1, Charles V had awarded his three brothers large appanages in order to maintain their loyalties. This leaving him with little for his second son, however, he had negotiated a marriage in 1374 between Louis and the king of Hungary's daughter, Catherine, who would bring the counties of Provence, Forcalquier, and Piedmont, and, more significant, the kingdoms of Sicily and Naples, as well as La Pouille, Salerne, and Monte San Angelo, over which Louis and Catherine and their heirs would rule.[33] The thrones of Sicily and Naples being contested, however, the deal was dropped.

Still, the Schism had created further possibilities for a French entry into Italy.[34] In 1379, Clement VII, attempting to entice the French into the peninsula, had infeudated Louis of Anjou with papal lands situated on the Adriatic, north of Rome, and, soon afterward, as we have seen, the duke was named heir to the throne of Naples, adopted by the childless Jeanne, queen of Naples, in defiance of the Roman pope Urban VI.[35] The idea was that Louis of Anjou would rout Pope Urban VI and leave the Avignon pope Clement VII as the single pope. Although the duke failed, the dream of an Italian kingdom continued. The Schism had freed the Visconti, Valentina's father, Giangaleazzo, and his uncle Bernabo, rulers over much of Lombardy, from papal interference, because the claimants to the Apostolic See were too preoccupied with each other to pay attention to anyone else. When Giangaleazzo, just after succeeding his father as lord of Pavia, heard of the Schism, he celebrated by calling for a three-day feast.[36] To take full advantage of the situation, however, he had to rid himself of his uncle Bernabo, which he did in 1385. The murder of Bernabo earned Giangaleazzo the enmity of Queen Isabeau and her branch of the House of Wittelsbach, for Isabeau's mother, Taddea Visconti, had been Bernabo's daughter. The queen and the duchess were daughters of first cousins; their parents, Isabeau's mother, married to Stephen III Duke of Bavaria, and Valentina's father, Giangaleazzo, shared a grandfather. Hence Giangaleazzo's eagerness to place his daughter Valentina at the French court as a counterbalance. The French court split over the murder, some, centered around the house of Orleans, supporting Giangaleazzo, and others supporting Giangaleazzo's rival for control of Tuscany, the Seigneurie of Florence, centered around the queen.

The winter of 1391 saw Charles VI planning an expedition to Rome to help the Avignon pope Clement VII and Naples press the claim to the throne of the young Louis II of Anjou, already crowned king of Jerusalem and Sicily by Clement VII. Froissart writes that it was the king's intention to head for Lombardy, accompanied by armies led by Louis of Orleans, the dukes of Berry and Burgundy, the Duke of Bourbon, *connétable* Olivier de Clisson, the sire of Coucy, and the Count of Saint Pol.[37] The king sent Louis and Philip ahead to seek an alliance with Giangaleazzo. They arrived in Pavia in March. But although Louis reached an agreement, when he returned to Paris he found the situation altered. The English—prodded by Boniface IX, successor of the Roman pope Urban VI, who did not want the French in Italy—suddenly began to pursue peace. An accord with the English was more advantageous to Charles VI than immediate expansion into Italy. And yet plans for an alliance with Giangaleazzo were renewed eighteen months later, when Charles VI requested that he refrain from joining the anti-Clementist league that Boniface IX was starting among the Italian states.[38] Giangaleazzo's ambassadors explained that their lord could not overtly recognize Clement VII for fear that his subjects would be attacked, unless France sent an army adequate to fend off potential enemies. Thus the idea of the kingdom of Adria resurfaced. In December 1392, Giangaleazzo's ambassadors arrived in France with a proposition for returning Clement VII to Rome.[39] Louis would reign over Adria, because not only was he "best qualified for the task, but most suitable as a close relation of the ruler of Milan. Independent of France but supported by the might of a French army, independent of Milan but duly submissive to Giangaleazzo's parental guidance, Louis would help the Count to annihilate his enemies."[40] The advantage to Milan was that, "hemmed in by Venice to the east and Florence to the south, Giangaleazzo looked strategically to the papal state, which was particularly vulnerable given the spectacular failure of the Avignon papacy to convince Italians that it was a viable political entity rather than a staging area for a shifting cast of warmongering legates."[41] Charles VI put Louis in charge of the project, the success of which would provide Giangaleazzo with a port in a friendly city.

Further proof of trust and affection toward Louis can be seen in Charles VI's commissions to the Parisian goldsmith Hermann Ruissel in the years before the onset of his madness. In seventeen of his thirty-two total commissions from Ruissel, the king included a request for his brother for the same item.[42] Had the double requests begun only after the king's insanity, it would be difficult to attribute the impetus with certainty to the king, but the fact that such commissions were already common indicates that Charles VI instigated the gift giving himself.

The Calamity

All was disrupted in August 1392 by Charles VI's insanity, an affliction from which the king would suffer for the rest of his life. The initial episode occurred en route to Brittany, toward which he was leading an army to avenge Clisson, at that point the victim of a failed murder attempt at the hands of Pierre de Craon, exiled from court a year earlier by Louis of Orleans.[43] Craon had fled to Brittany, where he was protected by the duchy's leader, Jean. After the initial incident, Louis and the uncles gathered in Creil with the raving Charles VI, who recovered his senses within a few days, raising hope that the incident would be isolated.[44] Still, Philip seized the opportunity to reestablish himself as the head of the government with the assistance of the Duke of Berry, wreaking vengeance on the marmousets, who again fled for their lives, as we have seen, and attempting to distance Louis from power.[45]

Louis could no longer be pushed aside. Although it is true, as Michael Nordberg writes, that Philip did not interfere with Louis's plans for Italy, even working with him, accusations surfaced in 1393 that Louis was bewitching the unfortunate king, which suggests trouble.[46] Given the suddenness and severity of the episodes, suspicions of sorcery were inevitable. Although Pintoin reports explanations ranging from an excess of black bile brought on by anger to divine displeasure over French sinfulness, most of the nobility and the masses believed the king to be the victim of a spell.[47]

As we saw in chapter 1, in January 1393, the king promulgated an ordinance naming Louis regent in the case of his death. Although he would plunge into another seven-month stretch of madness later that year, the king had made a relatively full recovery, suggesting that the ordinance reflects his own will.[48] It is not clear when the king ceased to be functional; surely, after a certain point he was never capable of reasoning, although ordinances continued to be promulgated in his name. The regency ordinance in any case reflects Charles VI's fear that he would die early, but it also indicates his desire to clarify the regency situation.[49] Around the same time, Pintoin describes an official attempt to cure the king through witchcraft in 1393: anguished counselors brought a charlatan magician named Arnaud Guillaume to court. Arnaud assured the queen and the nobility of the kingdom that the king was being bewitched by "certain" actors. Earlier in the passage, Pintoin indicates that Louis's wife was a prime suspect. According to Pintoin, the king preferred Valentina to everyone, even the queen. Valentina went to see him daily, Pintoin remarks.[50] Froissart, who in contrast to Pintoin is not sympathetic toward Valentina, assumes that she was bewitching the king with spells because she coveted the throne for her husband.[51]

Although Froissart and Pintoin depict Valentina as the target, I would suggest that these chronicles in fact preserve traces of Philip's accusations of Louis, with Valentina functioning as a double for Louis. It was a common practice to attack a powerful lord through his wife, one that reappears in chronicles over the years.[52] As we will see in more detail in chapter 6, Jean Petit's justification, in 1408, of Louis's assassination on the order of Jean of Burgundy accuses Louis and Giangaleazzo Visconti of conspiring to kill the king. Petit also accuses Louis of trying to poison the dauphin, an attempted crime attributed to Valentina by other sources.[53] This interchangeability of husband and wife suggests that although both were accused by the Burgundians, Louis was the real target.

The next incident of witchcraft recorded by chroniclers also includes Valentina, and it occurs just as French relations with Valentina's father, Giangaleazzo Visconti, break down completely, and the French enter into an alliance with his rival, Florence. The chronicles record Valentina's fleeing from court under the pressure of vicious slander. Pintoin writes that in addition to the king, many others throughout the kingdom began to suffer from the same disease, blaming magical spells. At court, too, both men and women circulated gossip about the Duchess of Orleans. Finally, the Duke of Orleans was persuaded to send his wife from court to avoid scandal, ushering Valentina from Paris in a magnificent cortège to another of their properties.[54] With Louis trying to create a kingdom in Italy with the help of Giangaleazzo, attacking Valentina would have been a means of getting at both men. Froissart reports that Giangaleazzo, apprised of his daughter's danger, sent messengers to the king and his Royal Council to plead on her behalf. However, the king answered very curtly, Froissart reports.[55] He had withdrawn his favor from the Visconti.

The next episode of witchcraft Pintoin recounts depicts the conflict between the dukes in 1398. Pintoin explains that Louis of Sancerre, then *connétable* of France, sent two Augustinians to cure the king with magic. Most interesting about this episode is that Pintoin explains that the pair frequented the Duke of Burgundy, whom they informed that the king was certainly the victim of some outside black magic. But, unable to restore the king's health, they fingered the Duke of Orleans. This accusation provoked a brutal reaction: degradation from their offices and decapitation. While Pintoin does not say so explicitly, he makes it clear that the Augustinians were in the pay of Philip of Burgundy.[56] The chronicle of Juvénal des Ursins gives a somewhat different story, describing the arrest of the Augustinians as one more blow in a cycle of attack and counterattack between the uncle and nephew, and adding that the attacks were motivated by the jealousy between the two dukes.[57]

A solemn *determinatio* published by the university on September 19, 1398, condemning twenty-eight articles related to magic, seems related to the dukes' war of words.[58] All magic is blameworthy, according to the *determinatio*, even when practiced with good intentions. But as much as it tries to halt the use of magic to cure the king, the document seeks to dampen the ducal dispute by stressing the gravity of the charges of witchcraft. Some sermons of Jean Gerson, chancellor of the Faculty of Theology at the University of Paris, are further evidence of the anxiety that the ducal rivalry was causing during the 1390s. In his sermons, Gerson tries to control the dispute by asking his listeners to be less sensitive to the culture of *médisance* (slander) that marked the court. Secret slander and deceitful flattery posed a genuine danger, he warns in several sermons preached before the Duke of Burgundy, whose chaplain he became in April 1393. In a sermon on the feast of Saint Anthony in 1393, Gerson laments defamation, attempting to arouse shame in those guilty of it and righteous anger in the innocent. The only solution, Gerson advises, is for a prince to disregard everything that he hears from a person who speaks ill of others ("mesdit d'aultrui"); anything worthy of being said should be spoken aloud in public. A person who listens only to those who flatter his wisdom and virtue, without heeding the counsel of others, is headed for trouble.[59] And it is very dangerous for a prince to create a situation wherein others cannot speak their minds openly for fear of him. In one of his "Poenitemini" sermons, also preached before Philip of Burgundy on the feast of Saint Anthony in 1396, Gerson explores the meaning of charity in the context of the active life.[60] Surely, he says, charity arises from love of the common good of the body politic, which means the harmonious functioning of the three estates. But these days, he warns, greed and self-love, the enemies of charity, are destroying the body politic.[61] Such self-love makes a seigneur proud, envious, and hateful toward all others of his estate. At court, counselors motivated by self-love care nothing about the common good; they produce only flattery and false adulation, lies and other vices with which they can deceive seigneurs and take what is theirs.

Some of Gerson's sermons also suggest a growing perception of the queen as peacemaker. In "Ave Maria gracia plena," preached at court on the feast of the Annunciation, March 25, 1397, he works to arouse love for women by addressing the Virgin in terms that evoke the queen: as the mother of God, Mary "has authority and natural dominion over the lord of the whole world and by the strongest right over all that is subject to such a lord." The hierarchy is natural, and thus "Notre Dame is called our advocate, our mediator, our queen." Gerson complains of deplorable treatment of women in general, insisting that "the nature of the noble and royal heart" is to be compassionate toward the afflicted. The greatest "courtoisie" is to give, and there is no greater "vilenie" than to steal and plunder. He concludes the sermon by calling on the Virgin for salvation, by the "natural love" that must exist between brothers and sisters of the same blood and flesh.[62]

Gerson loathed political dispute. In October 1396, undone by the stress of navigating his way between the two dukes, he accepted the deanship of the chapter of Saint Donatian in Bruges, set up by Philip, and spent little time at court thereafter. Appointed chancellor of the University of Paris in 1395, when his mentor Pierre d'Ailly abandoned the position to become bishop of Puy, he also let that go in 1400, although he soon returned.[63] In 1399 or 1400 he composed a letter complaining of having to please two rival masters whose names he need not mention.[64] Why should he live in the midst of envious crowds who misinterpret his words?

Gerson's lament about courtly backbiting is mirrored in Christine's courtly verse. Lori Walters has strengthened the case for a close literary relationship between Gerson and Christine by showing that Christine's "seulette" persona, that is, the name by which she refers to herself in numerous works, is borrowed from Gerson's use of the term in his own work.[65] It is not surprising, then, that Christine takes up Gerson's discussion of the terrible treatment of women. But if Gerson does not explicitly point the finger, it is important to note that Christine often praises Louis for speaking well of women, something she never associates with Philip. In the *Fais et bonnes meurs* she writes that Louis was renowned for refusing to listen to injurious language, taking "care not to hear anyone speak dishonorably of women, nor slander against anyone, and did not easily believe the bad of others that was reported to him, following the example of the wise, and speaking these noteworthy words: 'When someone tells me something bad about someone, I consider whether the person saying it has a grudge against the person he is speaking against or whether he speaks from envy.'"[66]

Louis of Orleans is depicted in Christine scholarship as greedy and lustful. I revisit the charge of greed in detail in chapter 3, showing that it stems from Burgundian propaganda. As for lust, the charge seems to derive from a much later myth of a love affair between Louis and the queen, now thoroughly debunked.[67] What remains, then, of the charge? It is useful to return to the sources. First, Louis's mistresses and illegitimate son are only typical among his peers, including Jean of Burgundy.[68] Furthermore, Pintoin provides a contemporary impression of the duke's sexual behavior, writing that, like all young men, Louis may have been somewhat inclined to vice when he was young, but that as a mature man he carefully avoided such self-indulgence.[69] Given Pintoin's generally critical opinion of the duke, the notion that Louis had a reputation as a great philanderer is difficult to justify.

On his presumed bad reputation more generally, even Louis's contemporary detractors describe him as an attractive man of great intelligence and eloquence. Pintoin reports that Philip of Burgundy admitted that his nephew was "commendable for his affability and singular eloquence."[70] The monk further notes that Louis was the most fluent man of his day and that he had personally watched the duke out-orate even great orators, bested only by university doctors; in his manner he was extremely appealing, always genially responsive. A record of the arguments of the dukes of Bourbon, Orleans, Burgundy, and Berry regarding the Schism confirms Pintoin's opinion. The Duke of Orleans, sworn in, places the Schism in its larger context, then captures his listeners' benevolence by explaining that he agrees with his opponents in principle, that the "voie de cession," that is, the resignation of both popes so that a new one can be elected, is the only solution to the Schism. He is eloquent and self-effacing, excusing himself for lacking the "prudence, sense and learning" required to speak well on the subject, but promises that he will speak his conscience, without bias or hatred.[71] He then goes on to enumerate why he believes that withdrawing obedience from the Avignon pope will not result in the resignation of the two popes. His self-representation accords with Christine's effusively positive view of the duke's good nature and manners in the *Fais et bonnes meurs,* noted in chapter 1.

Historians take for granted that Louis was unpopular with the Parisians. But Paris was not monolithic. Werner Paravicini explains that the city was too large and the Burgundians' power too fragmented to make Paris exclusively theirs, noting that Louis of Orleans, residing in the city permanently, had firm roots there.[72] Arnaud Alexandre, too, remarks on the effect of the constant presence of the Duke of Orleans. Louis was visible in Paris, receiving in 1397 (in addition to the Hotel de Boheme near the Louvre, which he had been awarded in 1388) a residence right next to the Hotel Saint Pol, and fashioning himself as an extension of royal power.[73] For Alexandre, Louis was too secure to need to create an Orleanist section of Paris similar to the Burgundian section.

Having begun in chapter 1 to question the common assumption that Christine supported Philip as regent, in the rest of this chapter I start to build the case that she supported Louis's regency.

The Political Poet: Christine's Courtly Lyrics

Christine's courtly verse, like Gerson's sermons, describes the strife-ridden court of the 1390s: even when the subject is romantic love, all texts are "in the last analysis political."[74] More specifically, Christine composes in a "cultural context where the discourse of love and friendship had long functioned to mediate political concerns," as Elizabeth Elliott has noted about Machaut, where the "amatory" served as a "surrogate for the political."[75] Christine's love poetry, with its narrator deprived of her leader or head ("chief"), jealous courtiers who delight in destroying reputations, married women waiting hopelessly for attention from busy lovers, men who feign love to seduce, jealous husbands, lovers unable to gauge the depth of a partner's commitment, and promotion of Boethian resignation, transcodes the power dynamics that structured the courtly community for which she wrote, a leaderless community in which factions jockeyed for power. This love poetry, therefore, is an important source for gauging her attitude toward the feud. I argue that through it she attempts to shape opinion in favor of Louis of Orleans. But, equally important, the love poetry exposes the ideological contradictions of Christine's community, in the form of what Fredric Jameson calls the "political unconscious." In the conclusion to this chapter, I examine the contradiction between French support for the king and the need for a functioning government that is inherent in Christine's proffered solution of Boethian resignation.

In this analysis, I follow the order of writings proposed by the poet herself in the *Livre de Christine*, today MS Chantilly, Bibliothèque du Château, 492–93, composed for the queen and completed on June 23, 1402.[76] This manuscript records the poet's trajectory from lyric verse to her first assays at "serious" writing, the *Epistre d'Othea a Hector* and her contributions to the literary debate over the merits of the *Roman de la rose*. The present chapter covers the cycles and the rhymed love narratives, in their manuscript order. But before tracing how Christine's lyric verse engages with contemporary politics, I consider the debate culture of early fifteenth-century Paris within which Christine composed these works.

Poetic Debate

The elite of Paris around the turn of the fifteenth century enjoyed literary debate. Two major types of debate, associated with separate spaces, can be discerned. The first space is the court, royal and princely. In 1358, Charles V, distressed by the murder of several of his counselors in his rooms in the Palais de la Cité, part of the complex on the Ile de la Cité that today houses the Sainte-Chapelle and the Palais de Justice, sought a new residence safe from urban turbulence. He chose a group of buildings between the Seine and the modern rue Saint Antoine, north to south, and the rue Saint Paul and the rue de Petit-Musc, east to west. Connecting the buildings with a series of corridors and courtyards, he created an enormous complex, which he protected by extending a wall originally constructed by Philip Augustus along the Seine.[77] Known as the Hotel Saint Pol, the complex dominated the right side of the Seine, forming the center of court society, along with other great hotels, like Louis of Orleans's Hotel de Boheme, on the site of the current Bourse.[78] Poetic competition, through formal and informal contests, was part of courtly cultural life. But this poetic activity was not uniquely oral: studies of the manuscript as a performative space suggest that much of what exists today only on the page was theatrical, part of a "hybrid" culture "in which various oral performances . . . co-existed with exuberantly literate productions."[79] Within such an environment, poets worked "competitively (but in collusion with one another) to acquire forms of symbolic capital" through the composition of interactive poetic anthologies, as Emma Cayley writes.[80] Christine's sometime evocation of "Prince" in the envois of her lyrics, recalling the arbitrating prince of the *puy* (although it probably refers literally to the princes at court), attests to her consciousness of poetry as a form of competition, regardless of whether hers was "performed" before an audience.[81]

The other circle was associated with the Royal Chancery, which had remained on the Ile de la Cité when Charles V moved to the Hotel Saint Pol. Several literary quarrels were waged during the last years of the fourteenth century and the first years of the fifteenth by secretaries or notaries in chanceries, men committed to diffusing humanistic learning. Through her father or husband, Christine would have known of the debate between Petrarch, scornful of French Latin literary practice, and Jean de Hesdin, defender of the French. Angered and demoralized by Petrarch's attack on their outdated Latin in 1367, French orators had responded by developing their style to accord with Italian humanistic practice.[82] The silver lining in the cloud of the Schism was the French papacy's contribution to the spread of Italian humanism in Parisian chanceries through networks of men associated with Avignon: Jean Muret, Nicolas de Clamanges, Laurent de Premierfait, and Galeatto Pietramala.[83] By 1394, a letter by Clamanges, then secretary at the University of Paris, to the Avignon cardinals, warning them not to elect another pope to replace the recently deceased Clement VI, was praised for its Latin by Pietramala, an Italian cardinal at Avignon, who was astonished that a Frenchman could write so impressively. Pietramala's letter provoked further debate in 1395–96. Joining Pietramala was Laurent de Premierfait; the opponents were led by Clamanges and Jean de Montreuil, objecting that there was nothing surprising about a Frenchman's lovely Latin.[84] Ezio Ornato has described a friendly debate between Jean de Montreuil and Gontier Col as motivated primarily by the desire for stylistic practice. Jean composed several letters refuting Gontier's contention that as a married man he had less time to devote to humanistic studies than his single friends. In the voice of Gontier's wife, Marguerite, Jean teased Gontier by claiming that the real reason for his lack of production was his love of taverns, games, and women.[85] Grover Furr sees in this debate a continuation of the defense of the intrinsic value of classical learning that characterized much epistolary exchange among these humanists: they shared a common interest "in the spread of a classical Latin style and its acceptability and admiration for it, as thoroughly bound up with the advancement of their careers."[86] When Ambrogio Migli intervened in the quarrel between Jean and Gontier, however, the tone turned hostile. Ornato professes confusion at this turn; Furr sees the apparent anger of the participants as motivated by Migli's transgression of what judges of the debates, as opposed to participants, were permitted. The quarrel over the *Roman de la rose*, in which Christine was involved, is another example of a literary debate, as we will see.

The debates that took place within the circles of the court and chancery were different in theme, style, and purpose, yet both "fed on earlier intellectual, legal, and literary structures," and both participated in an "economy of exchange," as Cayley notes, drawing on the terminology of Bourdieu.[87] In addition to this intellectual commonality, interaction between the two fields sometimes took place through individuals who functioned in both. At least since the time of Guillaume de Machaut, the roles of secretary, court functionary, and poet could overlap. Eustache Deschamps and Guillaume de Tignonville were poet-administrators associated with both the royal court and that of Louis of Orleans. Various interactions among figures like Gontier Col, Jean Lebègue, Jacques de Nouvion, Ambrogio Migli, Jean de Montreuil, and Nicolas de Clamanges, some of them diplomats, some court functionaries, some theologians, but all involved with the chancery at some point, indicate fluid networks. Carla Bozzolo and Monique Ornato have described how the *cour amoureuse*, or Love Court, of Charles VI, which I discuss later in this chapter, brought together members of the different circles. The officers of the *cour amoureuse* were members of the nobility. However, the ministers of the court represented a socially mixed group: great lords rubbed shoulders with royal secretaries, assigned the job of organizing poetic competitions.[88]

Of course, those who participated in both circles were male, or at least this was the case until Christine worked her way in. It is surprising but not unimaginable that Christine would have found entry into the circle of courtly debate, arousing wonder and admiration, because the crowds that gathered at the Hotel Saint Pol and the Hotel de Boheme contained men and women. At the same time, it is quite amazing that she enjoyed some access, however marginal, to the chancery circle, slipping into a field theoretically closed to women by taking part in a quarrel over the merits of the *Roman de la rose* with Jean de Montreuil and the Col brothers, all associated with the chanceries. This skillful move opened up opportunities for exhibiting her erudition to a different public than would have been possible otherwise. As I noted above, recent scholars have emphasized that the court and chancery represented two different fields within which cultural capital circulated and prestige was gained. Developing a reputation in these two fields allowed Christine to increase her influence in the groups whose support was important to Louis of Orleans.

The *Cent balades*

The *Livre de Christine* begins with a cycle, the *Cent balades* (not to be confused with Jean le Seneschal's *Cent ballades*). Through this meditation on the duties of subjects in a kingdom whose king is afflicted by inexplicable bouts of madness (see poem 95, on page 95, for the lamentation of the king's disorder), Christine works to arouse a loving sense of obligation toward authority and anger at those who disrupt social hierarchies through jealous quarreling.[89]

But the first thing to stress about the *Cent balades* is that the cycle is a protreptic, a consolation, encouraging identification with the narrator as she undergoes consolation, so that the same effect will occur in the reader. After a long iteration of traumas relieved by some moments of joy in verse, the cycle culminates in poem 97, where the narrator evokes Boethius. Available in various French versions from the late thirteenth century onward, Boethius's *Consolation of Philosophy* was widely read.[90] However, Sarah Kay suggests that the prose sections of this prosimetrum, propounding the austere vision of Lady Philosophy, offered little comfort to later medieval readers. Rather, they found comfort in the work's verse sections, which resisted Lady Philosophy's command to rise above earthly pleasures by offering glimpses of the "particular" in a "world dominated by contingency rather than necessity, where the possibility is held open that things could have happened otherwise." The verse, in other words, both "sustains the need for consolation and remedies it."[91]

By the time the narrator reiterates in poem 97 that "sense and discretion, / intelligence and consideration" protect against Fortune, noting that "Aristotle much approves memory" (97, 21–23), consolation will have taken place in the sensitive reader. These qualities, to which Christine will return in slightly differing variations throughout her career, seem to refer to the parts of the soul or brain popular made popular by theologians like William of Conches, the powers of intelligence, discernment, and memory, which Julia Sims Holderness argues Christine encountered in William's gloss of Boethius.[92] On how the consolation takes place in the cycle more specifically, Holderness sees an Augustinian influence in Christine's emphasis on memory, explaining that the readers are consoled as they progressively work through the material in the theater of their own memories.[93] Also important, Lori Walters suggests that in this cycle Christine reads Boethius through Aristotle (or, more specifically, I would add, through Aquinas's commentary on Aristotle's *Metaphysics*).[94] Poem 98 begins with a reference to the *Metaphysics* ("All men desire knowledge"), which itself begins with a discussion of memory as the seat of experience, in that it is through memories that one establishes the basis for "experience." Experience is practical, but it gives rise to art, that is, theory induced by the experience. Walters explains that poem 98 justifies Christine's use of memories of love in the cycle: the readers derive universal ideas about the dangers of Fortune from the individual details of the poetry. Poem 99, with its Christian perspective, then gathers the previous two poems beneath its umbrella, foreshadowing the climax of the *Advision*, as we will see.

The hundred poems of the *Cent balades* can be visualized as a series of concentric rings. The outermost contains the first and last poems. In the first, the narrator explains that although she did not wish to compose this cycle, when asked to do so by "some people" she agreed to do their will (1, 1). In the last, she announces that she has fulfilled her promise and gives her name in an anagram. Moving inward, the next ring includes poems on the loss of the narrator's head or boss ("chief"), the malevolence of Fortune, and the degradation of chivalry. Numerous relationships can be seen, for example, between poem 5, lamenting the death of "the head or leader of all my good and of my sustenance" (chief de tous mes biens et de ma nourriture) (5, 6), and poem 95, on the madness of Charles VI. The object of the narrator's sorrow in poem 5 is vague (husband? king?), effecting a symbiosis of personal and communal sorrow occasioned by the king's situation. These poems in turn embrace a core of two series of love poems. The first, running from 21 to 49, recounts a passionate love affair from the perspective of a woman. The second, running from 66 to 88, brings her lover into a dialogue with her. This structure invites reflection on the loss of leadership as manifested at the individual, communal, and universal levels.

Exploring the connections among the cycle's poems in more detail, we see that in the opening *balade*, the narrator shows herself to be a model subject, submitting her will ("voulenté") to those more highly placed than she in the social hierarchy. In so doing, Christine establishes one pole of the binary that will structure not only this cycle but her love writings in general: the emotion common to those who humbly accept their position, loving those whom they are bound to love, as opposed to the self-serving simulation of love. Asked to write some lovely words, "beaulz diz," she emphasizes that she is acting to please others rather than herself. She further shows her virtue in her fidelity to a man whom readers take to be her husband—"he who had all of my good" (2, 20)—although she never specifies this. Love is both an act of will, the fulfillment of an obligation to a higher power, and a naturally occurring, or innate, emotion. Presupposing humility and loyalty, it binds spouses and lovers, the people and the king. This emotion is missing from the current noble ethos, as Christine laments throughout the cycle. Also established in this first poem is Christine's pose as a "stranger to love," her distance from love in the present (although she has loved in the past), which guarantees her sympathy while assuring the reader of her ability to judge from an objective position beyond the prison house of love. The significance of this stance is revealed near the end of the cycle.

Christine engages with difficulties particular to late fourteenth-century France in the second ring of poems, which deplore the widespread neglect of the reciprocity upon which the healthy body politic is based. Absent its center, the court cannot properly reward the deserving. The second poem of the cycle attributes contemporary moral decline to this failure. In Rome, people were honored for their prowess; at Charles VI's court, the system of reward is out of kilter, with too much emphasis placed on "grant heritage." The third poem reinforces passionate love as a figure for genuine emotion with its description of the tragic drowning of Leander during one of his nightly visits to Hero. This great love, like the devotion of the cycle's narrator, serves as a standard against which to measure the false and dangerous versions of love that the poet sees at court. The emotion is one to celebrate, even though it is inevitably touched by loss. The fourth poem turns once again to court life, lamenting the devastating envy that reigns there. As envy led the Greeks to destroy Troy through treachery, so it will ruin the French kingdom.

Set against the backdrop of the ducal rivalry, the poems of the second ring reflect concrete experiences of daily court life: envy, rumor, treachery, and attempts to exclude the relatively low born from reward. The third ring, the love poems at the center of the cycle, serves as the affective substratum or microcosmic version of Christine's analysis of the court. Offering a vision of what is wrong with the realm, the cycle construes relationships, including love relationships, as hierarchical carriers of reciprocal obligations. Amour is the lady's superior, and thus her submission is positive. And yet it brings her pain because she cannot ascertain whether her love is fully reciprocated. Although Amour demands submission, he is fatally incapable of giving lovers the assurances they deserve. The distress of the lovers of the *Cent balades* reflects that of the good people of the realm, obediently loving their ruler, Charles VI, who, like Amour, is unable to appease his people's anguish. Poem 95, lamenting the madness of Charles VI, reads France's sorry state as the result of "our sins." Christine's response is to urge restoration of the values of the classical past: poems 93–97, surrounding the Charles poem, exhort the powerful to be less covetous of worldly goods and to demonstrate loyalty, and they mourn Charles's deception by disloyal, duplicitous courtiers, who upset hierarchies for their own gain.

Despite the distress to which it gives voice, the cycle as a whole is a consolation. Christine's suffering narrator goes through several emotional phases, rehearsing and mastering woe under Fortune's regime but always exemplifying the virtue necessary to achieve consolation. When Poem 97 explicitly brings Boethius into the discussion of Fortune, the problems of the kingdom are turned over to Philosophy through the figure of the narrator, who is consoled, along with the court, analogically. For many of the characters of the poems, their troubled private history is the work of Fortune and the unethical courtiers who torment them. But in evoking Boethius, and in the Christian-themed poem 99 especially, Christine suggests that history, both personal and communal, is governed by Providence. Certain apparently futile acts, like loving naturally, have the power to redeem, even though the ultimate significance of what happens on earth is incomprehensible to humans. From her narrative position as a former lover, Christine fully sympathizes with the terrifying uncertainty of her characters. At the same time, however, she is removed, having found consolation.

The message that submission to higher authority is good, even if painful, resounds throughout the cycle, and in delivering this message to a court public involved in a contentious discussion of hierarchy, Christine offers a form of political commentary, all the more pointed given the debate culture animating the royal court. The *Cent balades* are followed in the *Livre de Christine* by several groups of lyric poems in a variety of forms that offer further evidence of Christine's engagement with contemporary issues. For example, Christine dedicates many poems written as New Year's gifts, *étrennes*, to members of the court, among them Charles d'Albret (208–11, 225–26), Isabeau of Bavaria (227–28), Louis of Orleans (228–29), Anne de Montpensier (229–30), and the Seneschal of Hainaut (245–46).[95] She writes three poems praising the seven-on-seven-man combat between Louis's officers and English officers.[96] The political poems and the love poems throughout occupy the same manuscript space, inviting us to let the two cycles gloss each other. Many of the themes of the different cycles will be taken up later and developed in her political allegories: the ship of Fortune sailing without a captain on the open seas, the lying that characterizes court life.

Le livre du debat de deux amans

A series of narrative poems follows the poetic cycles in the *Livre de Christine*, further developing the theme of obligation created by love and encouraging adherence to the principle of hierarchy. The first, the *Debat de deux amans*, invoking Louis of Orleans in the first lines and requesting that he decide the debate, asks whether love awakens a desire that, even when unreciprocated, calls forth the lover's best qualities and should thus be embraced, or whether it only arouses the lover's cupidity and should therefore be quashed. As we have seen, Louis was associated with love verse as a spokesman for fidelity in Jean le Seneschal's *Cent ballades*, and Christine draws on this association here. Requests for judgment seem to have been calculated to confer or acknowledge status; we see similar requests for verdicts on chivalric enterprises, as when Jean de Werchin, in the context of the war with the English, asked Louis to judge a joust between Jean and anyone who wanted to challenge him.[97] To emphasize Louis's qualities as judge, in the first lines of this debate poem Christine highlights his relationship with his father, the "sage roi Charles V": Louis is a "Prince royal, renommé de sagece" (84, line 1).[98]

The poem's setting is a harmonious group, firmly united (86, line 108) and assembled for a festival. The proponent of love in this work is a handsome squire; not only is he beautiful, but his grace is such that he seems to possess a greater store of complete joy than anyone else in the place (88, lines 165–69). As we have seen, Louis's attractive appearance and affability are well attested, as is his defense of faithful love even in the face of envious slanderers in Jean le Seneschal's *Cent ballades*. His detractor is a knight detached from the crowd who assumes the classical gesture of melancholy, resting his head on his left hand. He is not joyous or disorderly, although he isn't ugly or old (89, lines 215–18). The narrator Christine, here in her "former lover" persona, is the only one who notices the knight's pain. She watches him follow a certain young lady with his eyes, trembling. He then asks Christine why she isn't dancing. When the squire appears, laughing, to speak of this and that, the talk turns to whether love brings joy to true lovers (93, lines 359–61). The question is so interesting that they decide to take it outdoors where they can debate it joyfully (93, lines 379–81).

The knight begins, disparaging love as a desire that can never be satisfied (95, line 439); on the contrary, he says, it overwhelms reason (95, lines 447–51). This terrible longing brings no good, even when the lover is loved in return, for when that happens, gossips ruin everything, causing rumors and fights ("murmures et guerres") (97, line 550). The envious steal the lover's sweet goods. Love leads only to jealousy, and it fills a man's heart with the rage to do evil and destroy (98, lines 589–90).

The squire, however, is no victim of love. Rather, he accepts the emotion and becomes a better person for it. Those who die from love should blame their own crazy manner ("fole maniere") (118, line 1378). As for the jealousy that so torments the knight, bad husbands are jealous, not true lovers (116, lines 1294–96). According to the squire, jealousy arises not from love but from cowardice (117, line 1341). When a coward encounters attractive and happy young men, he is troubled because he believes himself to be the ugliest of all (117, lines 1342–50). The squire presents examples to support his case of which Christine is sure to approve: Guesclin (123, lines 1573–74, 1579–80), Boucicaut (123, lines 1586–87), Othon de Grandson, and Hutin de Vermeilles (124, lines 1615–22).

The debate reveals that the knight is a mean and jealous man, both covetous and violent. The squire, by contrast, is wise, eloquent, and loving. A woman brought along to observe the debate speaks out against the knight, doubting that the pain of love of which he complains is really so terrible (106, line 957) and recalling the *Roman de la rose*: she dismisses love, like Reason (the name of the character) in that work, as something that "is worth little and passes quickly" (108, line 967). The knight is indulging in "fole amour" (118, line 1378). The squire, too, deplores this emotion, but he handles love as something that induces virtue.

It has been written of this poem that it concludes that "love is definitely not the ennobling force that callow youth and most preceding poetry would hold it to be," and that this is "no surprise for Christine's readers, who can discern this attitude in many of her poetic works."[99] But why? The knight is the intruder, his speech a dissonant note in the discourse. Love in this poem, as in Christine's others, is a force to which the lover must conform and that entails obligations. Those who expect compensation and refuse to suffer for it, like the knight, are undone by the emotion, while those who act in accordance with what hierarchy demands, like the squire, increase their own virtue. The debate seems to have been envisioned as a hybrid manuscript-performative event of the sort noted above, for Christine sends the same poem to Charles d'Albret along with a New Year's poem, explaining that although the textual lovers had asked that Louis of Orleans judge their case, they also sought the opinion of d'Albret, if he would agree to read or listen to their story (21, lines 231–32).

Epistre au dieu d'amours

Presenting a set of arguments that presuppose an already existing debate over male versus female deception, the narrative poem *Epistre au dieu d'amours* is sometimes considered the first recorded remnant of the *querelle des femmes*. In this brief discussion, I situate this quarrel in the context of court politics. But first I consider how the poem reflects on the disorder at the royal court caused by Charles VI's madness through the figure of Cupid, the helpless god of love. This befuddled Cupid draws on the familiar trope that equates political disorder with the inability to maintain order in one's love life. He claims to be all-powerful and yet has no control over the love relationships of his courtiers. Surely, the one thing that Cupid should be able to do is make his subjects fall in love when and with whom he pleases. But this Cupid admits that he exercises no such control.

As its title suggests, the work takes the form of a letter from Cupid to his loyal servants. The salutation with which the letter begins evokes royal ordinances, which, read aloud, interpellated their public as a group of interested subjects who had solicited the king's help in solving a problem. After its salutation, Cupid's letter continues to follow the format of a royal ordinance, explaining the reason for the ordinance. Cupid claims to be almighty: "The king of lovers, . . . / Who reigns amid the space of radiant skies" (35, lines 2–3).[100] And yet, as we soon discern, he has no control over love at all. He is helpless before all lovers except those who are already loyal. Those who need to be controlled, devious men who assume courtly manners only to dupe women, are beyond his reach. Worse, Cupid cannot even distinguish the genuine from the false, for imitators of love are able to mimic the emotion so accurately that he does not know which are which (39, lines 87–88). Men who ruin their ladies' reputations with lies should be ashamed, but the impotent Cupid can only complain: "So I repeat, that a man too much distorts / His nature who rehearses ugly slurs / Or blames a woman, thus reproaching her" (43, lines 181–83). Later in the letter, he claims sometimes to chastise cheats by making them fall for unworthy women, but the typical outcome is that these men then criticize the women they have seduced (59–61, lines 507–32). Although he offers the positive examples of Hutin de Vermeilles and Othon de Grandson (44–45, 225, 233), he can do no more than note that only the worthy will find these examples moving, while the "mauvais," the bad, will not be interested.

In addition to unchivalrous men, Cupid denounces clerics. The ladies whose complaints he echoes feel themselves much maligned by this group, a closed circle propagating misogynistic literature among its youngest students to turn them against women (47, line 259). Ovid and Jean de Meun, too, are censured, while Cupid offers a series of positive examples of women from classical mythology to counter their misogyny (57, lines 437–66), culminating in a discussion of whether women are deceitful. If the odd woman is cunning, it is only because she is held in the vassalage of a man "filled with spite" (60–61, line 551). The Gospels are free of misogynist slander, presenting women as filled with "great prudence, great good sense, great constancy" (60–61, line 563). A long passage praising the Virgin Mary follows. Women should rejoice that they resemble the Virgin in form, Cupid exhorts, for nothing else (except Jesus Christ) is of "equal dignity." Cupid brings his letter to a close by announcing what should be done to the malfeasants he has just decried: they should be "banished from our court, chased out, brought low, / Banned from all rights and excommunicate" (73, lines 776–77).

Through the figure of this flummoxed god, the poem contemplates the distance between the French vision of the king and the reality of the present king's impotence. The court's center, Cupid/Charles, is no longer able to guarantee the protection of his subjects/institutions. And to return to the issue of the *querelle des femmes*, I propose that Christine's participation is from the very beginning a response to a concrete situation. After laying bare the reasons for the crisis, the poem evokes the Virgin, which seems to be a plea for taking Isabeau of Bavaria seriously as a pivotal figure for the restoration of order. As we have seen, the queen had been associated with the Virgin in her entry into Paris in 1389. Christine, like Gerson in his sermon "Ave Maria gracia plena" of 1397, taps the queen's potential as a unifying force. Cupid's ladies lament that France, once their protector, now dishonors them (34–35, lines 23–27); the conflict between the dukes during this period is reproduced in the letter's structure of a king unable to control a faction bent on destroying a group—in this case, ladies—that it had formerly protected. The period's most persistent problem was the breakdown of unity within the kingdom. A possible solution, hinted at here, is the promotion of a woman, the queen, as a new center.

The *Dit de la rose* and the *Cour amoureuse*

The *Livre de Christine* follows the *Dieu d'amours* with the *Dit de la rose*, a work still more firmly embedded in the *querelle des femmes*, contemporary politics, and, I suggest, the culture of debate. This becomes clear when we read this narrative as a response to the *cour amoureuse*. In January 1400, a charter declaring the foundation of a court to offer "honor, praise, recommendation, and service toward all ladies" was written up and signed.[101] The charter remains in only one manuscript, and evidence about the court is sparse; indeed, although the charter carefully outlines poetic competitions that were to be held regularly, historians do not know whether the festivities ever took place. However, I suggest that we regard the *cour amoureuse* as one of the hybrid performative spaces referred to above, which, in this case, served as a virtual battleground for the dukes. The charter is accompanied by a list of the members' arms, and five more manuscripts contain partial lists of the members' arms. Carla Bozzolo and Hélène Loyau have collated information from all of the manuscripts to offer a complete list of the participants, along with their identifications—approximately 950 in all from 1400 to 1440. Whatever the *cour amoureuse* may have been, it was significant enough that someone took the trouble to keep it up.[102]

Knowing who founded the *cour amoureuse* is central to my argument about Christine's reaction to it. Because the dates and the place of the court's establishment are noted in the charter, we can verify who was in the right place at the right time.[103] The document claims to have been published in Paris at the Hotel d'Artois, one of Philip of Burgundy's city residences, on Saint Valentine's Day in 1400.[104] But the final lines of the document, just before the signatures, specify that the institution was "granted humbly in the royal hall at Mantes," on January 6, 1400. This date is also referred to within the body of the charter, which notes that the excellent and powerful princes, Philip and Louis of Bourbon, requested on January 6, the feast of the Epiphany, that King Charles VI create the *cour amoureuse*.[105] Although the date 1400 is ambiguous because it may be based on the new style of dating (our 1400) or Easter style (our 1401), a set of internal and external factors make it clear that the date of the founding was our 1400.[106] Isabeau was at Mantes on January 6, 1400, and Philip is recorded nearby.[107] The chateau at Mantes seldom received royal visits, the queen's itinerary revealing how infrequently she was there, with only one other visit, in late February and early March 1389.[108] For this reason, the use of the chateau's name in the charter bears the ring of authenticity. None of the other figures having to do with the charter was anywhere near Mantes in January 1401. Two other facts support the 1400 date. The dauphin died on January 11, 1401, after an illness of several months. The week of January 6, 1411, thus seems an unlikely date for such entertainment. Also, the charter notes that an epidemic had caused the gathering. Isabeau was in Mantes in late 1399 and early 1400 precisely to escape the plague, which ravaged Paris in the summer and fall of 1399.

It seems, then, that Isabeau and Philip instigated the charter in January 1400. What was their intent? As we will see in the next chapter, both were political opponents of Louis of Orleans in two disputes: one over the struggle between Giangaleazzo Visconti of Milan and the Florentines, and the other over the Holy Roman Emperor, which was heating up at precisely that moment.[109] Although the list of members in its charter shows that the *cour amoureuse* was a predominantly although not exclusively Burgundian group, the hierarchy of officers named both attests to this Burgundian tone and reveals the institution's purpose.[110] The *grands conservateurs* of the court are noted as Charles VI, Philip of Burgundy, and Louis of Bourbon.[111] Isabeau's brother, Louis Duke of Bavaria, and Philip's son, Jean, head the list of eleven *conservateurs*, followed by Louis of Orleans. This violation of rank is an act of literary aggression by Philip, who placed himself alongside the king while relegating Louis to a position behind Isabeau's brother and his own son. Furthermore, the charter specifies that on the chimney in this chamber, the Duke of Burgundy's arms will hang next to those of the king's, with the Duke of Bourbon's to the left: the arms of the Duke of Orleans are not mentioned.[112]

Still, what was Isabeau's interest? Her accounts record her purchase in January 1399 of a book titled *Cent balades*. Although this book has sometimes been identified as the ballads of Othon de Grandson, it has been more convincingly identified as the *Cent ballades* of Jean le Seneschal.[113] As we have seen, this poetic cycle debates the question of whether a young man should be promiscuous or faithful in love, with Louis of Orleans as one of the contestants arguing for *loyauté* as opposed to *fausseté*.[114] Thus Isabeau would have been aware of Louis's reputation as a supporter of loyalty in this literary love debate when she helped to found the *cour amoureuse*, and she may have thought it amusing to offer him such a lowly spot in her own poetic hierarchy. As for her role in the *cour amoureuse*, although the poetic competitions were to be limited to men, women would serve as judges.[115] A rhymed Burgundian pastoral narrative known as the *Pastoralet* (1422), which uses allegory to justify Jean of Burgundy's assassination of Louis, depicts a shepherdess explicitly said to represent Isabeau in the act of judging a poetic contest between, among others, the characters said to represent Louis and Jean. Although this is not proof that Isabeau actually judged poetic competitions, it suggests a perceived link between the queen and political and poetic competitions. Although Isabeau had not yet been named mediator between the dukes when the *cour amoureuse* was established, as she would be in 1402, she seems to have been viewed as a force for peace, as I have noted. The *cour amoureuse*, then, allying verse, politics, and arbitration, would have enhanced her political authority to arbitrate. Like the competitors, she would have gained symbolic capital as a judge.

In the same way that poets responded to one another in the debates that Cayley has analyzed, I believe that Christine responded to Louis's demotion in the charter of the *cour amoureuse* by putting him at the center of the *Dit de la rose*, which she presented to him in February 1402, around the time that Tignonville would have returned from Milan.[116] This narrative poem dramatizes the goddess Loyalty, sent as a messenger by the god of love on a visit to a gathering at the hotel of the Duke of Orleans. The poem's female narrator explains that on the evening of Loyalty's visit, she had been with a group of like-minded friends dining together, doors tightly closed, with no *estrangiers* in their midst (94, line 67). Her description is a reference to court factionalism: the friends are Orleanists, the absent *estrangiers*, Burgundians. The goddess Loyalty, whose luminosity sets the room aglow, recalls the reference, as we have noted, to Louis, and to that virtue in the charter of the *cour amoureuse*, where the Prince of the *puy* explains that "the glorious virtue of humility and the constant virtue of loyalty shine clearly in all lands in which Christian faith rules and dominates, and thus divine providence nourishes in many pleasant ways all who embellish and adorn the understanding of their hearts with these two happy virtues."[117]

Loyalty enters Louis's hotel to discover a joyous group of people entertaining themselves in poetic competition, speaking of "honor and of courtesy," each vying "to write the best he could" (95, lines 68–75). This poetic contest, coupled with the feast that the guests are enjoying, echoes the competitions outlined in the charter of the *cour amoureuse*. Loyalty offers the crowd vases filled with fresh roses of vermilion and white. But anyone wishing to accept the gift must first pledge to treat ladies well:

> To keep each lady's reputation clear
> Forevermore, in every way I know,
> And to be sure no woman's name is smeared;
> And thus I take the Order of the Rose.
> (103, lines 197–204)

Loyalty then offers the willing, along with the roses, rolled-up copies of the *balade* that she has just recited. As we have seen, the *cour amoureuse* is dedicated to honoring women.[118] The Order of the Rose represents a counterpart.

Before departing, Loyalty offers the narrator a white bed in which to spend the night. But the goddess has not finished, for she later reappears to the narrator in the form of a glowing cloud and a charming voice, explaining that she has something to add to the message from the god of love. The god is troubled by envious slander at court, and he would like to see an end to this custom, which is "evil, ugly, low / And vulgar" (109, lines 319–20). Physical strength is of no value if not accompanied by inner goodness, "goodness coming from the soul" (110, line 359). Although the god of love strongly deplores slander against women, he departs from the *cour amoureuse* charter in condemning slander against men as well: motivated by envy, slander "dishonors more women than ever before but many worthy men as well" (112, lines 408–11).

Loyalty then comes to the point of her visit. She would like virtuous ladies, starting with the narrator, to whom she hands a bull, to spread the god of love's message throughout the world. This message can only be a reproach to the slandering Burgundians. Although their notorious propaganda machine would become all the more effective under Jean of Burgundy, Philip was already an adept, as we will see. The *Dit de la rose* urges a return to proper order by agreeing with the charter of the *cour amoureuse* that ladies must be honored, but it insists that slander against men must also stop. The *Dit de la rose* reveals further information about Christine's assessment of the combative situation at court. Unlike the charter of the *cour amoureuse*, which gives Charles VI a central spot between the dukes of Burgundy and Bourbon, the *Dit de la rose* depicts an absent authority figure who must rely on a female messenger to convey his wishes. The distressed god of love is as powerless as Charles VI to maintain control of his court. Like Isabeau, Loyalty has been assigned to bring accord to the warring factions. In contrast to the *cour amoureuse*, the charter of which associates it with the Burgundian faction, the *Dit de la rose* represents an opening to the world. True, the story originates in the hotel of the Duke of Orleans, but Loyalty's message is intended for wide diffusion. Its purpose, therefore, is precisely the opposite of that of the *cour amoureuse*. It is difficult to judge the tone of the work from our distance. Was it meant as a playful rejoinder to the *cour amoureuse*? Maybe. But the message is serious. Christine understands that faction and stigma lead to violence.

That the *Dit de la rose* was associated especially closely with the Duke of Orleans is indicated by its still visible excision from BnF, fonds français 835, one of the four parts that once made up what is today known as the Duke's Manuscript.[119] Intended for Louis, this manuscript was purchased after his assassination by Jean of Berry. The *Dit de la rose* was to follow the *Debat de deux amans*, also associated with Louis, as we have seen. And yet this work was allowed to stay while the *Dit de la rose* is absent: as part of a courtly debate, Christine may have feared that it was too controversial to include. Indeed, Philip appears to have responded to the *Dit de la rose* by ratcheting the menace up a notch. He gathered sixty men together to create a new order of his own, the Order of the Golden Tree, on January 1, 1403, presenting them with clasps (*fermaux*) adorned with a golden tree standing between a white enamel eagle and lion, with the words "en loyauté" spelled out in red enamel across the bottom of each *fermail*.[120]

Le livre des trois jugemens

The three cases that the narrator presents to Jean de Werchin for adjudication in the *Trois jugemens* reproduce many of the same concerns that animated the *Debat de deux amans*, particularly the problem of love and how to react to it ethically. In the first case, the central question is which of the several social bonds that two lovers create has priority. The story begins with a young man who pretends to be madly in love with a young woman and uses the typical arguments to woo her: "Before she loved him he suffered, / This he said and that he would rather die / Than endure any more" (156, lines 42–44).[121] Taken in, she responds positively. Her response is explained as inevitable: no one can resist Amour when she (Amour is a grammatically feminine noun in medieval French) lights the fire. The two promise loyalty to each other (160, line 198). But then the young man makes himself scarce. When the young woman confronts him, he replies that he is only thinking of her reputation, blaming his absence on the *médisans* at work (162, lines 297–302). In her loneliness, she accepts the advances of another loyal young man, and for a time their relationship goes smoothly. The omnipresent *médisans* reappear (167, lines 511–12), and, motivated by envy (168, line 520), they tell the first young man about his replacement. The first young man scolds the young woman as false (169, lines 559–60). But she scorns his reiterated declaration that his neglect was motivated by concern for her honor. The story raises the thorny issue of loyalty in a society where rumor could not be verified easily. First, how does one test whether betrayal has actually occurred? Second, does one remain faithful after betrayal is proved? And, finally, if one allies with another, to whom does one owe primary allegiance? The lady demands that they take the case before a judge.

The second case also takes on the tricky question of "natural love" and how to identify it. The story depicts an interfering husband, who, after confronting his wife's presumed lover, is assured by the young man that nothing has happened: it was just a conversation. The lady's honor is saved (175, lines 805–7). But the husband is not convinced, and his constant surveillance means that the lover must keep his distance. The lover remains faithful for a while, but he eventually forgets the lady, meets another, and stops sending messages to the first (182–83, lines 1117–19). Of course, he denies any misdeed to the first lady; after all, he could not see her at all for fear of *médisans*. Moreover, it wasn't right for him to shut himself off from love, because "without love no young heart could receive any joy" (185, lines 1199–200). Her response is to ask for a judge.

The third case asks that the judge decide whether a knight guilty of treachery and "fole amour" should be welcomed back if he repents. Initially, the knight promises to love his lady forever; she is "young of age, a simple maiden, pretty and sweet" (187, lines 1279–80). But nothing on earth lasts (187, lines 1298–301). As the narrator notes, "fole amour" is mere wind (187, line 1309). Eventually, the knight decides that he is too good for the lady and looks elsewhere (188, lines 1325–26), approaching a powerful lady to whom he promises his heart (188, lines 1331–32). However, he quickly recognizes that she thinks she is too good for him (190, lines 1408–10). Chastened, he tries to return to the lowlier but worthier lady. But she does not accept his sincere repentance as sufficient cause to take him back (191, lines 1452–53). She insists on a female judge and tries to recruit the narrator. However, Christine refuses, deferring to the judge.

In these cases, the givens are more complicated than any we have seen previously in Christine's work, and the correct response is not at all clear. Embedded in society, the lovers in the stories have concerns beyond the relatively simple situation of the squire of the *Debat de deux amans*, whose problem is principally his own inner peace. As the tension at court grows, questions of loyalty become more complex. The problems raised by the individual cases—rumors, conflicting loyalties, obligations when one has been treated badly, treachery, and repentance—are all as familiar to political actors as to lovers. The question has moved beyond whether one should submit to the compulsion to love when called upon to do so. The narrative now admits that the ethical situation is complicated because of the external mitigating factors that must enter into the calculation.

Le livre du dit de Poissy

With its central image of a terrestrial paradise inhabited by nuns whose delectable outer forms unproblematically reflect their goodness, the *Dit de Poissy* also ruminates on the reality of the dukes' dispute and imagines an ideal solution. This work, too, features a love debate, between a young woman whose lover died in Nicopolis and a man who has been betrayed in love. Who has the greater claim to sorrow? But the more important aspect of the narrative, I believe, lies in its depiction of the gorgeous royal convent of Poissy, which is stocked with lovely, young, white, peaceful religious women, enclosed between the story of the trip to Poissy and the love debate. Once again, Christine serves as the intermediary between the debaters and the judge; the narrative begins as a request to a valiant knight to judge a love debate. Why, then, the long description of Poissy?

The narrative discusses "weighty" issues in love verse, mixing delight and gravity. The opening verses evoke the images typical of the amorous lyric. Christine, explaining that she has decided to visit her daughter, a nun, at Poissy, sets off with "many handsome squires / Who came along with me out of the goodness of their hearts / For amusement, not for any other recompense" (207, lines 57–59). Their trip takes them through a sweet and beautiful landscape, where a gentle wind blows and flowers bloom. Thinking about the wind, she realizes that it is the work of Amour (210, line 163). But the narrative is also an early version of the *Cité des dames*, featuring a society of women that functions implicitly to criticize masculine society. The royal convent of Poissy, birthplace of Saint Louis, is a well-ordered space, abundant in natural love, as evidenced by the lack of strife. Run by women, it is a reversal of the male-dominated royal court, with its jealousies. The beautiful nuns are exactly as virtuous as they seem and far beyond the reach of rumors. After Mass, the visitors meet with the prioress, Marie of Bourbon, and the king's daughter, Marie of Valois. As they chat, Christine comments on how pleased they all were to see the "beautiful royal estate within" (213, line 298), noting that all of the inhabitants are ladies ("toutes dames") (line 299), because no man ever enters to serve them, nor do they ever speak to a man unless he is a parent or someone brought by a parent. This ensures the continued purity and legibility of the female bodies. Their fabulous outer trappings reflect the true beauty of austerity, just as the "beautiful clothes of Arras" covering their beds (213, line 317) conceal not indulgence and luxury but the hard canvas bedding appropriate to a nun (214, lines 318–19). We also learn that the ladies sleep fully clothed. They serve a rich lunch to their guests but do not partake. Negotiations with the outside world take place through intermediaries. Thus they are both rich and austerely pure, self-sufficient and under the care of the king, who paradoxically guarantees their freedom by allowing them to remain enclosed; they are at once earthly and heavenly creatures.

A new version of love appears in this section of the poem: maternal love. When they enter through the large gates, Christine discovers her beloved daughter, who approaches her humbly and kneels. Christine kisses her sweet and tender face (211, lines 223–24). When the time comes to go, Christine weeps as they say goodbye (223, lines 701–4). Responding to the demands of this love causes pain, but Christine leaves her daughter in a sort of heaven. The diffuse symbols associated with romantic love on the trip to the convent and the sexualized but sexless love of the convent create, together with Christine's maternal love, a fantasy of plenitude, a magical solution to the problems of life on earth, with its unending losses and rivalries.

The love debate that takes place the next day must be read in the context of the convent's otherworldly aura. After an evening of dance and a night spent at a hostel, the group heads back to Paris. En route, Christine sees a lady who seems so distressed that a squire attempts to get her to tell her story. She agrees on the condition that he tell her the source of his woe. In this exchange of grief that is in fact a contest—whose story is the more heartbreaking?—we learn that the lady's lover was taken prisoner at Nicopolis. The squire is sad about his rejection by a lady who had loved him for a time. Whereas earlier debates pitted the combatants against each other, meaning that one would win and one would lose, this debate is an exchange of stories between equals. Both the lady and the squire offer long, detailed portraits of their lost loves; the typical portrait of the idealized lady is balanced by that of an idealized knight. These perfect bodies serve as idealized representations of society, a double "body politic," where women and men, though they suffer as individuals, live in harmony. Christine is appealed to for justice, and although she defers to her patron, she quickly sets to work to write the case down.

Conclusion

Christine's culture viewed the human being as a microcosm of the universal macrocosm. The four humors as a basis for medicine, and astrology as a basis for military decisions, for example, depend on this fundamental structure of the human body and the events on earth as part of a cosmic system of influences. Similarly, the relationships between lovers, between lord and subjects, and between God and humankind reflected and reinforced one another, the highest not only serving as an analogy for the lowest but also concretely affecting it. The love between humans was a version of divine love; the order of the king's household participated in the order of the kingdom; the king's madness was a literal reflection of the disordered relationships among his subjects. Thus when Christine wrote about the love between men and women, she was also commenting on the state of the kingdom. If the order of the love poems in the *Livre de Christine* reflects the order in which they were composed, the questions about love, and therefore the state of court society posed within, become progressively more complicated until the *Dit de Poissy*, when they are relegated to the realm of fantasy for resolution. The *Dieu d'amours* puts Cupid, however incompetent, at the center of the action. In the *Dit de la rose*, however, he has vanished entirely and speaks only through the goddess Loyalty: the relationship between the dukes begins to require increasing intervention, and Charles VI's ability to mediate wanes. In describing sincerely if effusively loving characters and in commenting on the evil of slander and the moral necessity of speaking well of women, Christine strives to create a poetic community united by warm feeling toward the Duke of Orleans. Certainly, much in her verse is conventional. However, as Jenny Nuttall has written, the presence of conventions should not blind us to how "certain very familiar elements of language" take on "a contemporary synchronic significance of one kind or another, a connection to a particular event or argument or person."[122]

But Christine's verse reveals the contradictions inherent in her beliefs about kingship. I have been arguing that many of her love works manifest her society's anxiety over the absence at the center of things through the figure of the impotent god of love. In other poetry of the period, "at the summit of the hierarchy of ideas and emotions, at the center of the allegorical court, we always sense the power of a god reigning like a prince: Amour."[123] For Christine, however, the god of love is either benighted or silent. When he is silent, as in the *Dieu d'amours* and the *Dit de la rose*, the fault lies with the deceitful individuals who appropriate his work by masquerading as lovers so that he cannot reward his faithful followers. When he is not there, his absence is sig-naled by the lovers' uncertainty about whether they have been betrayed. This is the case in the *Cent balades*. Christine promoted adherence to hierarchy as a means of reordering her dangerously disordered society. And yet, in praising French obedience as evidence of France's supreme virtue, of its "natural" love for the French king, Christine reveals this peculiarly French virtue as the source of suffering, reproducing an ideology of kingship requiring that even an insane king remain on the throne, and, perhaps more important, that the insanity be handled as an open secret. Although all of Europe was aware of the problem, the French treated the king as if he were merely ill, capable from time to time of resuming his office. Chroniclers refer discreetly to his "absences," as the king himself does in his ordinances. Unable to admit that a permanent regent was necessary and allow the designation of one who would enjoy unambiguous authority, this ideology spawned a competition for the office, with each competitor masking what he was in fact trying to do, which was to control the government. But Christine does not see this. Rather, she encourages her readers to undertake the "symbolic violence" that she works upon herself in bowing to authority even when to do so is against their interests. Her blaming the social unrest on individual envy and backbiting while encouraging individual virtue must be "grasped as the imaginary reso-lution of a real contradiction."[124] The solution that she offered was no solu-tion at all.

3

THE POINT OF NO RETURN AND THE
POLITICAL ALLEGORIES, 1401–1404

By 1401, Philip of Burgundy and Louis of Orleans were opposed on every issue of the day.[1] First, England. The Truce of Paris, sealed by the marriage between King Richard II of England and the seven-year-old French royal princess Isabelle in 1396, initiated a quiet period, which was broken in 1399 when the Lancastrians deposed and incarcerated Richard II in favor of Henry IV.[2] The French were obliged to aid the king's son-in-law. Although Henry IV dispatched messengers to France to smooth relations, they were denied safe passage and a herald was taken into custody. However, when news came that Richard II had died mysteriously, the French did not invade England; the king was beyond help, and an invasion would only further menace the little queen. Instead, negotiations undertaken in June 1400 persuaded the French that the truce of 1396 still applied, because it had been an agreement between the kingdoms, not individual kings.[3] Although forced in this way to recognize Henry IV, the French did not acknowledge him, and, anxious for the safety of Isabelle, they "unofficially" encouraged privateers to harry English ships. The English retaliated. The "opening years of the fifteenth century," Christopher Phillpotts observes, "witnessed an outburst of lawlessness at sea of such intensity that legitimate commerce between the kingdoms of France and England, and their allies, all but ceased."[4]

This unrest was catastrophic for Philip, whose Flemish territories depended on trade with the English to prosper. Louis, by contrast, assumed the role of defender of his family's reputation. The insult perpetrated by Henry IV on the French royal family—their daughter demoted from queen and then held in captivity for more than a year—was unacceptable. In addition to inciting privateers to attack the English in France and England, Louis personally issued several challenges to Henry IV beginning in the summer of 1402.[5] In his righteous anger, Louis was in tune with many of the French, whose hatred of the English was implacable, according to Pintoin.[6]

Another source of conflict was the continuing Great Schism.[7] Friction between the king and the university had existed under Charles V, the university being reluctant to recognize the Avignon pope Clement VII. Shortly after Charles V's death, Louis of Anjou had quashed university dissent, tossing Pierre d'Ailly into prison for calling for a council to resolve the Schism.[8] When Clement VII died in 1394, Charles VI hoped that the problem would resolve itself, assuming that the lone pope, Boniface IX, elected in 1389, would now cede his chair, allowing a new election. Not only did this fail to happen, but the Avignon cardinals quickly elected Benedict XIII. Benedict pretended at first to be amenable to ceding the papacy, but he reneged once in office. The French thus withdrew their obedience from the new pope at the third Paris Council in May 1398, instigated by the University of Paris and supported strongly by Philip of Burgundy and Jean of Berry. Their hope was that Benedict finally would cede, with Boniface close behind, and that the election of a new pope whom all could support would follow. Their withdrawal of obedience did not yield this result: although nineteen of twenty-four cardinals abandoned Benedict and the Avignonnais rose up against him, he clung to power, shutting himself up in the papal palace. To break his will, a siege led by Geoffrey Boucicaut was undertaken.

Although the Schism was a source of anguish and confusion for the faithful, early Valois support (and its later withdrawal of support) for the Avignon pope was determined by the immediate political goals of the various members of the royal family and, crucially, by who wielded control at a given moment. Howard Kaminsky has described the Schism as "a political construction created by certain interests; it was kept going while it served those interests, and it was ended when it stopped doing so."[9] Noël Valois discusses the royal uncles' overwhelming and badly dissimulated political take on the Schism. Undoubtedly, they retained some vague notion that Benedict was a perjurer for going back on his promise to abdicate. But their language reveals their primary motivation in pushing for the withdrawal of obedience: money. With obedience withdrawn, the king became head of the church in France, meaning that *aides* formerly collected by the pope would go to the royal treasury, where the uncles had access to them.[10] It is difficult to understand why some modern historians have singled out Louis's position as blatantly political; Françoise Autrand, for example, writes, "Louis of Orléans remained a staunch adherent of the Avignon pope, while the Duke of Burgundy supported attempts to bring the Schism to an end."[11] In fact, Louis, along with theologians Jean Gerson and Nicolas de Clamanges, believed that the effort to so demoralize the pope through the subtraction of obedience that he would abdicate was doomed to fail. Gerson detailed his objections to the withdrawal of obedience in *De subtractione schismatis,* arguing that it made no sense to subtract obedience from one pope when the other's intentions were not clear.[12] To do so risked creating a rift that could never be mended because one side necessarily would be declared heretical. These were Louis's arguments as well.[13]

Still another source of disagreement, the question of which candidate for Holy Roman Emperor to support, was directly responsible for the near resort to arms in December 1401. Wenceslas of Luxembourg was deposed in 1400 by a bare majority of the German electors in favor of Robert (or Rupert) of Bavaria, a member of the House of Wittelsbach, with Louis supporting Wenceslas and Philip supporting Robert. The general complaint against Wenceslas on the part of the Germans was that he had not done enough to maintain peace in the empire: preoccupied with fighting in his Bohemian kingdom, he rarely ventured out.[14] More specifically, he was deplored for failing to prevent the French overlordship of Genoa and for legitimating the conquests of Giangaleazzo Visconti by making him Duke of Milan in 1395 for a hundred thousand gulden, then Duke of Lombardy in 1397, without the electors' approval. The Germans regarded Giangaleazzo with anxiety; he had taken over Verona, Vicenza, Padua, and Siena, and was working on Florence as well.[15] But it was Wenceslas's actions regarding the Schism that brought matters to a head. At a conference in Rheims in 1398, Wenceslas had agreed to pressure Boniface IX to abdicate while the French negotiated with Benedict XIII. Before Wenceslas set off for that conference, Robert of Bavaria warned him that if he agreed to subtract obedience from Boniface, the electors would depose him. Nonetheless, the French, that is, Louis of Orleans, persuaded the emperor to their side.

Wenceslas was indeed deposed at the Diet of Rhens in August 1400 in favor of Robert. But the newly elected Robert also lacked solid backing in the empire, which he attempted to remedy by traveling through Europe in search of material support. Although the Florentines were happy to welcome him as a protector against Giangaleazzo, they were no match for the Milanese. After Giangaleazzo's men inflicted a crushing defeat on Robert's army in Brescia on

October 24, 1401, support for the new emperor dried up. Even Boniface refused aid, still worried that Wenceslas might return to power. In April 1402, Robert returned to Germany.

Isabeau, a kinswoman of the Wittelsbacher Robert, promoted his cause. On September 3, 1400, her father, Stephen of Bavaria, arrived in Paris, seeking backing for the new emperor; when he returned to Bavaria in February 1401, he announced that Isabeau and Philip would procure aid if Robert attacked Giangaleazzo.[16] Robert, aware of the importance of Isabeau's approval, communicated frequently with her. Several letters to the queen and instructions to the ambassadors who were to approach her, including her own brother, Louis of Bavaria, reveal her intimate involvement with pushing Robert's case.[17] In May 1401, Robert's secretary, Albert, arrived in Paris charged with enlisting Isabeau and Philip to detach Amadeus VIII of Savoy from Wenceslas.[18] The cooperation of Amadeus, set to arrive in Paris later in the month, was essential to Robert, whose troops needed to cross Savoy on their way to Lombardy.[19] At the same time, Robert hoped to block a marriage between the dauphin and the newborn daughter of Louis of Orleans, suggesting Marguerite, Jean of Burgundy's daughter, instead.[20]

Throughout the spring and summer of 1401, Louis of Orleans appears to have been unaware of the dealings with Robert. Indeed, Philip and Isabeau took care to keep their negotiations secret even while the three spent much time in close physical proximity, eating together and meeting when they were in Paris.[21] The queen sent letters to both the Duke and the Duchess of Orleans throughout the period.[22] She also hosted a celebration at her Hotel Barbettte for Louis, when he returned in triumph from the eastern reaches of the kingdom, with one of Robert of Bavaria's vassals, the Duke of Guelders.[23] Louis had persuaded the Duke of Guelders to render homage to the French king, a boon for France that Charles VI rewarded by presenting Louis with the county of Dreux, but a slap in the face to Philip.[24] For decades, the Duke of Guelders had been harassing Brabant, a fief of the empire that Wenceslas claimed should revert to him upon the death of its duchess, Jeanne, but which Jeanne had promised to Philip.[25]

The intriguing threatened to become dangerous in June. Two embassies from Robert arrived in Paris, the first proposing to marry the emperor's youngest son to a royal princess and the second asking for an alliance with Isabeau, the dukes of Berry and Burgundy, and the counts of Savoy and Armagnac against the Duke of Orleans and Giangaleazzo Visconti.[26] If such an alliance were created, Robert promised, he would observe strict neutrality between the French and English.[27] The king was mad at the time. Philip seems to have realized what would happen if Louis discovered what he and the queen were trying to negotiate on the king's behalf, because he decamped on June 14. After a last meeting with the other princes in his hotel at Conflans, just outside Paris, he left for Artois, where he could deal with Robert without worry of arousing Louis's ire.[28]

On July 31, 1401, the little ex-queen of England finally arrived home in France. Philip, already in the north, met her in Boulogne. On August 5, Robert made more specific his proposal of a marriage between his son and a royal princess, asking for the newly arrived Isabelle. Charles VI did not reply to the request, inclined to Louis's foreign policy, as he always was when he was able to speak.[29] As mentioned in chapter 1, on August 14 he sent Boucicaut and Guillaume de Tignonville, recently appointed *prévôt* of Paris by Louis, as ambassadors to Milan. The ambassadors' instructions on how to approach Giangaleazzo reveal the king's and Louis's ignorance of the queen and Philip's dealings with Robert: whereas the queen and Philip had just promised to negotiate a deal to marry a royal princess to Robert's son, the king instructed Boucicaut and Tignonville to offer one of his daughters in marriage to a son of Giangaleazzo if the duke agreed to help end the Schism by withdrawing obedience from Boniface, as Charles VI had done from Benedict.

However, Louis discovered what was afoot. It appears that in September Philip promised aid to Robert against Giangaleazzo. Shortly after ambassadors sent by the Duke of Burgundy reached Robert, the emperor challenged Giangaleazzo and set out for Lombardy. It is not clear precisely how or when Louis discovered this secret promise of support. Jarry, his biographer, hypothesizes that one of Valentina's ladies, Catherine Angoussole, wife of Renier Pot, formerly Louis's *chambellan* but in 1401 in the service of the Duke of Burgundy, discovered the truth from her husband and told Valentina.[30] Philip became the enemy at court, the king furious that he had encouraged Robert to move against Giangaleazzo.[31] The battle lines were drawn. Louis refused to appear at a convocation scheduled for October 22–26, 1401, in Senlis to discuss the Schism.[32] As Françoise Lehoux explains, the reason for his abstention was that a number of important issues, including whether the pope would be forced to heed the decision, were left unresolved. But, Lehoux continues, this was only one motive: relations were so bad between the dukes that Louis would not sit beside his uncle.[33]

On October 26, Philip, in Flanders to help prepare the wedding of his son Antoine, tried to restore his good name by making Louis look bad. He sent a letter to be read before the Parlement de Paris in which he explained that the king had summoned him to Paris. However, the king was indisposed, he continued, and, in any case, he, Philip, was occupied, although he had gone as far as Senlis. He then explained that he had heard that the kingdom was being governed badly. It was a great pity to learn of this, he wrote, and he could hardly believe that things were in such a state. He would do his best as soon as possible to right things.[34] The Parlement responded evasively, assuring Philip that they would continue to watch over the realm.

What brought the situation to a head is not clear, but on December 1, 1401, Philip departed Arras, entering Paris on December 7 with six hundred combatants, arms covered, and sixty archers from Burgundy, Artois, and Flanders.[35] The Parisians were stunned at this show of force, which was clearly intended to intimidate the Duke of Orleans. Louis assembled his own troops to surround Paris. And yet the queen, aided by the dukes of Anjou, Berry, and Bourbon, prevented bloodshed, bringing the two princes together in a public reconciliation in January. The document recording the reconciliation is written in her voice. She calls the dukes of Burgundy and Orleans to her side: "We, the queen, call you to ourselves." Before the other princes of the blood, she asks them to state aloud whether they are reconciled. Taking each by his right hand, she asks them to swear to uphold their agreement.[36] Afterward, the accord was sealed with a dinner. Although this is the first recorded act of mediation by the queen, she appears to have had experience at the task, having been called upon for this purpose earlier.[37]

Isabeau's mediation averted that danger, but strife erupted over the Schism in March. The subtraction of obedience having failed to bring an end to the unhappy situation, pressure to try a different approach grew.[38] Although the University of Paris remained convinced of the wisdom of subtraction, others, including the University of Toulouse, agitated for the restitution of obedience, and on February 26, 1402, the University of Orleans also declared that it would restore obedience.[39] On July 7, the University of Angers followed suit. On August 30, Duke Louis II of Anjou declared his support for Benedict XIII, upon whom he relied for his own claim to Naples; the pope would find refuge in the Duke of Anjou's provençal territories when he escaped from Avignon in 1403.[40]

If the growing dissension proved Louis of Orleans right about the futility of subtraction, it only fueled tensions between the dukes and led to Isabeau's first official appointment as mediator. The king had assigned the task of guarding the beleaguered Benedict XIII to his brother while charging the Duke of

Berry, who had strongly favored subtraction, with watching over the College of Cardinals. But violence between the two sets of guardians and also among the Avignonnais intensified the bad blood between the dukes. On March 16, Charles VI attempted to mitigate the situation in a royal ordinance giving the queen the power to mediate in matters concerning the papal guardians.[41] To control the fighting in Avignon, the document explains, the king will send two knights, who "favoring neither one party nor the other will guarantee the safety of the said Benedict and the people and familiars living with him and in his company, as well as the said college of cardinals and the said town of Avignon and its inhabitants, and prevent any violence or oppression and distribute food and necessities to the said Benedict and his people and familiars living with him."[42] Furthermore, rather than proceed by force of arms ("voie de faits"), the dukes were to come before the king to have their differences resolved, and, during the king's absences, the queen.[43]

Discord between the dukes related to French hostilities against England broke out in April, leading to another royal ordinance naming Isabeau mediator. Throughout 1402 Louis issued challenges to Henry IV, menacing the fragile truce, and in May seven of his officers met seven English officers in combat in Gascony, winning glory for themselves along with a gift of one thousand francs apiece from Charles VI.[44] Around the same time, Louis levied a tax to fund an army to go into Aquitaine, which he was able to do because on April 28, while Philip was absent from Paris, the king had given Louis authority to collect war taxes in the northern part of France. A group of three governors, headed by Charles d'Albret, was already charged with assessing *aides* in this region.[45] Louis, as "souverain gouverneur," was placed at their head, increasing the prestige of the group, as Jarry points out, and presumably its legitimacy. When Philip discovered this appointment, he was furious, sending his council and a secretary to the Parlement de Paris to request that a letter objecting to the recent tax be read in front of the body. Presumably recognizing that the move was intended to inflame the population, the Parlement refused the request. Letters were then distributed to be read before the public at Châtelet, the *chambre des comptes*, and the merchants and towns of the realm. All of this bolstered Philip's image as a man of the people.[46] However, as Nicolas de Baye, *greffier* for the Parlement, recorded in a marginal note, Philip only objected to the tax because it was ordered by Louis.[47] The king attempted to appease Philip by appointing him to serve with Louis as the "souverain gouverneur," but this only further incited the rivalry. Baye reports that a small group of the Duke of Burgundy's men appeared to request the publication of the royal letter "by which the king made and ordained Monsei-gneur the Duke of Burgundy 'souvereain gouverneur des aides' and that also said that without him, the Duke of Burgundy, nothing could be done con-cerning the said finances . . . notwithstanding the letters given before to Mon-seigneur, the Duke of Orleans, the king's brother." In the margin, Baye cites Lucan's *Pharsalia*: "Nulla fides regni sociis, omnisque potestas impaciens con-sortis erit" (There is no trust between associates in power; all power will be impatient of an associate).[48] In light of this activity, an ordinance of July 1, 1402, reiterates Isabeau's role as mediator, explaining that the trouble this time relates to finances. In addition, the ordinance assigns her guardianship of the government during the king's absences: "She will handle both the appeasing of our Uncle of Burgundy and our brother of Orleans and the management of finances and other difficulties of the realm, until we can take care of them ourselves."[49]

The conflict can be further traced through a royal ordinance of April 26, 1403, in effect withdrawing the powers of *administracion* of the realm the king had assigned to Louis in 1393 in the case of a minority kingship (discussed in chapter 1). If the king dies leaving a minor heir, the ordinance states, the kingdom will have no regent at all. Rather, the new king will succeed imme-diately, "without anyone else, no matter how closely related, taking over the care, regency or government of our kingdom, and without any obstacle being put before our oldest son in the natural right that is due to him, through regency or government of our kingdom or for any reason whatsoever."[50] Until the new king attained the age at which he could govern in his own person, all deliberations and conclusions would be carried out by the queen, the princes of the blood, and the Royal Council.

This ordinance created a potentially powerful role for the queen mother as acting regent or co-regent. Historians have long disagreed over who instigated the change. However, the change is an exact repeat of that wrought by Philip just after the death of Charles V, when he forced Louis of Anjou from the regency and established a ruling council. Thus it seems clear that he was behind the ordinance. But Louis successfully fought this change, for in a let-ter patent of May 7, 1403, the king acknowledges that certain recent ordi-nances may have been damaging to his brother and that any portion of these recent ordinances that deprived Louis of his power was to be ignored.[51] The ordinance was not reinstated until immediately after Louis's assassination in 1407, and until his assassination, chroniclers continued to see the Duke of Orleans as the head of the government. Still, the ordinance would have far-reaching repercussions, as we will see. Naming the queen the head of a college that would rule without a regent, it suggests that Isabeau would make a safer co-regent than any ambitious male relative, a premise that would undergird Christine's vision and that of future female regencies.

In another success for Louis, on May 28, 1403, Charles VI, realizing that the subtraction had no chance of resolving the Schism, restored obedience to the Avignon pope. As we have seen, Benedict XIII had been holed up in the papal palace, and he remained there for five years, until 1403, when, with Louis's help, he escaped to the safety of Chateau Renard, just a few miles from Avignon but securely in the territory of Louis of Anjou.[52] A Strasbourger called Becherer living in Paris wrote a letter on June 10 describing the restoration and opining that Louis's next move, if the Germans refused to work to solve the Schism, would be to invade Rome with Milanese help, depose the Roman pope, and install Benedict XIII on the throne. In return, the pope would crown Louis Holy Roman Emperor. It is not clear whether Louis was seriously after that position; a tradition of campaigning by brothers of the French king and some French kings themselves existed, so the idea is plausible.[53]

When Giangaleazzo Visconti died, in October 1402, Louis decided to cross the Alps with an army, hoping to aid his struggling widow against the enemies who quickly appeared. He set off in October 1403, not to return until February 1404.[54] In the meantime, the war with the English was under way; on January 30, 1404, with Louis in Lyon, the king imposed a tax to which Philip agreed, the royal treasury being empty of funds to pay soldiers.[55] But while in Brabant, where he had finally secured the duchy for his son Antoine, Philip fell ill with the plague. He died on April 2, 1404.[56]

Had the Duke of Orleans remained incapable of holding his own against Philip, the factionalism that led to the feud would have caused little disruption. However, as the second in line to the throne after the dauphin and armed with a royal ordinance appointing him regent, Louis made an effort to acquire territories to spread his influence as a counter to Philip's. The large appanages that Charles V gave to his brothers meant that most of France was already attributed by Louis's time. But if Louis was never able to assemble an empire the size of his uncle's, he extended his influence into key areas in such a way as to alarm Philip. A challenge to Philip, for example, is suggested by Louis's 1402 acquisition of rights from Jost Marquis of Moravia over Luxembourg, which lay in the middle of Philip's holdings. Jost had earlier awarded the territory to Philip, but, needing to aid his cousin Emperor Wenceslas, he turned to Louis, an ally of Wenceslas.[57] Louis had already received in appanage the duchy of Orleans in June 1392 and the county of Valois in 1393; he added to this the purchased counties of Blois, the Dunois, Champagne, Luzarches, and Fère en Tardenois. During the period that concerns us, the king awarded Louis Château-Thierry and the counties of Angoulême, Périgord, and Dreux, as we have seen, and Louis purchased the counties of Porcien and Soisson.[58] He also bought the seigneury of Coucy, a serious blow to Isabeau's father, who had hoped to acquire the territory for himself through a marriage to Isabelle of Lorraine.[59] Most threatening to Philip was Louis's 1401 acquisition as vassal of the Duke of Guelders, who was constantly at war with the Duchess of Brabant, whose territory Philip finally procured for his son in 1404. During the period 1399–1402, the Duke of Orleans became approximately as powerful as the Duke of Burgundy.

Before moving to Christine's responses to the tension between the dukes during this period, it is important to add a few words on the queen. I have noted that Isabeau was appointed mediator between the dukes by a number of royal ordinances, and that already with her coronation her position was defined as analogous to that of the Virgin, as an advocate. She had long been sought as a mediator. In 1389, the ruling council of Florence furnished the ambassador to France, Philippe Corsini, with instructions for approaching Isabeau if he could not persuade the king to act on behalf of Florence. In case of refusal, he would go to the queen, the niece of Bernabo Visconti, and ask her to intercede with the king.[60] As we have seen, the kin of Isabeau and Valentina represented opposing sides in a Visconti family dispute. Because Valentina and Isabeau were political enemies, Isabeau and Louis may have been, as well.[61] Added to their support for different candidates for the office of Holy Roman Emperor, they disagreed on all possible issues. Christine would try to coax them into alliance.

Christine's Response

In her love poetry, Christine explores the power dynamic responsible for courtly strife and reflects on how to maintain order in a kingdom whose monarch is insane, mediating her exploration through a narrator persona who is an ideal subject, obedient and unconditionally loving. This narrator continues to mediate Christine's love verse narratives (as opposed to her love lyrics) in which appropriate behavior for lovers is debated. As the quarrel between the dukes broadens and becomes more visible, however, Christine tries to build support for the Duke of Orleans through a narrator more overtly erudite and intellectual. In the rest of this chapter, I point to some of the different narratorial strategies by which Christine promotes the primacy of Louis in the government: in the *Epistre d'Othea a Hector*, the documents associated with the quarrel over the *Roman de la rose*, the *Chemin de longue étude*, and the *Mutacion de fortune*. In the *Livre de Christine*, the *Othea* and the *Roman de la rose* quarrel documents follow the *Dit de Poissy*, the last of the love narratives, and these are followed by *Les notables moraulz de Christine de Pizan a son filz*; *Une oroison de Nostre Dame*; and *Les quinze joyes de Nostre Dame rimees*. The manuscript originally ended there. However, several other works were later added, including the *Chemin de longue étude* and the *Mutacion de fortune*. These two works are thus later than the *Othea* and the *Roman de la rose* documents. The chronology of Christine's corpus is not always certain: she must have worked on more than one piece simultaneously during her periods of great creative activity. However, because the order of the contents of the *Livre de Christine* represents the poet's own arrangement of her work, whether or not the arrangement is literally chronological, Christine is responsible for the narrative arc that it suggests, that is, for the increasing complexity of her narrator, who is both learned and acutely aware of the limitations of her earthly knowledge. Already confident in her ability to move an audience through her lyric persona and finely wrought verse (as noted above, by 1399 at the latest, when her son went to England, her works had begun to attract the attention of powerful patrons), Christine responds to the increasing tensions between the dukes in her political allegories by dissecting the conflict and then interpellates her audience as supporters.

The *Epistre d'Othea a Hector*

The narrator of the *Othea*, a work composed around 1400 and dedicated to Louis of Orleans, is prophetic, erudite, and prudent. Sandra Hindman notes that the work was read as a chivalric treatise, handbook of the virtues, and collection of mythology.[62] Suzanne Conklin Akbari has characterized the *Othea* as a contemplative work in which "enigmatic verse," which serves as the "oracular heart of the allegory," is expounded through prose commentary.[63] Although this complex and popular work (fifty manuscript copies survive) served many purposes, I focus here on the way in which it backed the regency claim of Louis of Orleans. Presented as a letter from the goddess

Othea to fifteen-year-old Prince Hector, the work reveals this purpose in the relationships that it sets up between its narrators, Christine/Othea and dedicatee Louis of Orleans, between Louis of Orleans and Prince Hector, and between Prince Hector and Othea.

The fact that Louis's dedication consistently appears in copies of the *Othea* suggests that it was central to the work. Christine, in her own voice, opens the dedication by exulting Charles VI, praising first God and then the king, "the very high flower lauded by all in the world" (195, line 1).[64] The king is of the Trojan stock of ancient nobility (195, line 9). Immediately after the king, the narrator Christine addresses her praise to Louis, the second-greatest man in the realm:

> And to you, very noble and excellent prince of Orleans,
> Duke Louis of great renown,
> son of Charles, fifth king of that name,
> who, except for the king, you know none greater.
> (195, lines 12–15)

As Larry Scanlon has noted, "direct address does not merely locate a *persona* but constitutes it as well." An author does not merely speak to "a prince all of whose attributes are available immediately outside the text, but a prince whom he makes high, noble and excellent by so addressing."[65] In naming Louis the second most important person in the royal hierarchy, Christine assures his position before Philip of Burgundy.

In addition to promoting Louis, Christine begins in the dedication to make the case for herself as political advisor. Following her address to the duke, she evokes her own relationship to the royal family, reminding readers of her illustrious father, Thomas of Bologna, the physician and astrologer so much appreciated by Louis's father. Christine may be an "ignorant woman of little stature," but she is also the "daughter of a late philosopher and doctor who was a counselor and humble servant to [Louis's] father" (196, lines 19–21). The reference to Christine's astrologer father is the first of the connections that the poet draws between herself and the goddess Othea, narrator of the main work, which opens with four short rhymed texts on the cardinal virtues followed by seven short texts on the planets, astrological interpretations that cannot help but recall Thomas's area of expertise and thus Christine herself.

In the body of the work, Christine positions herself, through the eponymous Othea, as advisor to both Hector, whose youth and need of instruction seem to associate him with the dauphin, and Louis, whose prominent presence as dedicatee links him to the young Hector, possibly as mentor, given the king's condition. Although the dauphin would have been only about eight when the work was composed, we need not take Hector's fifteen years literally: surely the *Othea* was not intended to be read once and abandoned but was meant to be consulted over the years as the dauphin grew. As for the relationships among Christine/Othea, Hector/the dauphin, and Louis, they are elucidated by one of the work's intertexts, the biblical book of Proverbs, to which Christine refers throughout her corpus and which would have provided an obvious model for a set of aphorisms. Proverbs addresses *adulescenti* (Prov. 1:4) in its introduction, along with the wise, *sapiens* (1:5). The purpose of Proverbs is "ad intellegenda verba prudentiae et suscipiendam eruditionem doctrinae iustitiam et iudicium et aequitatem ut detur parvulis astutia adulescenti scientia et intellectus" (for understanding the words of prudence and receiving the doctrines of justice, and judgment, and equity, and that astuteness and understanding be given to young men). Moreover, the already wise should listen in order to learn how to govern: "et intellegens gubernacula possidebit" (understanding will possess the helms of governments) (1:3–4). Through this intertext, the *Othea* calls on both the dauphin and Louis to receive the message of prudence, explaining that by being attentive, the dauphin will gain understanding, and Louis will gain knowledge of how to act as regent.

Prudence, a key quality for Christine throughout her career, is implicitly associated with Othea through the work's intertextual relationship with Proverbs, but also explicitly. The young Hector acquired his qualities from this older feminine figure of Prudence: "And because all the earthly graces that a good knight must possess were present in Hector, we can say, morally, that he received them through the advice of Othea, who sent him this letter" (200, lines 98–102). The most important of these graces seems to be prudence, the mother of all virtues, which is necessary for the perfection of the knight. Prudence and Wisdom ("Prudence et Sagece"), Christine explains, are the mother and director of all virtues, without which the others cannot be well governed (201, lines 146–48).[66] The trait is the necessary supplement to chivalry (202, lines 149–50). Claire Le Ninan observes that Christine, unlike Nicole Oresme— who in his translations of Aristotle's *Ethics* and *Politics* distinguishes between two sciences, one concerning individual morality and one administration of the kingdom—follows Giles of Rome in rooting politics in ethics.[67] Although Le Ninan focuses on what she deems Christine's overtly political treatises, her point is pertinent to the *Othea*, in which the young knight's future success depends on developing prudence, a virtue that the poet grounds in morality.

The mastery of classical mythology that Christine demonstrates in the work attests to her erudition. But in addition to her knowledge, as an Othea figure with visible successes on her record, she proves that she herself possesses practical understanding, or prudence. Everett L. Wheeler has drawn attention to Christine's frequent use of a female figure, a proxy for herself, as a "teacher and source of chivalry."[68] I would add that because Christine was an intelligent maternal authority figure, educating her own son, Jean de Castel, in her real life, the conflation of Christine with Othea would have been all the more natural. Those who knew the poet would have known that Jean was about fifteen when his mother composed the *Othea* and that she had composed verses of practical and moral advice for his benefit. They would have seen her success as a mother, knowing that Jean had been taken into the household of the Duke of Salisbury in England, an honor for both mother and son.

As we have seen, the turn of the century saw a sudden increase in the tensions between the dukes in response to several discrete political problems. Although Philip had accused Louis of bewitching the king earlier, relations had been relatively quiet throughout much of the 1390s. The *Othea* intervenes at the point when the effects of the ducal rivalry became widely noticeable. In her study of the different manuscript versions of the *Othea*, Hindman reinforces this interpretation of the work's political significance. Two examples in particular, one from 1400 and the other included in the richly illustrated manuscript Harley 4431 in the British Library (also known as the Queen's Manuscript, of 1413, which Christine presented to Queen Isabeau of Bavaria), support the House of Orleans, although for somewhat different purposes.[69]

When Christine supervised the creation of the first manuscript, from 1400, Louis was still alive. This manuscript, Hindman explains, was a presentation copy to Louis that contained only the *Othea*, illustrated relatively sparsely with six miniatures in grisaille. One of her earliest works, the manuscript illustrates in its presentation miniature a man standing behind Louis holding a ducal baton, signifying Louis's position as next in line to the throne.[70] This visual argument supports the message elaborated in the prologue, that Louis, not Philip, is the rightful regent of the kingdom. However, the miniatures are not detailed and offer little else to indicate their connection to Louis's cause. I would note only that the word *renommé* adorns the final miniature of Perseus on Pegasus, a reference to the dedication, in which the duke's renown is emphasized. Christine's brief for Louis's regency is accomplished, in this case, mostly through the words of the text rather than through its miniatures.

When the second manuscript was composed, Louis had been dead for several years. Thus *Othea* bolsters the authority of the Orleanist faction, or Armagnacs, as they were then called, under Louis's son, Charles of Orleans. The Armagnacs had just defeated Jean's Burgundians after the Cabochian revolt, which allowed them to retake control of the government of the kingdom. The work is richly illustrated, with a colored miniature for each of the one hundred stories. As Hindman demonstrates, many of the miniatures of Harley 4431 insist upon the identity of the then deceased Louis. In the opening miniatures, Louis wears a necklace with his emblem, created for the Order of the Porcupine. But the political message comes through most clearly in a miniature portraying Hector with his shield. This shield represents the Order of the Gold Shield, founded by Louis's maternal uncle, Louis Duke of Bourbon, who died in 1410.[71] This is crucial because Jean, the new Duke of Bourbon, a staunch Orleanist or Armagnac, having just won a key battle against the English at the time of the manuscript's creation, had been called back to Paris to celebrate the Armagnac victory over the Burgundians in the Cabochian revolt. From 1409 to 1413 the kingdom had been under the control of Jean of Burgundy.[72] When the Armagnacs took control of Paris in 1413, Christine would have rejoiced. It was in this context that she responded to the queen's commission of a new manuscript, offering, among other things, a lavish reworking of the *Othea* originally presented to Louis of Orleans, to commemorate the original Orleanist leader while celebrating the victory of his faction.

With the *Othea*, Christine continues to emphasize the importance of affective relationships to social order, presenting Louis as a figure eminently worthy of love, second only to the king, and making a living, breathing woman of Othea by accentuating the links between the goddess and herself, a real-life mother. But she also begins to portray herself as an exegete, a writer capable of producing works that reveal important truths. The *Othea* demands that readers draw connections in order to piece together its many meanings. Each of the hundred chapters consists of a verse quatrain recounting a story, followed by a prose gloss expounding the moral significance of the story and a prose allegory interpreting its religious significance. The work covers a wide range of moral and political topics. The opening quatrains deal with the four cardinal virtues, beginning with prudence. The following quatrains recount stories mostly from classical mythology, culminating in a story of the Cumaean

Sibyl counseling Augustus. The work's structure of short narratives and possible interpretations, which often contradict one another or at least propose different meanings, and which in some manuscripts are accompanied by elaborate cycles of miniatures offering their own interpretational suggestions, forces the listener or reader into an active role, presumably a role that would have required the guidance of a wiser mentor figure for young readers.

The presence of the sibyl in the last quatrain picks up a reference that Othea makes to herself as a prophet in the first lines of the poem: she notes that Hector's life has already transpired and that she herself is watching the past, present, and future all at once:

> And as a goddess, I know
> through true knowledge, not experience,
> what will happen
> (198, lines 46–48)

This is the first time that Christine associates herself with prophecy, which will become a theme throughout her corpus, a way of authorizing herself as a political voice.

The Quarrel of the *Roman de la rose*

While she was working on the *Othea*, or perhaps just after completing it, Christine became involved in a literary quarrel over Jean de Meun's section of the *Roman de la rose*, siding with Jean Gerson against Jean de Montreuil and Pierre and Gontier Col. In confronting Jean de Montreuil, Christine makes a bid for recognition from the humanist circle associated with the Duke of Orleans.[73] Although it is often assumed that Christine's response to the *Rose* was motivated by outrage, her reaction is in fact carefully modulated. Deborah McGrady has shown how the poet created exactly the literary debate that she wanted, making it turn on the roles of women as subjects and readers of fiction in the dossiers of the debate that she collected and dedicated to Guillaume de Tignonville and the queen.[74] I would add that Christine could not have presented herself in any other way than she does in the debate and gained prestige through the exchange. This is not to say that she did not believe what she wrote. However, Jean de Montreuil's letter praising the *Rose*, the starting point for the debate at least as far as Christine's participation was concerned, was a serendipitous occasion for Christine's gaining entry, however circumscribed (Jean de Montreuil ignored her almost completely), into the chancery circle, and she seized the opportunity. As Emma Cayley has observed, members of the chancery involved in literary debates were deeply interested in the activity as an exercise in style, cultivating their writing facility in Latin and often composing in groups.[75] Christine's grasp of Latin may have been very good, but understanding a language is one thing, and writing well in it, another. Not possessing the specialized training necessary to participate in Latin, Christine sought access to the chancery culture by entering a quarrel in an area in which she was competent to speak, adapting to this new situation the themes and persona that she had already been developing for several years. In the quarrel letters, Christine presents herself as a discerning scholar, capable of separating substance from surface dazzle, looking beyond rhetoric to the meaning of things, or, as McGrady argues, as a talented reader whose skill encompassed that of the learned community of university men and elite lay readers.[76]

In what follows, I discuss two examples of how Christine showcases her carefully cultivated literary persona: through her skillful application of arguments that had circulated in earlier literary debates, and through her much-discussed defense of women, which, I contend, must be examined as part of a more general discussion of politics by means of stories of gossip and slander at court.

Christine's attack on Jean de Meun followed a line of argument employed by French humanists in earlier debates. From the time of Petrarch's infamous proclamation that "oratores et poete extra Italiam non querantur," Jean de Montreuil and others had argued that Italians were guilty of separating eloquence from *sapientia* (wisdom), prizing the former exclusively, whereas the French combined the two.[77] In insisting on the relationship between eloquence and wisdom, went the argument, the French had transcended Italian tradition.[78] Jean de Montreuil relies on this argument in a letter to Nicolas de Clamanges praising Pietramala for a style that, while imbued with the mellifluous dew of Lactantius, conveyed meaning yet "more ornate than his words."[79]

This becomes Christine's primary argument against Jean de Montreuil's treatise on the *Roman de la rose*. Jean de Meun's contents do not promote virtuous behavior, even though the writer himself may be a fine writer and a subtle thinker.[80] He uses "very beautiful terms and in elegant verses with rich rhymes" (13; 52) and he is a "very great cleric, subtle and eloquent" (20; 61).[81] But for this very reason he could have produced "a much better work, more profitable and with a more elevated sensibility" (20–21; 61). She dismisses with scorn the idea that the *Roman de la rose* teaches young women to distinguish the good from the bad (15; 54). Much in the work is good. But Jean de Meun's very excellence as a writer poses a danger to readers who will be unable to tell the good from the bad in the work, in other words, what is true from what is seductive but false. Christine protests first against Jean de Montreuil's approval of Reason's reference to the private male parts by their name (13; 52). God made nothing evil, says Reason, and therefore anything that God made can legitimately be called by its name. Christine disagrees: one should be embarrassed to speak inappropriately, referring to embarrassing things only when necessary and then soberly (4; 54). Just as the Francophiles had argued, Christine claims that the moral quality of language depends on the moral quality of that to which it refers. She then goes on to complain, giving several examples, that simply putting bad ideas in the mouths of bad characters does not mitigate the ideas' evil effects. Once again, her point is that meaning prevails over words, even words that may reflect the viewpoint of a character that the author means to serve as a bad example.

The second aspect of Christine's contribution to the *Rose* quarrel that seems particularly pertinent to the contemporary political situation is her spirited defense of women. That Christine would defend women seems so natural that her motivation has been taken for granted. And yet, just as the poet weaves her autobiographical details into the contemporary history of the kingdom, presenting them as microcosmic versions of the larger problems created by the feud, her interest in slander against women reaches beyond her personal experience to a larger issue. I have suggested that slander in her love narratives condenses the very real dispute between the dukes into an accessible problem, a means for discussing the dynamics of the power struggle. Slander of women is an especially poignant symbol for the attacking of vulnerable figures. In her letter to Jean de Montreuil, she alludes to her *Epistre au dieu d'amours*, recalling that in this work she had raised the issue of overkill—women are too feeble to merit the enormous opprobrium heaped on them (17–18; 57–58). A strong defense of women as capable of seeing through the obfuscation of a male authority, as having no motive but "advocating the pure truth," was valuable when the queen of France was being called upon to keep the peace between the dukes (19; 60). Anything that reinforced a woman's image as an intelligent discerner of the world around her was useful.

We do not know precisely how the literary quarrel over the *Roman de la rose* began or under what circumstances Christine joined in; in her response to Jean de Montreuil's initial treatise, she thanks him for sending her the piece but offers no details. Jean de Montreuil recounts in a letter to an unnamed friend, probably Pierre d'Ailly, that several clerics and others, including a certain Christine, had abused him for his positive assessment of the work and its author in the treatise.[82] What were the dimensions of the original quarrel, and how central was Christine to it? Although Jean mentions her by name, this may be because the participation of a woman was unusual. Christine created the record of the quarrel, and in her collection of the documents relative to it she includes only her own letters to Jean and to Gontier and Pierre Col, along with the letters of the brothers Col. But Jean de Montreuil's words seem to imply that the quarrel was somewhat larger than Christine's documents suggest.

The quarrel as we know it, then, is Christine's creation. That she mentioned the *Roman de la rose* in at least one work before she read Jean de Montreuil's positive treatise on the work suggests that she grasped the chance to display her already well-known persona. Surely, this goal was not compatible with Jean de Montreuil's. Cayley notes that such debates took place within closed networks and that in going public with the quarrel, Christine moved it from the space within which Jean de Montreuil normally operated to an area into which he refused to follow.[83] Why would she do this? Christine's publication, in the form of dossiers containing the quarrel documents given to the queen and Tignonville of what normally would have remained a literary debate among a restricted circle of colleagues, suggests that she was moved at least as much by the desire for recognition among influential people as by moral indignation.

In her letter to Isabeau introducing the debate documents, she draws attention to the wisdom and nobility to be found in the queen's power of discernment (these virtues, Christine writes, "sagesce avec noblesce," are to be found in her "noble entendement"), supporting Isabeau's arbitration between the dukes (5–6; 98–99). She characterizes the debate differently in the letter to Tignonville, treating it like the lovers' debates that she had already composed and asking Tignonville to judge the "amiable, and not spiteful" exchange (7; 100). She is eager to make clear that she is a "player," that she understands the rules of literary debate among humanists. She finishes by explaining why she has written in prose rather than her accustomed rhyme: she wants to write in the "style of [her] assailants" (8; 101). Thus she has positioned herself carefully to gain further recognition as a political voice.

The *Chemin de longue étude* and the King of the World

Even as a participant in a humanist literary debate, applying to the *Roman de la rose* the tried and true French humanist arguments about the relationship between beautiful style and meaning, Christine's debate persona is emotional, prone to interjections like "Ha!" This enthusiasm underlines the forceful moral tenor of her arguments. Still, she backs her indignation with substance. In the *Chemin de longue étude*, Christine emphasizes her erudition yet more insistently, as she promotes Louis of Orleans by proposing him as a candidate for Holy Roman Emperor.

The *Chemin* opens with the narrator Christine in the grip of emotion, lamenting the trials imposed on her by perverse Fortune. As she had already done in the *Cent balades*, she calls upon Boethius in her time of distress, representing herself engaging with the text and signaling common ground between his and the contemporary situation: the danger of jealousy. Boethius was brought low by the envy of those who "hate the life of the good, the truthful, the *non-médisans*" (100, lines 233–34).[84] In the modern day, too, envy continues to destroy peace. Even Christians kill each other, incited by covetousness (108, lines 351–57).

In the reading, she feels some of her own burden lifted. Still, Boethius's story continues to work on her even after she falls into an uneasy meditation. Obsessing over the state of the kingdom, the wars of the world, the Schism, and even the cruelty of nature, she nods off, drifting into a dream where she meets the Cumaean Sibyl and embarks on a journey along the "road of long study" into the heavens. Guided by the sibyl, she attains knowledge that enables her better to understand obscure earthly problems (126, lines 649–58). Adrian Armstrong and Sarah Kay have noted the paradoxical status of knowledge for medieval readers of Boethius: "inevitably compromised in worldly contingency," it also "has the capacity to console and fortify against fortune."[85] Consoled and enlightened, Christine will return to earth to spread the word that the only solution to the terrible conflicts on earth is that the planet be governed by a single monarch, a king of the world (266, line 3044). But as enlightened as the solution may be, it has little purchase in a world where factions vie for power. Although Christine acquires substantial understanding of the way things work from the sibyl and from what she observes in the heavens, this prophetic knowledge is of little use back home.

Before following Christine on her journey, it is important to put the notion of the king of the world, central to her narrative, into its historical context. I believe, as Gilbert Ouy and, more recently, Gilbert Ouy and Christine Reno have argued, that the king of the world to which the *Chemin* refers is the Holy Roman Emperor and that Christine has Louis in mind for the office.[86] To make their case, Ouy and Reno argue backward from evidence of the Duke of Orleans's ambitions to the imperial throne in two poems by Ambrogio Migli. I will reiterate this case, but I begin with the deposition of Wenceslas of Luxembourg, son of the emperor Charles IV (whose visit to France Christine describes in the *Fais et bonnes meurs*), in August 1400. As we saw in chapter 2, this threw the office of Holy Roman Emperor into turmoil. Wenceslas's narrowly elected replacement, Robert of Bavaria, was vigorously opposed by many leaders in Europe, including Louis and Louis's father-in-law, Giangaleazzo Visconti, who sought the office for himself before his death in 1402.[87] Supported by Philip of Burgundy and Queen Isabeau, Robert solicited the French court for aid, although he received only their encouragement. He nonetheless managed to lead an army to Italy to defend his imperial throne, crossing the Alps in 1401. He soon ran out of funds and lost his troops, however, returning to Germany the following year. He allied himself with England through the marriage of his son to the daughter of King Henry IV, and, recognized by the Roman pope Boniface IX in 1403, he managed to retain the throne until his death in 1410. Because Robert's claim aroused such opposition, the imperial throne was, for all practical purposes, up for grabs in the first years of the fifteenth century.

How does Christine's long debate over the king of the world respond to this situation? A prophetic literary tradition associated world peace with the French king's assumption of the imperial throne and the recovery of the Holy Land. A short text known as the Second Charlemagne, composed just after Charles VI's accession in 1380, announced that the young king would fulfill the prophecy.[88] But long before the composition of this text, a thirteenth-century prophecy had proposed the king of France as guardian of all Christianity: "a king descended from the ancient French people will appear, and his power over land and sea will grow, and he will heal the Schism, and, with the errors of the Christians purged, the Church will be restored to its optimum state of good."[89] In 1306, in the context of the battle between King Philip the Fair and Pope Boniface VIII, Pierre Dubois, counselor to the king, proclaimed in a treatise called *De recuperatione Terre Sancte* that the French should lead a crusade to recover the Holy Land and then rule the world from Jerusalem.[90] The result would be world peace. Pierre's choice for the ruler of the East was King Philip the Fair's brother, Charles of Valois.[91] Following the Second

Charlemagne, similar prophecies continued to be written; Telesphorus of Cosenza, a Franciscan hermit and follower of Joachim of Fiore, composed the *Libellus fratris Telefori* in 1386. In this work, Telesphorus describes being instructed in a vision to go to Italy in search of prophetical books on the Schism. He obeys, and when he returns he writes the *Libellus*. According to Telesphorus, the German Frederick III and the antipope will enter into a fight to the finish with a French King Charles and the true pope. The inevitable victory of the French will usher in a new period of peace.

Such prophecies, whose history has been traced by Marjorie Reeves and others, provide the background against which the *Chemin de longue étude* gained its political significance. Faced with the reality that mad Charles VI would never become the new Charlemagne leading a crusade, the *Chemin* proposes a sort of consolation prize: Louis of Orleans will take up the imperial crown and recover the Holy Land. Christine was hardly alone in considering the brother of the king for such a position. We have seen that Pierre Dubois created a model for a world divided between the French king and his brother. But, in addition, Louis's candidacy for the office of Holy Roman Emperor had specific historical precedent. Besides Charles of Valois, brother of Philip IV, other Capetian kings, or brothers of the French king, had campaigned specifically for the job. These included Robert of Artois, brother of Saint Louis; Charles IV; and, later, François I.[92] In addition to the backing of his brother, Louis could have counted on the Avignon pope and the German seigneurs whose vassalage he had been cultivating along the German border since 1398.[93]

As for the crusade, a notion widespread in Europe held that a principal responsibility of the emperor was to lead a crusade.[94] As Chris Jones shows in his recent study of the Capetian claims to the imperial throne, the "key recommendation made by several ecclesiastical councils that met after the fall of Acre was that the first step towards the recovery of the Holy Land was to elect a new emperor," a notion that "was firmly established by 1291."[95] The crusade occupies a predominant place in the *Chemin*, as Claire Le Ninan's study of the theme in Christine's writings demonstrates.[96] With its long description of the marvels of the East (158–80, lines 1192–568) as the point of departure for Christine's ascent into the heavens, the *Chemin* presents in allegorical fashion the happy advantage that would accrue from Louis's succession. He would unify the West and the East. Thus the *Chemin* offers a way of fulfilling prophecies that had circulated at the time of Charles VI's succession.[97]

We return now to the *Chemin* to explore the situation evoked in this work. Christine has set off on a journey of long study, led by the Cumaean Sibyl into the heavens. When she reaches the skies, Christine listens to Earth, "Terre," complain of her children's "hard and mortal wars, / in which they engage without stop" (242, lines 2647–48). The reason for the constant strife is covetousness (244, line 2678). The discussion leads first to the decision that peace might be achieved if a "single prince alone were reigning" (268, line 3090), and then to a long debate among four celestial ladies, Noblece, Chevalerie, Richece, and Sagece, about which traits are the most important in this sort of king.

That the poem promotes Louis for the role is suggested in several spots, beginning with the history of the Trojan royal family recounted by Noblece. The king of the world must descend from the Trojans. All of the Valois, including Philip, supposedly descended from the Trojans. However, the mention of a cruel uncle who envies the legitimate heirs, Romulus and Remus, recalls the young Charles VI and, later, Louis harassed by their jealous and ambitious uncle Philip.

> Once Remus and Romulus,
> . . . were stolen from their mother
> By their cruel uncle,
> Who greatly envied them
> (296–98, lines 3581–84)

Noblece later describes the aptitudes of the present-day Valois dukes. First, she recounts the fiasco of the deceased Duke of Anjou's attempt to claim the kingdom of Naples, which he had inherited from Jeanne of Naples, as we have seen (302, lines 3657–74). Following this story, Noblece describes the triumphs of the Duke of Orleans in Germany, where he had recently acquired lordship over several key regions. Noblece's argument is that Louis's "noblece" is the reason for his recent success. She explains:

> We now see again
> That this fact [that nobility is the most important trait] is notably
>   proven
> By the noble descent of the Duke of
> Orleans. How can it be that
> His holdings in Germany are such

> That at the moment there is no
> Town, land, castle or fortress
> In the Duchy of Luxembourg
> That does not do him homage?
> Is it not because of his high lineage?
> (302–4, lines 3675–83)

The new subjects of the Duke of Orleans think themselves fortunate to be governed by the son of a king (304, lines 3688–90). As for Philip of Burgundy, Noblece continues, he went off to Brittany, whether people liked it or not ("[a] qui qu'il plaise ou qui qu'en grongne"), where he mediated peace among the warring barons (304, lines 3697–708). The depiction is positive, but, in contrast to her glowing description of Louis's capacity to govern, she says nothing about Philip as a leader.

A debate among the four celestial ladies leads to the conclusion that the only way to achieve peace below is to choose a single king under whom all the world will be united. Although a heavenly council is called to help choose this king, the ladies fail to reach an agreement upon the critical question of who this should be. During the course of the debate, it emerges that Richece is unnecessary, even harmful, her words "ugly, proud, and insane" (328, line 4086), but that each of the other three attributes is essential. Sagece makes the point unambiguously in her final speech, which is the text's last word on the matter. The king must possess *noblece* and *chevalerie*, but these are to be guided by *sagece*. As we will see in chapter 4, these same qualities, in the same order, will characterize the ideal prince, Charles V, in *Fais et bonnes meurs*, structuring the work's narrative and associating Louis unmistakably with his wise father.

But despite this fundamental consensus, the ladies cannot decide who will be the king, so they send responsibility for the decision back to earth. The work's closing lines refer to the "Judgment of Paris" scene as an example of conflict resolution, which does not bode well for a successful outcome. Chosen to present the four ladies' recommendation for a king of the world to her friends, the princes of the earth, and ask them to decide who it should be, Christine appears unlikely to succeed. Still, she has made her point. The *Chemin* proclaims the duke's superiority to his challenger, Philip of Burgundy, for supremacy in the government. The election of Louis would resolve the conflicts tearing the government apart by forcing acknowledgment of the priority of Louis's rank. As we saw earlier in this chapter, the topicality of Louis as a candidate for the office of Holy Roman Emperor is evidenced by a letter cited by Ouy from a Strasbourger residing in Paris in 1403. The Strasbourger, who supported the Roman against the Avignon pope, assumed that Louis's strategy would be to enter Rome, depose the Roman pope, and install the Avignon pope, who would in turn crown Louis emperor.[98] This neatly summarizes the content of Telesphorus's text.

That the *Chemin* supports the case for Louis as candidate for the imperial throne is given further credence by the two poems by Ambrogio Migli, with whom Christine must have been acquainted as a visitor to Louis's Hotel Boheme. In the first of these poems, composed in 1404, Migli puts the case for Louis's candidacy for the office of Holy Roman Emperor in the mouth of the god Mercury, who begins his narrative with a description of the chaotic state of Europe. The situation could be improved, Mercury suggests, by the election of a single king.

> I am Mercury, sent from the heavens to set up among you, Christian people, a universal king. Listen with respect to the order that I have been charged with transmitting to you and do not think of disobeying the gods.
>
> Celestial majesty has been watching your internal wars, your feuds, your disorder, and the division of this empire of the Caesars, once so glorious, from on high. Alas, Caesar, light of your world, how you have been eclipsed today!
>
> The causes of this great sorrow are discord and tyranny, but also favoring of one's own land, each land worried only about itself and demanding imperial prerogatives for its prince. This is why the glory of the European Kingdom is so tarnished, and why the menace of slavery hangs over you.
>
> What insanity has blinded you, unhappy ones? Regain your senses and keep the world empire afloat. Come to an agreement over the choice of a single prince distinguished from all by the brilliance of his lineage and his line, and, under his rule, you will return to your former glory.[99]

Mercury shows none of the discretion of Christine's narrator, but he clarifies that "single king" refers to the office of Holy Roman Emperor and that he is promoting Louis of Orleans for the job: "To Louis then belongs accession to the imperial throne, he who is filled with sacred love for the public good."

Beyond proposing Louis for emperor, Migli's poems serve another purpose, one that becomes clearer in the second. This is the same purpose served by the *Chemin*. "Get a grip on yourselves," Mercury exhorts the public, "and give up your folly. Give the king's brother the rank that is his and make the other princes respect the hierarchy: order keeps kingdoms happy."[100] In other words, with public support rallied behind Louis, the menace posed by Philip would lessen and the danger of civil war would be diminished. Mercury, like Christine's narrator, is sent back to earth to preach the desirability of a king of the world.

The similarity of purpose between Migli's poem and the *Chemin* is so striking that it seems safe to assume that Migli had read or heard of Christine's poem. A detail in his first poem suggests that he had close knowledge of the *Chemin*: it refers to the three goddesses, Juno, Venus, and Pallas, who brought Louis his gifts, recalling the last lines of Christine's work. Such a scenario is all the more likely given that Migli and Christine must have known each other.[101] Ouy's assessment of the *Chemin* as a fictional account of a contemporary scenario that is repeated in Migli's poems seems fully plausible. Migli's poem also suggests the esteem in which Christine's *Chemin* was held.

The *Livre de la mutacion de fortune*

With its meditation on the relationships among fortune, history, and virtue, the *Livre de la mutacion de fortune*, completed in November 1403, represents another important step in Christine's career as a political commentator. In this work, Christine's narrator undergoes a transformation brought on by the distressing events of her personal life, from an emotional figure mourning her fate into what Kevin Brownlee describes as "a new kind of *clerc*: a learned poet historian."[102] This trajectory mirrors the one discernible across the major works of Christine's corpus, as she moves from courtly poet to author of political allegory and finally political treatises.

In the *Mutacion de fortune*, Christine returns to the Boethian theme of the *Cent balades* and the *Chemin*: the theme of Fortune as the force to which the kingdom's woes must be attributed, and the possibility of overcoming Fortune through knowledge and virtue. Equally important, in this work Christine continues to develop her vision of women's place in her society. As in the *Epistre d'Othea a Hector* and the *Chemin de longue étude*, a crucial part of her plan is to give shape to a complex political situation and assert her own capacity to advise. However, Christine's narrator has now become a figure through which universal history unrolls, who reveals how the contemporary situation fits into universal history in veiled but insistent terms. The role of women in this history, as Christine represents it, is no longer essentially mediatory but active, at least in cases where a male figure is lacking. This shift mirrors the one in Isabeau's role as outlined in the ordinances of 1402, where the queen is assigned the job of arbitrating between the princes when the king is absent, and of 1403, where the queen mother becomes the acting regent or co-regent with the immediate ascension to the throne of the young king, even if a minor, and the elimination of any explicit regent. As noted above, in 1403 the queen's authority was greatly augmented, at least potentially, with a royal ordinance abolishing regency altogether in the case that the king should die leaving a minor heir.[103] With no one administering the realm, the queen, already guardian of the dauphin, would exercise total regency through her son. Louis fought the 1403 ordinance successfully, but it left a blueprint for imagining female power as a check on male aggression.

The *Mutacion de fortune* begins by asserting Christine's credentials, offering a view of the conflict between the dukes in its universal historical context from the perspective of a woman well qualified to pronounce on such matters. Misfortune had sharpened Christine's understanding of how the world works. I will tell of the things, she writes,

> That happened to me
> Through her [Fortune], for which reason
> My sense became quite a bit more subtle
> Than it had been in the past.
> (1:8, lines 37–40)[104]

Fortune brings troubles, but she also teaches (1:8, line 46). Thus Christine has an important message for anyone who has ears to hear and wants to know the correct ending ("droite fin") toward which the work is heading (lines 47–50). This message is the story of her great adventure, a *mutacion* effected by Fortune. This mutation, of course, is the story of Christine's transformation from a woman into a man, from a *femelle* into an "homme naturel et parfaict" (1:12, lines 142–45), when, during a sea voyage in the land of Fortune, her husband is knocked overboard by waves, leaving Christine alone.

The notion of human life as a ship tossed by the winds of Fortune is one that Christine had already broached in *balade* 12 of the *Cent balades*. But in the *Mutacion de fortune*, the ship travels without a captain; the image evokes France making its way without a king. Christine now gives the image a narrative, offering a solution to the maritime emergency of the loss of the captain. She begins by establishing that it matters that her message comes from a woman. Before getting to the point, she explains, she needs to tell who she is; a person who wants to present him- or herself must begin by offering qualifications (1:12–13, lines 157–65).

Christine's credentials include her parental heritage: riches, although intellectual rather than financial, on her father's side, and a keen gift for discernment on her mother's. Her father, she explains, possessed two magnificent precious stones: astrological and medical knowledge. He desired a son to whom to pass on his riches. But her mother, Nature, to whom God gave "the authority to expand and maintain the world," wanted a child who resembled her. The result? Christine was born, resembling her father in manner, body, and face—in everything but gender, her "sexe tant seulement." Nature constrains men and women to different roles in the world, and for this reason she cannot inherit her father's riches. This does not mean that a woman is any less competent than her male counterpart to fulfill the tasks from which she is excluded by sex. On the contrary, Christine places natural gifts above acquired ones, explaining that her mother, Nature, surpassed her father, despite his erudition, in sense, strength, and worth (1:18, lines 342–44). As a daughter of Nature, however, Christine has no treasure of "science," and so her mother places her in the service of Fortune—an ominous choice—to complete her education. In preparation, Nature equips Christine to deal with that lady of "strange origin" by giving her a fine set of traits in the form of a *chapelet*, a crown or garland studded with the jewels of *discrecion, consideracion, memoire*, and *retentive*, a reference to the parts of the soul or mind, as we saw in chapter 2. These jewels are available to everyone, although few make use of them, and they grow when the body is stricken with illness; indeed, the body, the empire, the kingdom, and even the world are governed by the jewels (1:32, 739–54). By virtue of these jewels, Christine will be prepared to guide the ship when her husband is swept overboard, although her gender would normally have prevented this. When Fortune turns on Christine, she is at first devastated, but, guided by the *chapelet* that she keeps with her at all times, she returns the ship safely to port in the court of Fortune, where, still directed by the *chapelet*, she learns to "govern" ships and manors ("pourpris"). As she grows accustomed to her surroundings, she begins to understand in a new way how things work. And this is what she recounts in the rest of the story: the workings of Fortune, whose mutations never cease (1:55, line 1460).

Christine's tale of her transformation from female to male is an allegory that continues to move us even today as a narrative of initiation into the hard world. It reveals much about her attitude in the face of adversity. But as much as the allegory adds a new layer of emotion to the story of the loss of her husband, it serves another important function as a political allegory: in a period when the dukes were fighting bitterly over political influence, it reminds readers that a woman, too, can take over for a lost captain.

Christine now turns her attention to the bizarre castle of Fortune, suspended by four chains and turning in the wind. She describes the inhabitants of the castle in their seats of power. First come the two popes trying to squeeze themselves into one chair, a symbol of the Schism. The next seat represents the Holy Roman Emperor, which Christine claims is empty at the time of her writing (1403). In this way, she sets up a relationship between this work and the *Chemin*, where she promoted Louis of Orleans for the post of Holy Roman Emperor. As we have seen, the seat was not in fact empty, but because of the difficulties Robert encountered in pressing his claim, Christine describes the seat as effectively empty and in need of a new occupant.

But it is the seat of the French king, the seat of Frige (1:24–31, lines 4911–5130), that is the most interesting for this discussion of Christine's political views. This seat has been buffeted by bitter Fortune; still, it holds many advantages. The head has remained with the body politic, instead of being cut off, as elsewhere, surely a comment on the situation in England. There is little cruelty; the princes are too frightened by stories of what happens to cruel lords to do much harm. And yet there is no truth left in the land: "What a vice in great lords!" (2:25, line 4959). The rest of the section on France is a complaint about the covetousness, lying, and injustice that characterize the kingdom in the present age. Christine brings the passage to a close by noting that no one prizes *sagece*, or science, anymore. Aristotle taught Alexander to listen only to wise counselors, but this has changed. Now those in power are surrounded by lying, scheming ministers who look only for their own advantage. The section echoes Christine's lyric poems on courtly envy but gives the courtly backbiters a narrative framework. The kingdom still holds together, but not, Christine suggests, for long.

The poet remains silent about which French lords she is targeting, as we would expect. The complaint of lying and greed is sufficiently vague to be applicable to anyone. But Christine restricts her complaints about rebellious princes, which are more likely to be interpreted as pointed criticisms, to her section on the Italian seats. The perpetual conflict between the Guelph and Ghibelline factions serves as a caution about the dangers of the division that prevails at the French court. In such a land, no prince, no matter how powerful, can keep the warring lords in peace. "Long live the conqueror" is their watchword, which guarantees a constant state of unrest (1:18, line 4732). Philippe de Mézières had earlier associated French factionalism with the Guelphs and Ghibellines. In the allegorical scheme of the *Songe du vieil pelerin*, the queen uses the game of chess as a metaphor in instructing Beau Filz on the dangers of envy and factionalism. Beau Filz, who represents the French common good, the glory and joy of the French ship ("la nef Francoise"), must guard carefully against enemies. But because of the kingdom's sins, the ship has become, in part, Lombardy ("en part est devenue Lombardie"), where there are Guelphs and Ghibellines.[105] Christine, too, will liken the Armagnac-Burgundian conflict to the Italian one in the *Lamentacions sur les maux de la guerre civile*. Here in the *Mutacion de fortune*, like Philippe de Mézières, she uses the image to warn of where the rivalry will lead.

Christine's narrator has shown that the inhabitants of the earth live within the castle of Fortune. After describing them, she moves to a description of the history of the world as it is painted on the walls of the castle of Fortune. First, however, she pauses to describe Philosophy, whom she sees seated high on the wall in such a way as to appear mistress of all science (2:104, line 7195), whose categories she details. Philosophy is the mother and nurse of all science (2:133, lines 8065–67) and thus mediates between the narrator and her interpretation of the history depicted on the walls of the castle.

The history of the world as recorded on the walls shows the mighty repeatedly plunging into the depths. Christine describes fall after fall, until she finally arrives at the present day. The reign of Charles VI had been going beautifully, she explains, until Fortune struck Charles with illness. Still, his people continued to obey him and peace prevailed, all the more so because of the "belle chevalerie" (4:77, line 23561) that defended him. Just after Charles VI, as always, comes his brother (line 23567), on whom Fortune has shone thus far. The dukes of Bourbon, Berry, and Burgundy follow Louis. For the moment, good fortune is smiling on them, too, despite many past adversities. May their good counsel keep the country safe.

Christine concludes by asking the princes of the high tower of Fortune to consider whether they are indeed secure in their positions. She has warned against factionalism, revealing its cause to be envy. She has again asserted the royal hierarchy: Louis follows the king. To return to the lines with which I opened this section, the *Mutacion de fortune*, with its meditation on the relationships among fortune, history, and virtue, represents another important step in Christine's career as a political commentator: reading the history of the world with the support of Philosophy, the narrator warns loudly against the coming disaster.

Conclusion

Modern scholarship sees Christine's movement from love poetry to political allegory as a reflection of her maturation as a thinker. The poet herself seems to encourage this perspective, describing in the *Advision* how she came to compose beautiful things, lighter ("plus legieres") at the beginning, to distract herself from her troubles.[106] With practice, her style grew in subtlety, until she was capable of creating works with weighty content ("haulte matiere"). As one scholar summarizes Christine's career, the poet shifted "from the subject [of love] to the more serious matters she wanted to study and write about. Among her more serious concerns was France. That is, she turned from lessons of self-interest for women in love to enlightened self-interest for the good of the nation as a whole."[107] I suggest, by contrast, that Christine's love poetry was already reflecting on "serious matters" like the breakdown of monarchical authority and related vicissitudes, and that the alleged shift in her interests and subject matter is exaggerated. That she included her love verse in her major collections suggests that she considered it capable of conveying weighty ideas. The poet's own meditations on poetry suggest as much. In the *Dit de la pastoure*, for example, she insists that light works that seem to be nothing but "truffe" or "fable" sometimes contain important material.[108] In the *Fais et bonnes meurs* she draws no distinction between verse and prose but seems to consider both capable of conveying truth. Generally speaking, she explains, "the name poetry [poesie] is taken to mean some kind of fiction, that is, any narrative or introduction that on the surface signifies one meaning, but covertly signifies another or several others, although it is more exact to say that poetry is that whose purpose is truth and whose process is learning dressed up in words of delightful ornament and fitting colors."[109] She adds that poetry is the clearest and the most delightful way to communicate truth.

However, Christine works significant changes in her verse by enhancing the complexity and erudition of her narrator as she attempts to shape the course of the feud. The works that I have considered in this chapter require the effort of intellectual engagement with the narrator. As the bad blood between the dukes became more threatening to the kingdom's security in the first years of the fifteenth century, it was no longer sufficient to stir her audience emotionally, inciting love for the Duke of Orleans. Apart from the *Roman de la rose* documents, the works that I have considered so far are written in verse.[110] As we saw, Christine explains her shift to prose in the *Rose* documents as an attempt to write in the style of her opponents.[111] In the next chapter, I consider a series of works written in prose, which becomes Christine's preferred medium, though she never entirely abandons verse.

4

JEAN OF BURGUNDY AND RECONFIGURING REGENCY, 1405

Having secured the succession of Brabant from the duchy's estates for his son, Antoine, Philip of Burgundy traveled to Brussels, where the nearly eighty-two-year-old Jeanne of Brabant handed the government over to him. There, Philip was stricken with the plague and, not wanting to impose on the hospitality of Jeanne for care, headed for Arras, but made it only to Halle before he expired.[1] Christine mourned the duke's death in a *balade* exhorting the different members of the royal family and the people of France to lament his loss. Each verse of the *balade* begins with the command "Plourez" ("pleurez," or weep). All would soon realize, as the ominous refrain intones, that "eussions affaire du bon duc de Bourgongne" (we really could have used the good Duke of Burgundy) (256, lines 11, 22, 33, and 37).[2]

As Alfred Coville observed in 1901, this *balade* generated a number of imitations, and, as Nadia Margolis suggests, it may have had a long backstory as well.[3] Margolis observes that Christine borrows the anaphoric command to weep from Eustache Deschamps, whose *balade* "mock-honors a gallant solider and leader," Guillaume d'Angle. This Guillaume, "who had unfortunately defected to the English," was "a great lover and courtier to be mourned by all subjects of Love and Pleasure (Amours, Deduit), instead of a hero mourned by some more fitting gods like Mars and Minverva." This *balade* itself borrowed the "weep" from Catullus's Carmen III, which "subverts the rhetoric of lament through biting irony."[4] As for the subsequent references to Christine's *balade*, Coville writes that the abbot of Cérisy, Thomas du Bourg, who will respond to Jean Petit's justification of Jean of Burgundy's assassination of

Louis of Orleans, will draw on it by repeating its "weep" structure in a prose demand for justice. Then, in his second justification, Jean Petit will use the same formula sarcastically, to mock-lament the assassination of Louis of Orleans.

The "lugete" or "plange mecum" or "flete" topos is common in the Bible and also occurs in Latin religious drama, so its use may have been suggested to Christine by one of these perfectly serious sources. Or she may have borrowed her poem's anaphoric "weep" from Deschamps. Certainly, she was familiar with his work, and the possibility that she drew on a form previously used for parody is interesting.[5] Fearing that with the advent of Jean of Burgundy the Orleanist-Burgundian conflict would intensify, Christine had good reason to mourn Philip's death. The causes that she offers in the *balade* for mourning the old duke are ambiguous. The king mourned his uncle, Christine explains, out of familial obligation: Philip deserved his love because of the right of lineage (256, lines 5–6). Louis of Orleans's reason to mourn was that much fault had been covered over because of Philip's good sense ("mainte faulte est couverte") (256, line 15). "Faulte" could mean flaw but also a cleavage or fault line: because Philip was less ruthless than Jean, the divide between the House of Orleans and the House of Burgundy was not as profound as it might have been, or as it would become.

But most interesting is the exhortation to the kingdom itself to mourn. To describe the situation in which the kingdom found itself because of Philip's death, Christine turns to the game of chess, a popular metaphor for discussing political strategy during the Middle Ages.[6] In particular, she draws on the move of "open check" (eschec à descouverte) (256, line 27). The essence of this move is that the king is shielded from attack by a piece from the *attacking* side. When the shielding piece is lifted—say, a white piece, masking the defending black king—the defending black king is left in check. In other words, Christine creates the image of a white piece shielding the king from the attacking white side. Jean of Burgundy, previously restrained by his father, is now free to attack the king and take over the kingdom.[7] After the kingdom, Christine turns to the common people, warning them, "you will lose much, and everyone will witness it, / Whereupon you will often say 'check'" (256, lines 31–32).

It is not unlikely, then, that Christine too uses the "weep" motif ironically, in the sense that the chief reason for mourning Philip's death is that it has unleashed his son on France. Jean spent more than half his time in Paris with his father between 1398 and 1404; he would have been a well-known figure.[8]

In this chapter we will consider Jean's emergence as Duke of Burgundy and see that Christine's fears were well founded.

The New Duke of Burgundy

As we saw in chapter 3, although the truce with the English was renewed after the deposition and murder of Richard II, war continued, unofficially, from 1402 on. Enraged by the new king Henry IV's alliance of April 27 of that year with Holy Roman Emperor Robert, who referred in the document to the king of England as the "King of England and France," Louis of Orleans issued the first of several personal challenges to Henry on August 7.[9] Despite a series of conferences designed to maintain the fragile peace between the kingdoms in Leulinghem in 1402 and 1403, French privateers plundered the coasts of England, provoking retaliation that lasted throughout 1403 and into 1404.[10] In April 1404, the counts of Foix and Armagnac threatened the English in Guyenne and Bordeaux, and, in June, Louis was named lieutenant for the king and captain-general for war in Picardy and Normandy. Soon afterward, the Royal Council ordered the Count of La Marche to negotiate an alliance with Owen Glendower, hoping to incite the Welsh to revolt against Henry IV. Beginning in 1405, *connétable* Charles d'Albret and the Count of Armagnac led French offensives in Guyenne and Saintonge, while at the same time the Count of La Marche headed a naval expedition to Wales to aid the Welsh revolt. At the front of an expedition in Calais, the Count of Saint Pol was defeated at nearby Marck on May 20, 1405.[11] While the count and some of his men retreated inland to Thérouanne, those remaining were slaughtered, leaving Calais in the hands of the English. In the meantime, the Boulonnais and Flanders were threatened. The French kingdom had entered into a state of constant high alert against "ravaging, pillaging and destruction, permanent and ruinous warfare," a situation arguably worse for morale than defeat.[12]

This is the context for Jean's entry onto the Royal Council and his antitax position. As we noted in chapter 3, shortly before his death, Philip had approved a tax for the defense of the kingdom, along with the Royal Council. Pintoin explains that with the royal treasury exhausted, the king and the princes were not able to pay their debts, let alone fund the defense against incursions from the English. After much deliberation, Philip, who had long opposed such taxes, was persuaded by the rest of the Royal Council that a tax was necessary.[13] This is the tax for which Christine praises Philip so warmly in the *Fais et bonnes meurs*, as we will see below.

The new Duke of Burgundy first entered Paris on May 23 to pay homage to the king for his newly inherited lands.[14] Although he did not remain long during that trip, continuing on to Dijon, he had wine distributed to merchants of Paris and royal officials in an effort to gather support on which to draw when he returned.[15] Although he stopped in Paris in August on his return north, he did not take his place on the Royal Council until February 1405. Richard Vaughan suggests that his appearance at that point was strategic, corresponding to deliberations on a new tax for the war.[16] At that time, Pintoin notes, Jean did not have much clout, ranking only fifth in deliberations of the council.[17] This chronicler's report of Jean's refusal to support any tax suggests that it was staged as a way of garnering popularity in Paris. Pintoin complains, "The military expeditions that I have written about this year, whatever they brought to the glory of the kingdom, they were not able to curb the pride of the English, who prowled freely through the kingdom along the maritime coasts, making trouble for people, and, when they engaged, they often came out on top." Everyone suffered from these depredations and the taxes imposed to defend against them: the clergy, the nobility, and the lower classes. All laid the blame for their suffering, the chronicler continues, on the queen and the Duke of Orleans, who were governing inefficiently. After this report, Pintoin announces that Jean refused to approve a new tax because it would be tyrannical: his territories would not be subject to it. Indeed, if he could be convinced that funds truly were lacking to maintain the honor of the kingdom, he would make up the shortfall with his own money.[18] Just days later, Jean announced his position before a group that included two presidents of the Parlement de Paris, two of the *maîtres des comptes*, and the *prévôt des marchands*.[19] Furthermore, he was courted in May in Artois by an embassy from the University of Paris seeking his support in the Schism. We recall that obedience to the Avignon pope had been restored in May 1403. When the Roman pope, Boniface IX, died on October 24, 1404, officials at the University of Paris hoped that Benedict XIII would reach out to them to end the Schism. The Avignon pope did not do this; still furious about the restoration, the university men called on Jean to support them against Benedict.[20]

With Philip dead and Jean threatening, Isabeau allied with Louis. The way for this alliance may have been paved by the death, in 1402, of Giangaleazzo Visconti, Louis's father-in-law and the enemy of Isabeau and her kinsmen; as we saw in chapter 3, although Louis and Isabeau were in contact, the queen's family politics were opposed to Louis's. But if her politics had been compatible with Philip's, she was suspicious of the new Duke of Burgundy, her apprehension obvious in a treaty that she signed with him the day before the double marriage of his daughter Marguerite to the dauphin and his son Philip to the royal princess Michelle on February 14. In the treaty, Isabeau promises to defend Jean's interests as far as permitted by the family hierarchy, where the interests of those more closely related to her than Jean (this would be Louis) must precede his.[21]

Pintoin's chronicle offers evidence of the deterioration of the relationship between Isabeau and the Burgundians. A report of a sermon preached at the court by the Augustinian Jacques Legrand in May 1405 demonstrates that the Burgundian propaganda machine had begun to include Isabeau in its attacks on Louis. The text of the sermon no longer exists; we have only Pintoin's description, according to which Legrand preached that "Lady Venus" occupied the throne in Isabeau's court and that she was followed by "drunkenness and debauchery," "turning night into day, with continual dissolute dancing."[22] Pintoin's account of the sermon, which the monk characterizes as critical of Isabeau and Louis of Orleans, is the primary cause of a misperception that Paris buzzed with rumors of a romantic liaison between the queen and her brother-in-law. Although the suspicion that Louis and Isabeau were lovers has been laid to rest, Pintoin's interpretation of the sermon as an attack on the financial management of the two continues to be accepted as true. However, the monk's take on the sermon misses its central point. Legrand's sermon specifically targeted the English war: May 15, 1405, saw the disastrous expedition of the Count of Saint Pol against a garrison at Marck. That this is the point of the sermon is clear from Pintoin's own reiteration of the sermon's content. He explains that the king, having missed the sermon, summoned Legrand and asked him to repeat his words. The sermon reported by Pintoin this time around is not an indictment of the queen's immoral court but of the badly managed war with the English.[23] Legrand compares Charles VI unfavorably to his father, who had also imposed taxes. But Charles V had used them to increase the glory of France. The taxes imposed by Charles VI, by contrast, funded expeditions that were not glorious.[24] Thus the criticism reported by Pintoin that Venus reigned at court was the traditional one of ineffective fighters as knights of Venus rather than Mars, a complaint against Louis and Isabeau that the war was going badly.[25]

This entry, coupled with the passage noted above in which Jean refuses to approve a new tax for defense, shows that Jean considered Isabeau a genuine threat. Until this point, Pintoin's chronicle has never referred to Isabeau as a powerful figure: indeed, she receives scarce mention; control of the government is attributed to Philip of Burgundy and Louis of Orleans. And yet Isabeau suddenly appears as a ruling figure, alongside Louis, just after Jean's succession. Her sudden promotion can only be the result of her support of Louis. Jean will now characterize her as an enemy until he disposes of Louis in 1407.

Despite Jean's posturing about taxes, he was in search of royal funds to finance Burgundy. Philip of Burgundy had received about half of his total yearly revenues from the royal treasury in the form of ordinary pensions, gifts, and *aides* for military ventures conducted in the interests of the French kingdom by soldiers from Burgundian territories.[26] But Jean, whose family relationship to the king was much more distant than his father's, was excluded initially from similar access to funds.[27] In April 1405 Jean sent a request to the king through Jean Chousat, his treasurer and receiver-general of finance, for the usual military *aides* and the annual allowance for the upkeep of the Sluis garrison. Chousat apparently received sealed letters from the king authorizing payment. Still, Jean could not collect the money, because Louis held the purse strings.[28] Although Jean sent ambassadors to the king, queen, and Royal Council to plead his case, nothing came of it.[29]

Jean responded aggressively. Advised by his counselors to take his case directly to the king, he left Arras for Paris on August 15, 1405, accompanied by eight hundred soldiers bearing hidden arms. Although he later claimed that he intended only to render homage for his maternal inheritance and that he had been invited by the king to discuss reformation of the kingdom, no other evidence suggests that the king wanted his opinion on reform.[30] Moreover, the eight hundred covertly armed soldiers are difficult to explain if Jean wanted only to pay homage. Rather, his entry appears to have been a threat designed to provoke the intervention of the king to restore the position of influence within the government formerly enjoyed by the House of Burgundy. In addition to threatening violence by entering Paris with his army, Jean planned to gather support from the Parisians. He had set off from Arras carrying a document detailing a set of demands for reform of the kingdom, which he would produce later for a public reading.[31] As we have seen, the new Duke of Burgundy had already begun cultivating connections in Paris, and he possessed a store of good will among the Parisians inherited from his father.

When Louis learned on August 17 that Jean was approaching Paris, he understood the significance of his cousin's challenge. On August 16 or 17, the king slipped into madness, which meant that Jean could seize the eight-year-old dauphin, his son-in-law since February, as a pawn.[32] Thus the boy had to be protected from Jean. Louis departed for Melun, one of the queen's fortified chateaux, where he called his men to arms, while Isabeau, joining Louis in Melun, ordered that the dauphin, his recent bride, Marguerite of Burgundy, and the other royal children be sent to her there. The guards of the children's convoy included the queen's brother Louis of Bavaria and the king's *grand maître de l'hôtel*, Jean de Montaigu. Arriving in Paris on August 19, Jean was informed that Louis and Isabeau had departed two days earlier and that the children were on the road to Melun. He did not even stop but continued on through Paris, overtaking the children and guardians in Juvisy, about twenty kilometers south of the city and thirteen kilometers from Corbeil, where Louis and Isabeau had come to meet the children. Jean forced the convoy to return to Paris. The guards protested but acquiesced, not wanting to alarm the children, one of them riding to inform Louis and Isabeau.

Jean, conscious that in seizing the dauphin he had laid himself open to charges of a coup attempt, moved immediately to mitigate the damage. That same day, he sent a justificatory letter to the cities of France, claiming that he had been summoned to Paris by the king.[33] As for the dauphin, he pretended not to realize that Isabeau had summoned the boy in response to his own march on Paris. Upon his arrival, he writes, he learned that the king had fallen ill and that the royal children had been transported from the city. Suspicious, he had gone to investigate. Louis quickly countered in a closed letter to the Parlement de Paris. The Duke of Burgundy had committed an act of *lèse majesté*, he claimed, requesting that the Parlement "not suffer the dauphin to be moved, nor more soldiers to enter the gates of Paris for fear of violence."[34]

The Royal Council forbade joining forces with either Louis or Jean.[35] Nor was Jean's call for reform, expressed in letters to the Parlement and the Chambre des comptes, received favorably by either of those bodies. The Chambre des comptes declined when requested to consider it, the president intimating that the Duke of Burgundy was overstepping his rank: "the gentlemen of the Chamber are the natural subjects of the king, and obligated to protect his rights and to serve him loyally because of their offices and for many other reasons, and they will keep their loyalty forever towards him, the queen, and their children, and they would always do their will and offer them service and heed all of their wishes."[36] The princes of the blood were also deeply suspicious, as we see in a letter from Chousat to the Chambre des comptes of Dijon recounting the obstacles that Jean's proposal faced with them. The

Duke of Berry had immediately demanded that the dauphin be turned over to him, which Chousat described as a "very bad beginning for our task."[37]

Still, that the "kidnapping," in what has come down through history as the "kidnapping of the dauphin," refers to Louis and Isabeau's attempt to keep the dauphin out of the hands of Jean rather than Jean's seizure of the boy indicates how effectively the Duke of Burgundy was able to sell his version of the story. True, Louis responded in a letter of September 2, addressed to the Parlement and sent out to the cities of France, that Jean's actions were illegal, and he reminded his audience that the king had named Isabeau guardian of the royal children. The queen and the children would never be safe as long as such thuggery was allowed; all authority would be lost. Most serious, Louis claimed that Jean's goal was nothing less than custody over the mad king.[38] But the Duke of Burgundy continued to control the discussion, indicting Isabeau as a mother in a letter of September 8, in which he claimed that he had stopped the dauphin on his way to Melun because he could not believe that the queen had authorized the transfer, given that the boy was haemorrhaging from the nose.[39] No other account mentions this. Ferrando de Robledo's account of the incident to the king of Castile explains that Louis of Bavaria showed Jean letters from the queen ordering that the dauphin be sent to her.[40] The Duke of Burgundy concluded by insisting again on his selfless motives. He had no desire for power for himself, and none to stir dissent and division in the kingdom.

Françoise Autrand has observed that as the foremost of the princes of the blood, the Duke of Orleans felt no need to pander to crowds.[41] But Jean made his case publicly and thus easily controlled the representation of the dispute.[42] Traces of this control abound. The Orleanist-inclined chronicle attributed to Guillaume Cousinot claims that the Duke of Burgundy, seeking to turn the people against Louis and Isabeau, spread lies in taverns.[43] Other incidents are recorded in Pintoin's chronicle, which mentions that during the standoff between the dukes, gossip flew back and forth between the factions at court: one could not say anything without the other being informed about it by false courtiers, whose hateful words only augmented the animosity between the two.[44] A Burgundian pamphlet of 1406 called the *Songe véritable*, which I discuss in the next chapter, presents Fortune vowing to ruin the queen's reputation within the year. In this case, Jean's counselor Jean de Nielles told members of the Parlement, the Chambre des comptes, and the university, at a gathering at the Louvre on August 21 presided over by the dauphin, that the Duke of Burgundy sought only the good of the kingdom.[45] The discourse, prepared, as I have noted, before Jean departed Arras, claimed that the king was not being well cared for; that the king's *officiers* were corrupt; that the domain was dilapidated; that the church was weighed down with taxes; and that the Duke of Orleans was spending on himself the taxes collected for the war against England.[46] The university supported the proposals outlined by Jean de Nielles.[47]

Although Jean of Burgundy would lose the university's backing when he took over the government in 1409, in 1405 he maintained the support that his father had enjoyed. Louis's supporters worried, with reason, that he was on the defensive. Cousinot's Orleanist-leaning chronicle says that the Burgundians' letters suggest that they truly wanted to reform the royal domain and defend the kingdom, and they sent these letters to the cities, which, because of high taxes, were inclined to favor the Burgundians. As for the Parisians specifically, the Burgundians won them over by persuading the king to return their chains (the chains with which they closed off the city for security against attack had been taken from them after their rebellion of the early 1380s). Thus the *menu peuple* supported the Burgundians more and more ("Dont lui adhérèrent le menu peuple de plus en plus").[48]

During the month of September, the armies of the two factions waited while soldiers for both sides pillaged, angering the Parisians. Eventually, Jean moved first, calling in more soldiers, which caused Louis to prepare for attack. But after his initial advantage, Jean hit resistance. Although he called upon the Parisians to join him against the Duke of Orleans, Pintoin reports that on September 24 a group of the ruling men of Paris announced their refusal to take up arms against Louis: they did not answer to Jean but to the king or the dauphin.[49] Describing the same event, Juvénal des Ursins asserts that the Parisians honored all but one of Jean's requests. When he asked that they gather in the fields with him, they responded that they would defend their city but would not take up arms and follow him.[50] The Parisians' refusal to fight for Jean marked the beginning of the end of the adventure. Jean's situation degenerated as the cost of keeping his army in Paris mounted. Nor did the Royal Council heed Jean's call for reform, putting him off again and again.[51]

Peace Restored

After a brief period of lucidity, the king had slipped back into madness on September 23 or 25. As we have seen, when the king was mad, Isabeau was authorized by royal ordinance to arbitrate between the dukes, and she took action when he lapsed in late September. She and Louis headed for Vincennes to begin peace negotiations. Their arrival was delayed, however, by Jean of Burgundy, who went out to meet them for reasons unknown, accompanied by four hundred men bearing lances, causing them to halt in Corbeil. Isabeau sent letters from Corbeil to the dukes of Burgundy and Bourbon on September 29, presumably to inform them of her desire to settle the conflict.[52] She and Louis then departed for Vincennes, according to Pintoin, on October 8.[53]

Buoyed by Christine's letter of October 5, the *Epistre a la reine de France*, the queen undertook to mediate, but little progress was made initially, for the dukes remained stubborn on Jean's demand for reforms. Juvénal des Ursins explains that the Duke of Burgundy insisted that his proposed reforms, or at least some of them, be accepted as a condition of reconciliation. The Duke of Orleans, seeing this as another Burgundian ploy to cultivate the favor of the Parisians, refused to allow his cousin any advantage. Instead, he summoned the *prévôt des marchands* and other important bourgeois of Paris and made his own case to them. He laid out the argument in "beautiful and gracious words" that he was closer to the throne than Jean and that he desired only the good of the kingdom. When Jean learned of this, he threatened to put the Chateau of Vincennes under siege, although he was talked out of the plan.[54]

On October 12, the Royal Council promulgated an ordinance from Vincennes reiterating the queen's authority over the dukes. Written in the voice of the king, the ordinance refers to the regency ordinances of 1402, explaining that by "the very weighty deliberation of the Council, we long ago gave the power to our very dear and well-loved companion the Queen to attend to, work on and take care of the important needs and affairs of our kingdom during our absence, or when we were too occupied to work on or attend to them, and if there occurred problems, disagreements or discords between some of our blood and lineage." The king, discovering that Louis and John had called up men-at-arms, ordered them to submit immediately to the queen's arbitration: "And whatever our companion wants to be done, let it be done with the same rigor as if we had ordered it ourselves." If the dukes did not obey the queen, they would not be permitted to reenter the kingdom, "on pain of physical forfeiture and the forfeiture of goods."[55]

Negotiations lasted until October 16, writes Pintoin, when an agreement was concluded, announced by heralds in the Parlement de Paris and at Châtelet.[56] Lehoux, citing Chousat, explains that Jean agreed to peace because at least some of his reforms would be enacted.[57] The next day, the dukes made their entry into Paris together and sent their troops home. Afterward, before the Duke of Berry and the queen, to whom they gave thanks for their work, the dukes saluted each other and, having clasped hands, exchanged a kiss of peace and swore to each other to remain henceforth in concord.[58]

Christine and the Appearance of Jean of Burgundy

With the *Chemin de longue étude*, Christine continued to create authority for Louis against the challenges of Philip, laying out the three qualities most necessary to a leader—noblesse, courage, and wisdom—and suggesting that the Duke of Orleans possessed all of these. Christine chose the same trio of qualities to structure her panegyric to Charles V in the *Livre des fais et bonnes meurs du sage roy Charles V*.

Philip's death in April 1404, while Christine was in the midst of composing the *Fais et bonnes meurs*, brought the ascendance of Jean sans Peur, and with the new Duke of Burgundy's apparent success in winning support for himself, Christine seems to have reevaluated how best to support Louis's regency, deciding that associating him with the queen would enhance his authority. Thus Christine begins to fortify the queen's reputation as peacemaker, as manifested in Isabeau's entry and coronation and made explicit in Charles VI's regency ordinances. Just as Mary offered the church an approachable human face, so would Isabeau represent the monarchy. We have noted that regency consisted of two separable offices, guardianship (sometimes called *tutelle*) of the dauphin and administration of the realm. During certain regencies, the two positions were held by different individuals; during others, they were invested in a single person. Christine does not advocate replacing Louis with the queen; she continues to support him as administrator of the realm. In 1405 and 1406, however, she composes, along with the *Epistre a la reine*, the two great treatises on women to which she owes her rediscovery by feminist scholars of the 1970s and 1980s. These works, which must be read in the context of Jean's attempts to seize control of the government, reinforce Isabeau's position as peacemaker, saving the throne for her son. In the rest of this chapter, I examine Christine's first four major works of prose: the *Fais et bonnes meurs*, and the "feminist" works, the *Cité des dames*, *Epistre a la reine*, and the *Livre des trois vertus*. I conclude with a reading of a hybrid verse-prose love story, *Livre du duc des vrais amans*, arguing that in this narrative of *médisans* tormenting a pair of lovers, Christine returns to a tried and true genre of love narrative to deplore Burgundian propagandists.

In this study of Christine's engagement with the Armagnac-Burgundian feud, I cannot adequately analyze the interesting and much-noted poetic phenomenon of her shift from verse to prose. However, the shift cannot be left entirely without comment. As I noted in the previous chapter, and as E. Jeffrey Richards and others have detailed, Christine characterizes her use of verse or prose as a stylistic choice, explaining that both can be vehicles for truth.[59] Still, as Adrian Armstrong and Sarah Kay demonstrate, Christine's own assessment of the effects of her work may not be adequate, because "poetic form plays an important role in shaping knowledge and in grounding the relationship between author and public."[60] Suzanne Conklin Akbari offers another perspective, seeing Christine's movement to prose as participating "in an effort to integrate some of the rational and argumentative structures found in late fourteenth-century French translations of philosophical and scientific writings within the originally poetic forms of medieval allegory."[61] In full agreement with these perspectives on the effects of Christine's choice of verse or prose, I would draw attention to another issue relevant to Christine's poetics, a shift that cannot be associated entirely with her choice of verse or prose: her narrators. On the one hand, the narrators of Christine's lyric verse and verse allegory are avatars of Christine herself, their narratives filtered through this autobiographical character. This Christine also directs the reader through some of her prose works, forming the subjective site of the stories of the *Cité des dames* and the *Trois vertus* as well as the *Advision*. The continuation of this character from verse to prose lends credence to Richards's argument that Christine herself imagined these binaries not as constitutive of separate genres but as a stylistic choice, although this does not deny that the effects of this choice were more profound than she understood.[62] On the other hand, in many of Christine's prose works composed after the rise of Jean of Burgundy, the narrator plays a minimal role, a phenomenon I discuss in chapters 5 and 6. It seems that Christine chose prose to make her increasingly urgent arguments, as Akbari proposes. But I would add that because Christine's narrator persona was well known and was associated with the House of Orleans, her presence had to be curtailed in some works, replaced by a narrator less grounded in concrete detail. A prose work filtered through an unmarked narrator was appropriate to a work intended to work intellectually on a politically divided public, and thus protected Christine.

The *Livre des fais et bonnes meurs du sage roy Charles V*

Scholars have suggested that the *Fais et bonnes meurs* should be read as a mirror for princes, a guide for the dauphin, Louis of Guyenne.[63] The work also has been regarded as a move on Philip's part to "to reinforce his own political influence," that is, to establish "himself as the most fitting person to direct the kingdom's future."[64] Certainly, in this panegyric on her beloved Charles V, Christine creates a mirror for the young dauphin. However, as for the notion that Philip sought to build his reputation with the commission, although he may have intended this outcome, Christine seized the opportunity to circumscribe his role, praising him only in his role as Duke of Burgundy, never as regent. Moreover, the work, completed after Philip's death, warns readers discreetly against the new duke Jean.

Most interesting, given the circumstances of its production, the work promotes Louis. This is clearest in the attribution to Charles V of the same three principal qualities that Christine had recently given the king of the world in the *Chemin de longue étude*. *Noblece* (*de corage*), *chevalerie*, and *sagece* are the qualities necessary for the king of the world, and these also structure the narrative of the *Fais et bonnes meurs*, each quality serving to organize one section of the work. In addition to drawing attention to the similarities between Louis and his father in this prominent way, Christine encourages other resemblances and echoes throughout the work. One of the most obvious is the remarkable youthful success of father and son. As Christine points out in the first section of the *Fais et bonnes meurs*, Charles V was renowned for the uncommon good sense and strength of character that he had shown as a young man directing the kingdom during King Jean's imprisonment in England. At the time of his coronation, "despite the tumult of his young age," Charles "was luminous with clear knowledge, which let him distinguish the clear from the cloudy, the beautiful from the ugly, the good from the evil, by which he was inspired to follow the way of salvation, casting aside youth blinded by streams of ignorance" (1:20–21).[65] As for Louis, in the sketch in the *Fais et bonnes meurs* that she devotes to him, Christine describes his capacity to assume heavy responsibilities at a young age. The duke possessed "natural sense that none of his age surpassed," she explains (1:172). She further casts Louis's youth in a positive light by noting that he attracted people from all over with his "beautiful youth and hope of good action" (1:172). If he lives to old age, she writes, "he will be a prince of great excellence through whom much good will be accomplished" (2:175).

With this basic comparison established, a series of passages on Charles V's youth in the first section of the work takes on new meaning. Christine consecrates passages of general interest to "the youth of King Charles, and why it is dangerous when the children of princes are not instructed in good doctrine," followed by passages on "coronation," "youth and its conditions," "more of the same," "still more on youth," "the time of discretion and the perfect age," and finally, "the age of maturity" (1:2). Why this emphasis on the state of youth? That the *Fais et bonnes meurs* was intended as a guide to raising and training the young dauphin may partly explain the inclusion of these passages. But I believe that the passages serve a dual purpose, as defenses against Philip's complaints that Louis was too young to be given responsibility. As we saw in chapter 2, the chronicles of Pintoin and Juvénal des Ursins reveal that Philip of Burgundy exploited a narrative of Louis as a rash youth. As I noted in chapter 1, Charles had been subject to criticism during his youth. Christine thoroughly rebuts the Burgundian accusation that Louis's youth, such as it was, was a disadvantage.

Christine begins the section on youth by noting cryptically that Charles V's youth had been "more perverse than appropriate for such a prince" (2:17). The king's biographer Roland Delachenal, puzzled by Christine's statement, sought fruitlessly to corroborate it: "What do such vague allusions hide? Disordered morals? Possibly, but unsubstantiated insinuations—sometimes simple 'they say' ['on dit']—are a very fragile basis for authority, even for conjecture."[66] But in the context of Christine's extended comparison of the defunct king and his son, the mention of Charles V's youthful folly looks like an attempt to make Louis look even better than his father. Christine first points out that the wise Charles V led a "perverse" youth; she further notes that his youthful faults could be attributed to his bad training: "I suppose that this could be due to bad administrators" (1:17). In contrast, the young Duke of Orleans never passed through a period of youthful folly, according to Christine, a happy fact that she attributes to his excellent training. King Charles V, she writes, "committed administration and care of him [Louis] to a good and wise lady, called Madame Roussel . . . and this good lady, as soon as he learned to speak, the first words that she taught him were his 'Ave Maria'" (1:169–70).

Christine throws her emphasis on the youth of Charles V and his son into yet greater relief in a section praising men "of mature age," for here she points out that nothing is more dangerous than an old man who is *not* wise. In Roman times, she explains, youths honored their elders. On the one hand, it is good to honor old men in a "well-ordered body politic" (1:35). On the other, she hastens to add, she is talking only about "wise and brave old men," not "men grown old in bad malice," because "in the world there is no greater peril [than they], or those who reach a great age without knowledge of virtue or prudence" (1:35). That she means to compare the old Philip unfavorably to the young Louis becomes manifest in what follows immediately after these words. There are many "old men without wisdom," she says, contrasting them with "other men rather young and filled with virtue and wisdom, as was the wise King Charles, about whom we write, the same who at a very young age wished to know the effects of virtue, which was a gift of God beyond nature; and also they [virtues] are greatly influenced by such graces, but there is no doubt that if such chosen men can live into maturity, in them the perfection of their graces doubles." As noted above, Christine writes nearly the same thing about Louis: that if he lives to old age he will be a prince of great excellence.

A further resemblance between father and son is their facility with language. Christine praises Louis's "beautiful speech naturally adorned with rhetoric," referring to the moving discourse that Charles V presented before Emperor Charles IV. "And then the wise king, who in his understanding possessed science and in his language a sovereign rhetoric, began his speech with a preamble so beautiful and remarkable that it was a lovely thing to hear" (2:116–17).

Finally, the structure of the sketch of Louis in the *Fais et bonnes meurs* also reflects the tripartite structure of the text as a whole, as Françoise Autrand has noted.[67] Christine mentions first that "this prince is of great courage" (1:170). Next she discusses his chivalry: "He is today the retreat and refuge of all chivalry in France, of which he holds a noble court with very handsome and refined young men, beautiful, attractive, and well refined, all prepared to devote themselves to the service of good" (171–72). She brings the section to an end by noting Louis's wisdom, his "sagesse," offering examples of his own words to demonstrate it (175).

Christine also praises the Duke of Burgundy in the section devoted to him, but only for carrying out his duties in his own territories, never as regent of France. First, she comments on his valor at remaining at his father's side in the Battle of Poitiers (1:144–45), then on his advantageous marriage to Marguerite of Flanders (145). Next in line is his wise governance of his territories, followed by praise for his augmentation of the French Crown by arranging profitable marriages—including that between Charles VI and Isabeau (146–47). This leads to mention of the princess Isabelle's marriage to Richard II, that king's overthrow, and a warning against treason (147–48). More praise for arranging useful marriage alliances follows, along with the comment that in this way ("ainssi") Philip helped the French kingdom; he also did his best to help the present king in his illness (149). The section concludes by commending the duke for permitting a tax to be collected for the war with the English just before he died (150). Christine acclaims those of Philip's actions carried out as Duke of Burgundy. As she had striven in other works to highlight Louis's proper place as second to the king, so she situates Philip as Duke of Burgundy in his place.

While circumscribing Philip's role, the *Fais et bonnes meurs* also criticizes Burgundian politics. In her study of Charles V's version of the *Grandes chroniques de France*, Anne Hedeman discerns the careful program undertaken by scribes and illuminators to control the representation of the reign of the wise king. As we have noted, Christine read the *Grandes chroniques*. Indeed, it was one of her major sources for the *Fais et bonnes meurs*, which borrows several of the chronicle's arguments: the legitimacy of the Valois; French rights over the English territories in France; royal support for the Avignon pope. Christine draws upon these arguments to support Louis's position, showing how he furthered the program set in place by his father, and to criticize the actions of Philip, who had no legitimate claim to head the government.

Regarding the legitimacy of the Valois, the *Grandes chroniques* needed to justify the rupture between Charles IV, last of the Capetian kings, and Philip VI of Valois, to verify that the crown had been passed down from father to son in a direct line, and, when that became impossible, to the closest male relative. Obviously, that had not happened; as we saw in chapter 1, many had contested the crown's passing to Philip VI, great-nephew of Philip IV, instead of Charles of Navarre, grandson of Philip IV through his mother. But peaceful succession was a tremendous source of pride for the French, who compared themselves to the English, whose Richard II had been deposed by a usurper. Charles VI's malady was dangerous because it had allowed Philip to reinstall himself at the head of the government fewer than four years after Charles VI had forced his uncle from power to take control for himself. We have noted that in other works Christine insists on Louis's precedence over Philip in rank, systematically placing the young man ahead of his uncle. The single work in which Louis follows his uncles is the *Fais et bonnes meurs*. In this case, however, Charles VI also follows his uncle. Christine explains why: Charles VI and Louis are the fruits issuing from the noble tree, whereas the brothers of Charles V are its branches. Logically, the branch comes before the fruit; therefore, the brother will be mentioned first (1:134). In the *Fais et bonnes meurs*, Louis is matched up with Charles VI: "Now we will speak of the fruit issuing from this noble stem and tree, that is, the two noble sons" (1:161).

In contrast, when Christine mentions Philip in the context of the government, it is never to place him next to the king. On the contrary, her point is always to recall that he seized power from his brother, Louis of Anjou, after the death of Charles V. In her sketch of the Duke of Anjou, Christine explains that after the death of Charles V, although the Duke of Anjou was granted regency of the realm until the young king was old enough to be crowned, he left everything in the hands of the other brothers and left France (1:138). Although Christine does not overtly criticize the Duke of Burgundy for having pushed Louis from the regency, in the third part of the *Fais et bonnes meurs*, she discusses Charles V's ordinances on the regency designed to prevent Philip from seizing power after his death, that is, the new laws that the *Grandes chroniques* makes a point of mentioning, as we saw in chapter 1. In a chapter titled "On the prudence and skill [art] in the person of the king Charles, and what this is" (2:21–25), she explains that Charles V, recognizing that he would not live to old age, wished "for the good of the French crown and common utility" to guarantee that his son would receive the royal dignity at the age of fourteen. This ordinance thus created a new law, one that set a new precedent; furthermore, "the king instituted other laws and establishments regarding the guardianship of his children and the finances" (2:22). Christine acknowledges that some would deny a king the right to change custom by imposing a new law to suit his own purposes. But Charles had the right to make this change, she explains, and such new laws should be honored, even if they contradict old laws. It is impossible not to see here a reproach to Philip for his refusal to honor the regency laws of Charles V by wresting regency from Louis of Anjou and insisting on a regency council.[68] Moreover, as we have seen, Philip ejected the marmousets, whom Charles had charged with watching over the royal children and the finances of the realm. Once again, Christine cannot overtly chastise the duke for this. But she is lavish in her praise for one of his victims, Charles V's most trusted counselor, Bureau de La Rivière (1:101), as we saw in chapter 1, and refers to Jean de Montaigu as a true friend (1:179).

In her description of the conflict with England, Christine further praises Louis while quietly criticizing Philip. She approves Louis's efforts to defend the French against the English after the assassination of Richard II. She praises his courage in sending letters to England challenging the usurping King Henry IV, "with his own body" and by "many valorous challenges to a duel," which Henry IV did not dare accept (1:171).[69] Philip, whose territories in Flanders depended upon untroubled trade with England, wanted only to keep peace with the English, and for this reason he raised obstacles to the taxes that Louis attempted to assess for the war with England. It is in this context that we must read Christine's frequent insistence on the right of a king to collect taxes to support a war, "which, for such a use, is an ancient right and custom in all lands, that is, for arms to vanquish enemies of the country; as everyone can see, this tax is being used for armies, which are there on the borders of the realm" (1:149–50).

Maurice Rey has shown that the taxes that Louis raised for the war did not actually go into his own pockets, as Burgundian propaganda claimed.[70] Indeed, Christine cites with approbation the single case in which Philip gave his support to a tax assessed for the war. In describing the Duke of Burgundy's virtues, she mentions that although he was much loved, no one escapes some criticism. Philip was criticized for approving a tax, even though it was "just and not excessive, however much some complain about it" (1:149).[71] At the very moment that she was writing the *Fais et bonnes meurs*, Jean of Burgundy was inciting the Parisians against Louis of Orleans by proclaiming his opposition to all taxes for the war.[72]

Finally, as we saw in chapter 2, the conflict between Louis and his uncle was largely rooted in their positions on the Great Schism. Louis, who favored restoring obedience to Benedict XIII in 1403, had never ceased to support the popes of Avignon. Philip, in contrast, had helped to bring about the withdrawal of obedience in 1398, a position in which he remained steadfast. Christine does not hide her preference, writing that Louis "has given himself great pains to restore peace to the Church, even going to see the Pope" (1:175).

The description of Philip in the *Fais et bonnes meurs* has been described as a panegyric on the duke, while the portrait of Louis is allegedly "much more rapid and less laudatory."[73] But when we look closely at the text, it is difficult indeed to understand how the depiction of Louis, so similar to that of his father, can be regarded as anything but laudatory. The assessment undoubtedly derives from an old prejudice against the Duke of Orleans as a foolish and debauched young man.

Female Regency: The "Feminist" Works

The practical virtue of prudence that Christine attributes to Othea and to Charles V receives even fuller treatment in her defense of Isabeau. By the time that she composed the *Cité des dames* in 1405, Christine had already been tapping Isabeau's image as a figure of peace. In this work she goes further, inserting Isabeau into the constellation of queen-regents: French, biblical, and mythological. Female regency had a long history in France. In the *Cité des dames*, Christine fortifies the role that Isabeau had been assigned in royal ordinances by creating for the queen a genealogy of prudent and skilled female regents. In the *Epistre a la reine* and the *Livre des trois vertus*, she lends further authority to the queen's position, showing it to be one that required great prudence to navigate.

In the *Cité des dames*, Christine's argument for Isabeau is based on female exclusion from the throne, which itself emerges logically from the construction of gender that the poet details throughout her corpus. We saw in the *Mutacion de fortune* that women are barred from certain positions, held back by "Nature," who maintains a divinely ordained hierarchy. But this does not mean that a woman is not as competent as her male counterpart to fulfill the tasks from which Nature excludes her, if she possesses prudence, the quality necessary for governance and mediation or diplomacy. True, women do not normally engage in public careers. But this is because "as a wise and well-organized lord divides his household into different offices to take care of different tasks . . . God wanted that man and woman serve him differently, that they help and support each other mutually, each in his or her way" (92).[74] This is not because of women's insufficient understanding ("entendement," the quality that Christine attributes to Isabeau in her dedicatory letter to the *Roman de la rose* quarrel) (94). Those who believe that women lack natural sense ("sens naturel") for government will be proved wrong by Reason's examples of great female rulers of the past.

Nicaula, or the queen of Sheba, "who governed with marvelous prudence," is the first example (94–96). She is followed by Fredegonde, who prudently appeased the barons by showing them the baby king Clotaire, and who "raised [Clotaire] herself until he was big and, because of her, wore the crown and the honor of the kingdom, which never would have happened except for her prudence" (98). The appearance of Fredegonde as a positive French forebear is interesting, as Colette Beaune has noted: "After a long and chequered literary past, the queen appears in a new and modified form in the first decade of the fifteenth century, her private life, described as scandalous in earlier versions, nearly completely erased and her public qualities exalted."[75] The regency of Blanche of Castile in the mid-thirteenth century had necessitated some positive forebears, Beaune writes, and Fredegonde, as regent, offered one possibility.[76] The problem was her reputation, but this difficulty was overcome thanks to one episode that became iconic in the late fourteenth century, and that Christine drew on: Fredegonde's display of her baby to the warring barons. The story appears in Charles V's regency ordinance setting the age of accession, although Fredegonde is not named (she is "the queen his mother"), and the baby is identified incorrectly as well.[77] This is the Fredegonde who figures at the head of Christine's genealogy of regents.

Nicaula and Fredegonde, then, lead the list of French noblewomen who "governed themselves and their jurisdictions well in their widowhood": Blanche of Castile, Jeanne of Evreux, Blanche of Orleans, Bonne of Luxembourg (wife of Jean Le Bon), Marie of Blois, Countess of Anjou, and Catherine, Countess of La Marche and Vendôme (100).[78] Behind this illustrious group, we find many female regents from mythology who ruled for their husbands or brothers (94–150). In the discussion of these mythological regents, Christine returns several times to the quality of "entendement" (150–94) and then prudence (194–214).

When Isabeau finally appears at the end of book 2, it is neither her intelligence nor her prudence that is vaunted, but her goodness. Earlier, the allegorical figure of Raison (Reason) has commented that God and Nature were kind in making women physically weak, for this has spared them from perpetrating the horrible cruelties for which men have been responsible (104). Droiture (Rectitude), the second of the allegorical figures in the *Cité des dames*, reiterates the point in her description of Isabeau. Appearing among the living princesses and ladies of France, Isabeau is implicitly contrasted with the Duke of Burgundy by Droiture, who explains that in Isabeau there is no "cruelty, extortion, or any vice whatsoever, but rather great love and kindness towards her subjects" (422). Christine has already lauded the queen's mental gifts in earlier works. Here, Isabeau's peacefulness is her primary advantage.

This quality is also evoked via references to the Virgin Mary, the ultimate exemplar for female regents, throughout the *Cité des dames*, from its beginning in Christine's office to its ending with the Virgin's entry into the city, a scene that recalls Isabeau's own entry of 1389.[79] As the narrative opens, the narrator Christine is deploring the slanderous portrayals of women common in literature. As she wonders tearfully why God would have created such a miserable creature, a beam of light falls across her lap, and the story, like Jesus, is conceived through divine intervention. Also, the physical "city of ladies" that Christine will help to construct refers to the body of the Virgin, the City of God. Psalm 87, describing the new Jerusalem, the *Civitas Dei*, was commonly held to refer to Mary, in whom Jesus "resided" (the psalm is still sung today at celebrations of the Virgin).[80] The Virgin's presence in the *Cité des dames* is further underlined through the figure of the queen of Sheba, the first of a series of female rulers Christine introduces. The empress Nicaula, the queen of Sheba, was often associated with the Virgin Mary through her entry into Jerusalem in search of Solomon and his wisdom, which was interpreted as a precursor of Mary's assumption into heaven, or as a figure for the church. The queen of Sheba was also associated with the bride of Christ in the Song of Solomon.[81] Moreover, one sees her portrayed with Solomon, the pair representing Christ and the Virgin in the court of heaven.[82]

Book 2 of the *Cité des dames* presents the prophetic sibyls, ten women "filled with wisdom [sapience]" (218). The feminine models in this book manifest the qualities of love, loyalty, and patience, qualities traditionally associated with the Virgin, and they end with contemporary princesses, including Isabeau. In book 3, the Virgin Mary herself, who has dominion and lordship ("dominacion et seigneurie") over all things after her son, "whom she carried and conceived through the Holy Spirit and who is the son of God the Father" (430), arrives in the *Cité des dames* to become its leader. This queen, blessed among women, reaches the city gates with her noble entourage, like a queen entering the city of Paris for her coronation: the castles and houses are ready and decorated, the streets strewn with flowers (430).

The second of Christine's works to defend Isabeau's regency, the *Epistre a la reine*, was written in the late stages of Jean of Burgundy's coup attempt, on October 5, 1405. In this work, Christine continues to draw on the Virgin Mary and Blanche of Castile in making her case for the queen, who is needed to mediate between the dukes. Its purpose is to enhance Isabeau's authority as an arbitrator to bring an end to their standoff and restore peace to the kingdom. It precedes by one week the ordinance promulgated by the Royal Council threatening the dukes with bodily harm if they refuse to submit themselves to the queen's arbitration.[83] It seems to have worked.

In the *Grandes chroniques*, Christine would have read the story of Blanche of Castile and the child Louis IX harassed by the barons of the realm. The chronicle recounts how the barons did not believe that Blanche, a woman, was fit to rule a kingdom.[84] Hearing that the barons were planning to seize the young king, the queen mother asked the powerful men of Paris to come to her aid. She then sent letters throughout the kingdom asking for further support. A great army assembled at Paris to deliver the young king from his enemies. In the epistle, Christine draws a parallel between Blanche and Isabeau, both harassed by unruly lords (76).[85] Christine means to rally the people of Paris behind Isabeau, just as they once came to the defense of Blanche. Like Fredegonde, Blanche had taken the child Louis in her arms and, extending him toward the quarreling barons, commanded that they look at their king, reminding them that he would one day be old enough to do something about their unruliness (76). The episode reminds readers that Isabeau had responded to Jean's entry into Paris with his army by calling the dauphin to join her in Melun, but that the boy had been waylaid by Jean and forced back to Paris.

As noted earlier, the king was lucid from August 26 through September 23 or 25, that is, during most of this crisis.[86] We have no record that he asked Isabeau to intervene in the dispute during this period. When he recovered, according to Juvénal des Ursins, he helped the Royal Council compose the ordinance mentioned above, reiterating Isabeau's authority to mediate.[87] Isabeau, therefore, was not authorized to mediate throughout most of the crisis. Moreover, she had strategic reasons for refusing to negotiate with the Duke of Burgundy, who was still strong enough to force the Royal Council to undertake the reforms he was proposing. In addition to fearing the strength of Jean's position in September 1405, Isabeau must also have doubted her ability to negotiate efficaciously between the recalcitrant dukes. But Jean's early advantage diminished with each passing day, as we have seen. By the time the king relapsed, Jean's situation was such that he was eager to negotiate.

The third text in which Christine promotes Isabeau's regency is the *Livre des trois vertus*, which features a mediating princess at the head of a community of women of all social levels. Although the work is dedicated to the dauphine, Marguerite of Burgundy, the role model for princesses in the work conducts herself like Isabeau, trying to keep the peace between belligerent lords. Christine acknowledges the weak position of a princess like Isabeau relative to the dukes. If women want to be effective, Christine explains, they must pursue other means than domination: "And you, who are a simple little woman, who has no strength, power or authority except given to you by others, do you think that you can dominate and surmount the world at will?" (20).[88] Only a clever woman can impose her will, by acting through others and persuading them to follow her—but the princess will be expected to produce results. People will come to her when they want the wrongs of her husband righted. In these cases, the princess will be a good friend "in the petition that they are requesting and in all other things in her power" (26).

Most important, the princess serves as a counterweight to impulsive male actions. "Men are by nature hardier and hotter, and their great desire to avenge themselves does not allow them to think in advance about the dangers and evils that might come from this" (34). When their heat leads to social disruption, the princess will mediate. Christine even supplies pacifying words that the princess might use with the offending party: she will say "that she acknowledges that the misdeed that has caused the dispute was very serious and that with good cause the prince is angry about it and intends rightful vengeance; however, she is always desirous of keeping the peace, and, therefore, if the offenders would like to make amends or make suitable reparations, she will make an effort to try to find a way to appease her husband" (34–35).

Explicit in its theory of female prudence as the quality necessary to political action, the work as a whole is premised on the mandate to fear God above all. It begins by advising the princess to begin the day with a careful examination of her conscience. But Christine repeats this stricture in her section on what we might think of as courtly virtue, or *prudence mondaine*, beginning this too with the reminder to fear God above all. Practical virtue is thus grounded in spiritual virtue. *Prudence mondaine* is the set of rhetorical skills necessary for positive self-representation, or, as Christine calls it, "honneur" and "bonne renommee" (41), which are essential to the political action in which the princess is involved (those who attend meetings of the Royal Council will be treated as a "sage" mistress of great "auctorité") (49). Retaining one's "bonne renommee" requires that one speak in an "ordered fashion with wise eloquence," an echo of both Louis and Charles V, whose well-ordered discourse Christine praises (45). This skill will allow the princess to dissimulate convincingly when necessary. Later in the text, Christine explains that "discreet dissimulation and prudent caution" are not vices but virtues (64).

Describing the special problems faced by a widowed princess, Christine explains that the job of keeping barons in line will fall to her if her son is too young to take charge. In the event of war between barons over the government, the princess will depend upon her wisdom to guide them and to bring them to peace and maintain it (84). Foreign enemies are not nearly as dangerous to the minor heir as internal ones, Christine asserts. Apart from the risk that barons might go to war over government, even debates surrounding such struggles are dangerous. Thus the wise lady will maintain peace between warring lords, acting as "an excellent arbitrator between them with her prudent composure and knowledge—thinking of the evil that could come of their disputes, given the youth of her child—that she will be able to appease them. To do this, she will seek the most appropriate means possible, treating them with gentleness, and making sure that all is done according to good and loyal advice" (85). It is clear to whom and what Christine refers.

Conclusion

The narrator of the *Fais et bonnes meurs* is a relatively discreet variation on Christine's autobiographical narrator. She writes her presence into the opening folios of the work, recounting how the Duke of Burgundy called her and her people ("gens") (1:8) to the Louvre to commission a biography of Charles V. Still, she presents herself as following in the stylistic footsteps of moral "edifiers" in prose, although her own intellect is not bright. The work is a "compilacion," she claims (1:5), a collection of others' words, and thus she does not thematize her own narrative presence. By contrast, the *Cité de dames*, the *Epistre a la reine*, and the *Trois vertus* depend for their effect on the narrator, Christine, as a mediating presence, a woman who knows the value of women in general and the significance of the queen in particular. I believe that the difference in audience accounts for these divergent narrative strategies: the Burgundians had commissioned the *Fais et bonnes meurs*, while the female regency works can be seen as interventions in favor of the queen, who was at that moment allied with Louis of Orleans.

I close this chapter on Christine's first responses to the aggression of Jean of Burgundy by examining the *Livre du duc des vrais amans* (1405). Like much of Christine's love poetry, this work is an appeal against slander, beginning, like the *Cent balades*, with the narrator explaining that although she is not particularly interested in writing a love story, she has agreed to do so because she has been summoned by a lord whom she must obey. This story, then, like the *Cent balades*, is founded on an act of obedience, and, like that cycle of poems, it continues to thematize the primacy of obedience in its depictions of lovers' ceding to the demands of love. The duke voluntarily devotes himself to love, submitting himself in the abstract even before he encounters a real lover. He thus shows a positive inclination of the will to accept natural hierarchy, like the loving young squire of the *Livre du debat de deux amans*. When he finds a lady worthy of his devotion, he assumes a position of inferiority toward her as the more highly ranked and older party, assuring her that he is hers, body and soul (155, lines 2701–2).[89] Although this story has been read as an indictment of courtly love relationships, it, like Christine's other love writings, can fruitfully be considered an allegory of court politics, a narrative about the alliance of Louis and Isabeau after the death of Philip of Burgundy. Louis had long been targeted by the Burgundians, but Isabeau fell victim to the propaganda machine only in 1405, just after allying herself with Louis. Furious at being checked by the pair, Burgundians criticized them for mismanaging the kingdom. As we have seen, the gossip circulated by the Burgundians was treated as a serious problem in contemporary sources. Given Isabeau's proximity to power, the fact that the only extant criticisms of her issue from Jean sans Peur and his immediate faction bespeaks the high regard in which she was held.

The *Duc des vrais amans* continues Christine's long-standing tirade against *médisans*, exposing their modus operandi in a long letter of warning to the lady of the story from her *duenna*, Sebille de La Tour, whose name evokes the sibyl, a figure present in several of Christine's works, as we have seen.[90] That Christine uses this same letter in the *Trois vertus*, verbatim, suggests the gravity with which she approached evil gossip. Slander was a serious business. The two works in which Sebille's letter figures are very different from each other, one a collection of courtly love lyric poetry and prose and the other a mirror for female conduct. But both are obsessed with the matter of how to present oneself in order to avoid damaging gossip. In both, Sebille writes that rumors are circulating about the lady because she appears to be happier than in the past (173, lines 60–70). Looking happy is dangerous. A highly placed lady needs to monitor her appearance: even if she resists "seduction," she risks being ruined, because the appearance of wrongdoing is just as damaging as actual wrongdoing. Women, mercilessly scrutinized, cannot hide their emotion, which leaves visible traces upon on its victims. As soon as gossips notice such traces, they spread the news. Whatever the truth, when a lady gives the appearance of any kind of pleasure, gossips will assume not only that she is in love but that she is involved in an illicit affair.

The power of gossip to destroy is thus very real, and it does not matter whether it is truthful. Christine emphasizes this by avoiding the question of whether the duke and the lady are actually sleeping together. The lady attempts to manage her own desire and that of the duke, asking him to promise that he will guard her honor and good reputation. He will never ask her to do anything against her will (142, lines 11–17). The reader is never told whether the relationship is consummated; this is irrelevant, for gossip requires no verification. The lady eventually falls into despair, separated from her lover for long stretches, and the narrative ends unhappily for both parties. Although the lovers and Sebille appear initially to represent opposing positions regarding love, the lovers in favor and Sebille vigorously against, the letter should not be seen as a rupture of an idyllic relationship but as a prophetic restatement of the problem of which the lovers are painfully aware: that no matter what they do, they will be destroyed by gossip. Whether or not they consummate their love, they cannot win. This meditation on the impossibility of avoiding gossip reflects Isabeau's treatment at the hands of Jean sans Peur. She cannot do otherwise than support Louis, and thus she becomes an enemy of Jean. Factionalism, which naturally occurs wherever resources are in short supply, will result in slander. There is no higher authority to keep society in order. The god of love demands and receives submission, but he cannot guarantee the rewards of his lovers. The narrative expresses the sorrow of a realm whose center, the king, is absent.

5

HEADING TOWARD SHOWDOWN AND
THE PROSE TREATISES, 1405–1407

Although the peace treaty between the dukes, signed on October 16, 1405, had headed off bloodshed, it offered a short reprieve. The impact of Jean's coup attempt was significant, Bertrand Schnerb explains. In occupying Paris and its surrounding areas for more than two months, the Duke of Burgundy had shown his serious intent and proved his support in the capital, lending force to his demand for a central role in the government.[1] With the peace treaty, the princes of the blood (with the exception of Louis of Orleans) and the Royal Council had betrayed their intimidation and their willingness to compromise with Jean. And yet the treaty did not result in widespread acceptance of Jean's program for reform from the princes of the blood or royal institutions. The tension remained, with the Duke of Burgundy staking his reputation on the passage of reforms as agreed on during the negotiations, while Louis and the other princes of the blood resisted, recognizing that ceding to Jean in this area was tantamount to granting him equal status.

In this chapter, I examine the relationship between the dukes from the end of their standoff in October 1405 to Louis's slaying by Jean's hit men on November 23, 1407. The period, during which relations between the dukes often appeared calm, must be imagined in retrospect as the volcanic buildup preceding the explosive eruption of the assassination: although the accumulation of pressure was evident and worrisome, the explosion itself came as a shock. During the months immediately following the end of the standoff, Jean continued to press his reform program, and some institutions at least went through the motions of considering his proposals.[2] I frame this section of the chapter with Jean Gerson's sermon "Vivat Rex," of November 1405, which attempted to bring the dukes into harmony and preserve the peace, and the anti-Orleanist pamphlet the *Songe véritable*. The first work evokes the atmosphere of nervous hope in Paris during the fragile peace between the dukes in the first months after the standoff; the second embodies the resentment seething beneath Jean of Burgundy's appearance of cooperation, the resentment that led him to murder his cousin.

"Vivat Rex"

Juvénal des Ursins describes the Parisians' joy when the peace between the dukes was announced. With the dukes' men-at-arms departing, the queen and the dukes made their ritualistic entry: "Friday afternoon, the queen entered Paris in great pomp. . . . And in her company were the kings of Sicily and Navarre and the Dukes of Berry, Orleans, and Burgundy. On Sunday, the queen went to Notre Dame in a chariot, and her two sons with her, accompanied by the *seigneurs* mentioned above, which was a beautiful and noble thing to see." On Saturday a great council was held where the dukes renewed their vows, "for which the people and the council members were overjoyed."[3]

For many observers, the near miss between the dukes seems to have sounded an alarm, and because they were not willing to risk all-out war, keeping the peace between the dukes at all costs became a priority. A sermon known as "Vivat Rex," delivered by Jean Gerson before the royal court on November 7, 1405, embodies this perspective, attempting to appease the quarrelling dukes by affirming the most prominent arguments from each side and proposing a principle for moving forward. Gerson did not enjoy negotiating between warring masters, as we saw in chapter 2. However, as "chancellor [of the university], advisor to kings and princes, maker of popes, renowned international preacher, devotional writer, unquestionably the most renowned intellectual figure of his time," in the words of Daniel Hobbins, Gerson enjoyed unequaled prestige in the kingdom, and, under the circumstances, his intervention was needed.[4]

Some scholars have interpreted the "Vivat Rex," incorrectly, I believe, as critical of Louis of Orleans and favorable toward Jean of Burgundy. Even Michael Nordberg, whose scholarship explicitly attempts to correct the Burgundian bias in modern historical accounts of the conflict, analyzes the sermon in this way, casting Gerson as the university's mouthpiece.[5] On the one hand, Gerson, in the service of the dukes of Burgundy, in 1395 had been elected chancellor of the University of Paris, which as a body tended to support the dukes of Burgundy until the assassination of Louis of Orleans. But, on the other, as we have seen, Gerson did not represent the university's majority opinion on all issues, and as some of his sermons show, he could not be regarded as the toady of the dukes of Burgundy. Indeed, he fled Paris because he so disliked being stuck between two powerful lords. In the "Vivat Rex," he positions Louis as the legitimate head of the government and casts Jean as seditious. Like Christine, Gerson was a staunch opponent of revolts like the one that Jean had attempted to provoke, preaching at length about the sacro-sanctity of royal power and reminding his listeners of their obligation to support one king. But he also granted that Louis might not be the most popular of regents, and in his call for reform, he clearly appealed to Jean. As a whole, the "Vivat Rex" gives a shape to the conflict in a way that allows both sides to claim partial victory.

In the first lines of the sermon, Gerson assumes the voice of the university, the daughter of the king ("fille du roy"). This might seem at first glance an attempt to provoke the Duke of Orleans, who during the crisis had dismissed offers to mediate from university representatives, insisting that as knights tend to their own business, so should clerics. But in the polarized audience before which Gerson preached, he needed to restore the university to its position as the king's (and therefore Louis's) beloved and objective advisor. Thus he characterizes the university as the obedient daughter of the king, intervening with all humility and devotion. She is distressed by what she sees around her: trouble, cruel oppression of the people, violence instead of justice, rapine instead of mercy, destruction instead of protection.[6] Her response to such unrest is to cry "Vivat rex, vive le roy"—long live the king (1139). Why? Here, Gerson begins to court Louis; it is because it is well known that a single king is the best form of government, the most durable, the most appropriate, the most reasonable (1138). In contrast, "a plurality of princes or principalities is bad" (1138). Using the same model of the division of "seigneuries" after the death of Alexander that Christine would draw on in the *Advision* to describe the chaos among the princes as they fought for regency after Charles V's death, Gerson deplores the lack of unity in the kingdom. The problem that he describes, of too many men claiming power, or a plurality of princes, can only be intended as a reproach to Jean of Burgundy. Someone had to govern during the king's absences: that someone, according to the king's royal ordinance, tradition, and proximity of relation, was Louis. In this context, Jean's challenges to Louis's regency represent a proliferation of princes, whereas Louis's exercise of the position granted him by royal ordinance represents no such thing. But it is time to move on, Gerson asserts. Injuries may have been committed, he owns (as we have seen, Louis of Orleans characterized himself as grievously wronged by Jean of Burgundy), and yet one must forgive and start over (1143).

From the sermon's very beginning, then, Gerson maneuvers between the Scylla of Louis and the Charybdis of Jean. The organizing trope of the sermon is the tripartite royal body, divided into separable but nonetheless metaphorically, and to some extent physically, related aspects: corporeal, civil, and political—and theological. Gerson explains the university's duty to care for each aspect. As for the king's corporeal body, Gerson insists first on the need to keep the suffering Charles VI healthy. Then, in a reference to the recent challenges to royal ordinances regarding Louis's regency during the king's absences, he stresses that the dauphin is the same person as the king: "comme une mesme personne avecques le roy" (1147). This leads him to note the importance of guiding the young dauphin with the example of the role that Saint Louis's mother played in his upbringing (1148). Gerson here sidesteps Louis's right to regency, although he implicitly accepts it. Succession from father to son, with Louis filling in during the dauphin's minority as his closest male relative, is the construction upon which Louis himself based his authority (Gerson has already deplored the proliferation of lords). Gerson also gestures toward Isabeau (though Pintoin mentions that the queen did not attend the sermon) with a reference to Blanche of Castile, the figure on which Christine had based her appeal to the queen of October 5.[7] Still, Jean would find nothing objectionable in the notion that the dauphin succeeds automatically; as we have seen, this construction undergirded the Burgundian claim that during the king's absences the dauphin, even as a minor, ruled with the help of a council.

In discussing the civil or political body of the king, Gerson returns again to the need for social harmony in contrast to the present disarray. Citing Boethius, as Christine so often does, Gerson explains that the most effective social glue is love. Love is capable of uniting humanity just as divine love unites the universe (1149). Furthermore, just as the four humors must be balanced in the corporeal body of the king, so the four cardinal virtues must circulate in the body politic. The problem, however, is that the four virtues are stalked by four vices. But, Gerson wonders rhetorically, does he dare reveal this? Reflecting on the problems involved in speaking up as a public conscience,

Gerson retreats into an allegory, using the personification Dissimulation, who pretends that all is fine to avoid getting herself into trouble, and Sedition, who pulls a series of defamatory pamphlets from under her cloak, some with true and some with false charges. Here is sufficient material to provoke discussion about reform before the Royal Council, says Sedition. Luckily, Discretion, sent by the university, comes to Gerson's rescue (1154). Gerson will speak truthfully, but in such a manner as not to offend anyone, criticizing both dukes.

The gist of his truthful speech is that the king (or Louis, under the circumstances) may be a bit of a tyrant. It is tyrannical for a prince to ask his people for three or four times more than he needs, especially when the resources are not used for the defense of the kingdom or the common good. As we have seen, the summer of 1405 was a low point in the war with the English, with the French unable to halt English pillaging, despite heavy taxes for defense. But Jean is equally blameworthy. It is not right that if the head hurts a bit the hand should strike it; that would be the act of a crazy person. Nor is it right to cut off the hand and separate it from the body. Rather, the head should be cured in all sweetness, with good words as much as good medicines. There is nothing more unreasonable and harmful than attempting to avert tyranny by sedition. Sedition is popular rebellion, explains Gerson, without rhyme or reason. Often, it is worse than tyranny (1159).[8]

Gerson then turns to the pamphlets that Sedition has pulled from her cloak, offering two major reforms for the kingdom. These have been taken to represent support for Jean of Burgundy's program. However, if a comparison shows some overlap, we also see some difference of emphasis, which suggests that Gerson intends to both co-opt and redirect the Duke of Burgundy's call for reform. As we noted in chapter 4, not everyone accepted Jean's claims. He had claimed that the king was not being properly cared for; that his *officiers* were corrupt; that the royal domain was in a bad physical state, its buildings falling into ruin; that the church was being oppressed with taxes; and that the taxes supposedly collected for the war against England were lining the pockets of the Duke of Orleans. In contrast, Gerson proposes uncontroversial reforms. He proposes, first, that the king not alienate his lands (Charles VI had frequently given in to importunate counselors asking for favors), and second, that justice be restored to the kingdom, because without justice kingdoms change hands easily (1173). Included in the category of reforms to justice are proposals about the ways in which royal officers should perform their jobs. The scapegoating of royal officers was a time-honored tradition, circulating widely since the reign of Saint Louis. Such complaints were voiced by both factions and therefore implied no individual blame.

One of Gerson's themes is the importance of prudence, particularly concerning counselors. Counselors must be prudent; but, also important, prudence demands that a seigneur be wary of "secret" accusations, or those made with the intent to hurt someone (1166). The discussion of prudence, so crucial to good kingship, as we saw in chapter 4, cannot be meant for the insane king. Jean having no claim to be acting as regent, the discussion of prudence can only be meant for Louis. We have seen that in the *Fais et bonnes meurs* Christine describes Louis's caution regarding accusations, and, as we will see, Christine devotes an entire treatise to Louis's prudence.

Reform and Cooperation

Gerson's sermon, then, can be seen as an attempt to find common ground between the dukes, to bring Jean's reforms into public discussion without alienating Louis. Other reactions to the Duke of Burgundy's plan for reform were less promising. Juvénal des Ursins reports that the Royal Council met to deliberate reforms on the Sunday after peace between the dukes was established, but that although many "belles ordonnances" were promulgated regarding the restriction of the number of officers and pensions, these bore no lasting fruits.[9] The *greffier* of the Parlement de Paris, Nicolas de Baye, reported that on November 23 and 24 that body had worked on recommendations for reform that the Royal Council had returned to it for further examination.[10] But the Parlement would not revisit the issue until the following July. As for the princes of the blood, the Duke of Orleans, the Duke of Berry, and the queen reveal their continuing anxiety over Jean's ascendance in an alliance signed in Paris on December 1. The alliance explains that the three have vowed to come to one another's aid if anyone tries to cause trouble, damage, or dishonor to any of them or to the king or the royal children.[11] Shortly after the three-way treaty was signed, Chousat writes in a letter to the bailiff of Dijon, dated December 9 or 10 and translated by Vaughan, that Jean had been excluded from the networks of power in Paris. The previous Saturday, according to Chousat, the Duke of Burgundy summoned the constable of France, Charles d'Albret, and the royal *chambellans* to discuss the reasons for which he, Jean, had come to Paris in the first place and to remind them of the promises that had been made regarding reform of the kingdom during the recent peace negotiations between himself and the Duke of Orleans. Jean "made [the group] promise that they would dine with him the next day in his hotel, so that he could talk to them again about this."[12] But at the same time, a more intimate council, including among others the dukes of Orleans, Berry, and Bourbon and Jean de Montaigu, the king's *grand maître de l'hôtel*, had gathered at the Bastille Saint Antoine to discuss finances, never so much as mentioning the Duke of Burgundy, although they had sent him an invitation to dine that night, which he refused. When they discovered that Charles d'Albret and some of the royal *chambellans* were scheduled to dine with Jean the following evening, they forbade their going: such a gathering would create the impression among the people that Jean "had a perfect right to undertake the reformation of this kingdom, and that these *chambellans* were about to join his party."[13] A meeting of the Royal Council took place at the Hotel Saint Pol on Monday morning, Chousat reports. He did not know what happened there, but he did not believe that Jean's reforms were being taken seriously.

The Duke of Burgundy's itinerary shows him dining at the Hotel Saint Pol December 22–24, and specifically with the king (apparently lucid from December 25 until February) on December 25, 26, and 30.[14] During his time with the king, Jean persuaded Charles VI to grant him a position on the regency council equal to that held by his father; that is, in January 1406 the king revised the regency ordinance of 1393, transferring the place formerly occupied by Philip of Burgundy to Jean. The reason for the appointment, states the ordinance, is the king's entire confidence in Jean's "trez grans loyalté, sens & proudomie."[15]

As for the continuing story of Jean's reforms, the records of the Parlement de Paris indicate that on February 17, several were presented to the body. The king had decided to limit lifetime pensions to counselors who had served for twenty years; it was also proposed that the president of the Parlement be given authority to suspend without pay members who were not doing their jobs. A heated debate ensued, with members of the Parlement protesting that they refused to be treated like children: they were, after all, called "maîtres" by the king and "seigneurs" by others.[16] It was decided that the ordinance would need to be redone. On July 28, 1406, an ordinance was signed that aimed to remedy the problems surrounding the multitude of officers to whom the harassed king had granted pensions.[17] A group of advisors that included Louis, Jean, and the Duke of Berry had determined to cut back on the number of officers in the king's employ. However, R. C. Famiglietti explains that the ordinance changed little, because fifty-one officers were retained and very few were let go.[18] In fact, the Parlement refused to publish the ordinance, with Baye writing on August 14 that "ce seroit contre l'onneur du Roy."[19] The ordinance had little effect. The next reform ordinance, of April 28, 1407, was another story. Promulgated while Jean was in Flanders, this ordinance cut the number of royal officers to twenty-six and axed three of Jean's most vigorous supporters.[20]

Still, to all outward appearances the dukes began to get along in 1406, encouraging hopes for a calmer future. Jean's itinerary shows that they ate together on May 1, celebrating the holiday at Saint Denis; five days later they ate together again, and Jean presented Louis with a beautiful jewel in the form of a *rabot*, that is, a carpenter's plane, Jean's device or personal symbol.[21] In June Louis and Jean celebrated with ostentatious shows of friendship the weddings of the former queen of England, Isabelle, to Charles of Orleans, and that of the king's son, Jean, to Jacqueline of Hainaut, daughter of Count William IV of Hainaut.

The dukes also became military allies, jointly attempting to defend Pisa from the Florentines. Moreover, they came together to defend France against the English. Plans were set in motion in the fall of 1406 for Jean to attack Calais while Louis attacked Bordeaux.[22] The offensive would be funded by a special *aide*. However, Louis was forced to abandon the fight in January 1407; Jean never even began, although he convoked an army at Saint Omer in October. But his attack was called off, and on November 17 he was back in Hesdin. What happened to the grand offensive from two positions? Monstrelet claims that the king ordered Jean to halt plans, but this is doubtful. Jean sent messengers to Paris reporting that he had not received the funds promised. This was a lie: his accounts indicate that he did indeed receive his portion.[23] Cousinot's chronicle reports that in 1406, after the broken truce with the English, a tax was raised to halt the English warriors pillaging the coasts of Picardy and Guyenne. Part of the tax was accorded to the Duke of Burgundy for the purpose of raising a siege at Calais.[24] However, Cousinot continues, when he received the money, he retreated into his country of Flanders without raising the siege. Why would he do this? Schnerb hypothesizes that Jean was caught between conflicting interests: he was leading a French army as a French prince against the English, but as the lord of Flanders he was negotiating a peace with the English, which demanded neutrality on the part of the western Flemish border castles.[25]

The Hidden Tension

It was in this atmosphere of hidden tension that someone in the Burgundian circle composed the pamphlet known as the *Songe véritable*. Although its author is unknown, this long narrative poem centers on Jean's most common complaint and ostensible basis for calling for reform: that someone has been spiriting away the king's money. The poem attacks two men soon to be killed at Jean's order: Louis of Orleans and Jean de Montaigu, the king's *grand maître de l'hôtel*. The poem further attacks Jean of Berry, with whom Louis and Isabeau had signed a treaty against Jean in December 1406, and, to a lesser extent, the queen.

The story told in the poem concerns the people, represented by an allegorical figure called Chascun, or Everyman, burdened by taxes that never reach the king (233, lines 129–36).[26] The result is that the king is poorly cared for. How can this be? To solve the mystery, Chascun sends Povreté, Poverty, to discover the truth, Verité (237–38, lines 290–94). But Povreté returns when she discovers that Verité resides at neither Châtelet nor the Parlement, nor with "canons, deacons, cantors, deans, or archdeacons, or treasurers or generals, nor with religious orders or judges or secular clerics, lawyers, people of the church or merchants" (236, lines 227–78). Thus Commune Renommé, "Public Knowledge," is summoned to find out what is going on. Commune Renommé verifies Chascun's hunch that the king's funds are being appropriated by someone else (240–41, lines 367–94) and calls in Excusacion to testify that the king is not to blame; the poor monarch is just as impoverished as Chascun. To blame for the disgraceful situation is Faulx Gouvernement. Questioned, Faulx Gouvernement admits his guilt, followed by Experience, who in her mirror reveals at length and in detail the characters of the greedy culprits responsible for the situation (249–55, lines 716–930).

These culprits are Louis of Orleans, Jean of Berry, Jean de Montaigu, and the queen (257–65, lines 993–1308). When questioned by Commune Renommé as to how these individuals happen to find themselves in such a favorable financial position, Experience allows Fortune to speak. After warning the characters that she might spin her wheel, Fortune cedes to Raison, who scolds each of the guilty parties in turn (267–79, lines 1381–860). Finally, Dampnacion threatens them, before the "acteur," or author-narrator of the poem, issues a final warning.

The *Songe véritable* is an example of the renowned Burgundian propaganda machine, clearly not only showing that a campaign to impugn Louis and his closest associates was in place but revealing the social mechanism by which it worked. Commune Renommé is incited to spread "public knowledge" about the king's most intimate circle.

The *Livre de prodomie de l'homme*

Christine could not have missed the Duke of Burgundy's efforts to rally support in the months following his attempted coup. As we have seen, in January 1406, at the behest of Jean sans Peur, the king revised the regency ordinance dealing with the care of the kingdom during his "absences," transferring to Jean the place formerly occupied by Philip of Burgundy on the regency council, owing to the king's complete confidence in Jean's "very great loyalty, sense, and prudence" ("proudomie"). Christine reacted to Jean's progress with the king, composing within months of his coup attempt the *Livre de prodomie de l'homme selon la diffinicion de Monseigneur d'Orleans.*

She opens the treatise with a long prologue, praising the Duke of Orleans's great eloquence and wisdom in a sort of recapitulation of her laudatory passages on him in the *Fais et bonnes meurs.* She then moves into an analysis of the virtue of prudence ("prodomie"). Because the work contains several warnings to the duke against treacherous slanderers, the title of her work seems to refer to the new ordinance bringing Jean into the council that governed during the king's absences. The body of the *Prodomie de l'homme* is a glossed translation of a moral treatise based on a lost work of Seneca, the *Formula vitae honestae,* also known as the *De quattuor virtutibus.* This work was believed at the time to have been written by Seneca, but it was in fact the work of the sixth-century bishop Martin of Braga. Translated into French by the eminent member of the University of Paris Jean Courtecuisse for the Duke of Berry in 1403, the work was already popular in Paris when Christine adapted it.[27]

Before considering some topical allusions in this work that shed light on Christine's political agenda during this period, it is important to examine this text for what it has to offer more generally about the poet's state of mind during the years 1405–7. Suzanne Solente writes that the *Prodomie de l'homme* had to be composed after October 5, 1405, the date of the *Epistre a la reine de France,* because in the *Prodomie* Christine refers to a small epistle that she had written to the Duke of Orleans.[28] Solente identifies this epistle as a rondeau accompanying the letter to Isabeau. Obviously, the *Prodomie* had to be composed before the duke's assassination on November 23, 1407. Moreover, the work exists in two distinct versions. One is the effusive paean to the duke mentioned above, and the other a general discussion of the virtue of "sapience" (all instances of "prodomie" or "prudence" are changed to "sapience" in the first several folios), minus the prologue, that makes no overt personal allusions to a patron. The two versions are distinguished by their titles, the *Prodomie* and the *Prudence*. The *Prodomie*—that is, the version with the prologue dedicated to Louis of Orleans—is found in the presentation copy of the manuscript today housed in the Vatican Library, Reg. lat. 1238, and in a manuscript of the Bibliothèque nationale de France, today fonds français 5037, containing documents pertaining to Charles VII and Louis XI. The *Prudence* is found in five manuscripts, including a sumptuous manuscript presented to the Duke of Berry, BnF, fonds français 605, although it may have been intended originally for Louis, and the Queen's Manuscript, Harley 4431 of the British Library.[29]

Why were references to Louis omitted from these later versions of the work? As we will see, Jean of Burgundy's seizure of power terrified friends of the Duke of Orleans, including Isabeau, who fled with the royal children in the wake of Louis's murder. And the Duke of Burgundy quickly did away with Louis's followers, executing some and forcing others to take flight. Christine, known to be especially attached to the House of Orleans, would have felt threatened. Always circumspect, she would be cautious in her writings until the *Ditié de Jehanne d'Arc*. BnF, fonds français 605, belonging to the Duke of Berry, is particularly interesting in this respect. Initially intended for Louis, the manuscript shows traces of the transformation of the *Prodomie* into the *Prudence*, wrought after the young duke's assassination. Folio 22r bears a scratched-out allusion to the Duke of Orleans.[30]

However, at the moment of the original composition of the *Prodomie*, Christine seems to have been cautiously confident, having just observed the Duke of Orleans emerge victorious from the confrontation with his cousin. In the *Prodomie*, as in *Fais et bonnes meurs*, Christine describes herself listening to the duke speak and being moved by his words. *Prodomie* rests in the well-ordered heart, she explains, reveling again in the image of good order. Her purpose here, however, is to teach something about the "entendement," the understanding, of the wise man, and for that she needs to discuss prudence, which resides in the house of virtue (185v).[31]

With this, she moves into the body of the treatise, her translation of the *Formula vitae honestae*, which she glosses with frequently topical allusions. What does the man who wants to perfect himself do? He turns first toward prudence, "qui est mere des vertus" (186r). In introducing the four cardinal virtues, Christine gestures to the *Epistre d'Othea a Hector*, which also begins with an exposition of these virtues and where she explains that prudence is their mother and director. Although dedicated to Louis, the *Othea* presents itself principally as a guide for a young prince, possibly Louis's nephew, the dauphin, creating a mentor figure of the Duke of Orleans. The *Prodomie* might be seen as a guide to prudence for adults, and, in many of its glosses, it alludes to real dangers. Christine is profoundly worried that Louis has not responded forcefully and effectively in public to Burgundian slander. Glossing a text that warns against slander, she commands against speaking ill secretly or defaming covertly. The prudent man shows the vicious his courage boldly and in public ("baudement et en publique") (190r). A man who is strong of heart will show that he is right when he shows his precedence, "son droit," without fear. To a text that warns that speaking evil in secret, rather than issuing a public challenge, shows weakness, Christine adds the gloss that a man shows weakness when he covers himself with fraud and lies. In the context of the Burgundian propaganda machine, this seems to be a warning that Jean, although weak and cowardly and assaulting Louis without directly challenging him, has nonetheless gotten the upper hand.

Christine adds further counsel on how to achieve effective vengeance—the best way is to let one's enemy see one strong and prosperous and of good reputation. In other words, one should take control of the public discourse, something the duke had so far failed to do. In another gloss, she writes bitterly that those who defame or tell lies about others to get a laugh are suited to care for pigs. However, such men are often found beautifully dressed in the court of the powerful (192r). This leads Christine into a short text claiming that one should "praise sparingly, but detract even more sparingly" (192r). The text's gloss begins with this affirmation but then turns into a sharp criticism of destroying reputations: "What greater evil or prejudice or crime can be done to human beings than to defame them? Because in the whole world nothing is more beautiful or worthy than a good reputation" (192v).

The work praises Louis, explaining in the prologue that Christine is no false flatterer but a truth teller. At the same time, it anxiously admonishes the duke to care more for his reputation.

The *Livre de l'advision Cristine*

In chapter 1, we examined a number of autobiographical passages from the strange and striking *Livre de l'advision Cristine*, a three-part work that is a major source of biographical information on the poet; the last section is devoted to Christine's recounting the story of her woes and consolation. The fully fleshed-out narrator of this work offers a striking contrast to the discreet narrator-glossator of the *Prodomie*.

The *Advision* presents readers with many mysteries; these may have been intentional. The poet offers a gloss, a later addition, of the first part of the work in manuscript ex-Phillips 128, suggesting interpretations for some of the odd figures who populate this part of the story (xli).[32] That only a single manuscript contains the gloss, coupled with the fact that it was added later, indicates that Christine did not intend the meaning of her text to be transparent to her entire public. Three manuscripts of the work exist today, all from Christine's atelier (xli) and all dated 1405–6. One copy seems to have been owned by the Duke of Berry. Philip the Good of Burgundy, son of Jean, owned a copy. He may have inherited that copy from his father, although payments of 1406 and 1407 by the Duke of Burgundy to Christine for books do not prove this.[33] In the *Advision*, Christine complains of a great lord who had recently paid her very tardily for some of her manuscripts (115). This great lord was almost surely Jean, and the payment one of the 1406 payments for the *Fais et bonnes meurs*. The identities of the other books are unknown. But even if Jean of Burgundy did own a copy of the *Advision*, he did not possess the gloss that would have revealed the anti-Burgundian significance of part 1.

The first part of the *Advision* deals with the chaotic state of France, represented by the miserable Libera, whom the poet leaves in distress at the end of the section; the distress of this section is mirrored by the turbulent state of Christine's own life in the work's third section, which is resolved by Philosophy, whom the poet finally recognizes as Theology in a transformation recalling that of the *Cent balades*, as we have seen. A number of unmistakable references connect parts 1 and 3: the despairing Libera of part 1 and the plaintive narrator Christine of part 3 (both characters come from foreign lands to settle in France, both are widows, both are devastated by the death of Charles V, both believe that their tribulations were caused by Fortune, and, as I will suggest here, both suffer when Philip of Burgundy, despite the careful arrangements of Charles V's regency orders, seizes control of the kingdom).

The listening Christine of part 1 likewise resembles the consoling Philosophy of part 3. Forming the bridge between these figures of parts 1 and 3—or the macrocosm of France and the microcosm of Christine's life—is a strange allegorical figure called Dame Opinion.

Because the *Advision* begins by recalling the first lines of Dante's *Divine Comedy* ("I had already passed the midpoint of the road of my pilgrimage") (11), the section devoted to Opinion can be seen, like Purgatory, as a place of passage, where the pilgrim leaves behind the strife of earthly factionalism, in this case between the Orleanists and Burgundians rather than Dante's Guelphs and Ghibellines, to prepare for a divine vision. But why Opinion?

As has long been recognized, chapters 4–12 of Thomas Aquinas's *Commentary on the Metaphysics of Aristotle* furnished Christine with one of her most important sources for the *Advision*. Besides referencing the work in the *Cent balades*, Christine incorporates about twenty loosely translated passages from this commentary into the *Fais et bonnes meurs*. She uses the commentary again in the *Advision*, but here the material, which makes up about 10 percent of the total, is very closely translated; the only changes are intended to simplify or clarify material that would be unnecessarily complicated in its new home. The *Advision* also draws heavily on Thomas of Ireland's *Manipulus florum* for book 3: forty-six of the forty-eight citations of this text are located there.[34] These citations alternate with passages drawn from a French translation of Boethius's *Consolation of Philosophy*. The *Advision*, Christine Reno and Liliane Dulac conclude, is composed primarily of borrowed material, translated and commented upon.

Opinion is an important concept in Aquinas's commentary, appearing regularly in book 1, where Aquinas comments upon different philosophers' opinions, many of them faulty, on first causes.[35] Moreover, in Dame Opinion's section of the *Advision*, Christine the narrator makes a direct reference to a passage of the commentary (7.15.1610) that describes, among other things, the quality of opinion: "what can sometimes be true and sometimes false, is opinion, in the same way it is impossible that there should be demonstration or definition of those things which can be otherwise than they are; but about contingent things of this kind there is only opinion." This is precisely the description that Dame Opinion gives of herself: "I am never certain; for if certainty exists, I will not be there" (57).

Dame Opinion has other models as well. As Reno and Dulac observe in the notes to their edition of the work, Opinion is also an important character in the *Commentary on Scipio's Dream* (163). And yet, if Dame Opinion can count these figures among her ancestors, the question remains of how such a lineage prepares her to serve as the link between the woes of France and Christine's life. We find a clue to how Opinion works in another long-acknowledged source for the *Advision*, Boethius's *Consolation of Philosophy* in its fourteenth-century French translation, *Le livre de Boece de consolacion*. In book 1 of this translation, we see Philosophy alternately scolding Boethius and encouraging him, fixing on an opinion that he utters, an opinion that in this case happens to be truthful, as the spark that will bring him to his cure.

Philosophy first asks Boethuis whether he believes that this world is governed by chance ("avanture") or reason. He replies that he knows very well that God governs from on high and that he has never held any other "opinion" (113).[36] Philosophy presses on, confusing him with further questions: what kind of steering wheel does God use to govern the world; does he remember the end of all things; does he know the beginning of all things; does he know that he is a man? Boethius's answer to this last question being unsatisfactory, Philosophy explains that the reason for his distress is that he does not know who he is (114–15). But not to worry: Boethius has a good foundation for a cure, a little spark that is going to become the fire of life, the knowledge of truth: his belief that God governs the world (115). It is just that he is not yet ready for the cure, the strong medicine that is true opinion ("vrayes opinions") (116).

When he is ready, he will be led by Philosophy out of the turmoil created by the false opinions that are hampering his ability to see the brilliant light of truth. In the same way, Christine, whom Dame Opinion authorizes as one who writes the truth—"as long as I am founded on law, reason and true feeling inside of you, you will make no fundamental mistakes in your works regarding those things which seem obvious," she assures Christine, "in spite of diverse judgments" (57). Like Boethuis, Christine has much wrong, we learn in section 3, but she too is cured of her distress. As for the link between the consoled Christine and Libera, when Christine emerges at the end of the *Advision*, she, like Boethius, sees the truth, and she is therefore qualified to speak about France's troubles and show the way to peace. Like all humans, Christine is susceptible to fall victim to false Opinion, who has admitted that she feeds many erroneous ideas to Christine's contemporaries. Moreover, the opinions of many in France are wrongly held because they are clouded by envy, Opinion notes (57). But, the shadowy figure continues—and this, I believe, is the purpose of part 2 of the work—Christine's vision is not clouded by the shadows of false opinion. Rather, because she has closed her mind to the turbulence of passions, a point reiterated in part 3 when Christine describes how she turned from trifling to serious writings (110), and, ultimately, because she is visited by the radiant light of Philosophy/Theology (140–41), she is qualified to serve as France's spokesperson, rallying the French to support the Valois kingship.

Opinion, then, encompasses the truth that Boethius possesses through faith, but because Opinion can be wrong, the figure also represents the false ideas of those misled by their passions. The frighteningly similar appearance of good and evil is a continuing obsession with Christine—from her poetic cycles, where lovers cannot distinguish true from false lovers (and where, in the *Cent balades*, the troubled cycle comes to an end with an appeal to Boethian consolation), to her critique of the *Roman de la rose*, to the quarrels between the four celestial ladies of the *Chemin de longue étude*, each of whom is convinced of the unique worthiness of her offering. In a political work like the *Advision*, opinion is particularly problematical: France's problems are the result of the quarrel between two factions both convinced of the rightness of their cause. Surely, one is right, but which one is not easily known on earth. This is why Christine works so hard to convince her reader that she herself has been through a process by which she has been freed of the obscuring shadows of the passions.

Christine's consolation, then, proves that the problem of France as she has outlined it in the *Advision* represents an instance of true as opposed to false opinion. But what is the problem, as she sees it, and what is its solution? Let's consider briefly again that crucial intertext for the *Advision*, Aquinas's commentary on the *Metaphysics*. The prologue to that commentary cannot help but remind us of the *Epistre d'Othea a Hector*, introducing the project of the *Metaphysics* as describing the science that is the "mistress of all the others," that "rightly lays claim to the name *wisdom*."[37] What sort of science is this? This can be discovered through induction, writes Aquinas, "by carefully examining the qualities of a good ruler." More specifically, this science is the one that, first, considers first causes; second, comprehends universals rather than particulars, accessible through the senses (in other words, that comprehends being and those things that accompany being); and third, comprehends not only things that are abstractable from matter but things that are separate altogether from matter. What is this science called? Because it studies both universal and particular causes, it must be known by three names: it is divine science, or theology, inasmuch as it considers the aforementioned substances; metaphysics, inasmuch as it considers being and the attributes that naturally accompany being (for things that transcend the physical order are discovered by the process of analysis, as the more common are discovered after the less common); and philosophy, inasmuch as it considers the first causes of things. As Ben Semple, Glynnis Cropp, and others have shown, there are good reasons why Christine insists at the end of the *Advision* that Philosophy is in fact Theology, but here is a straightforward reference—Aquinas calls the science that is the mistress of all others Theology-Philosophy, and it is with reference to this science, I believe, the Christine links France to her private tribulations: both the kingdom and Christine manifest particular disruptions caused by a more abstract, or universal, transgression.[38]

What is this transgression? Problems arise on earth, it seems, because universal hierarchies have been transgressed—there is a very real connection between the universal and the particular. In the third part of the work, Christine relates a series of events that describe the effects of the strife related by Libera on an individual level: the distress that the poet reveals arises from her personal experience of the feud, unleashed by Philip's seizure of power in 1380. In part 1, after describing the death of Charles V, Libera explains that from that wise king's entrails arose two butterflies. Christine Laennec has shown the prophetic character of this scene: prophecy for Christine is primarily textual, requiring interpretation.[39] As Christine explains in her gloss, these butterflies might represent Charles and Louis. They grow up together, turn into falcons together, and then the one who bears the sign that allows him to be king is flattened by a devastating illness. At this point, furtive men, inhabitants of the forest, arrive, claiming that it is their right to distribute private and personal things ("departir les choses propres et privees") (24). This is a legal expression referring to the royal treasury; they appropriate for themselves things meant for common usage ("communs usaiges") (24). After recounting a long allegorical story of the woes that assailed the kingdom as a result of this wrongful appropriation, Libera stops to summarize: she wants to make sure that Christine has grasped the root of the bad feeling between the feuders. After the parts of her goods ("propres") were given to each of her children, according to the custom of Athens, she explains, the strongest declared the right of guardianship over the youngest. But her children said "never" (nequaquam) to the strongest, and this is the reason for her injuries.

This attribution of blame has been interpreted, incorrectly, I believe, to refer to Louis of Anjou's actions after Charles V's death. The problem with reading the usurper as Louis of Anjou, who was awarded regency of the kingdom during Charles VI's minority—although Charles V specifically placed the duke under the surveillance of marmouset Bureau de La Rivière—is that the scenario Christine describes would then make no sense. For one thing, it is misplaced—the story describes what happens to the kingdom after the madness of Charles VI. Moreover, Christine never accuses Louis of Anjou of seizing power. On the contrary, as we have seen, she sees Philip of Burgundy as the usurper. Louis of Anjou departed for Italy, and Philip ruled, unimpeded, aided by his brother, Jean of Berry. Once revolts against the taxes that Philip imposed were put down, the kingdom entered a phase of prosperity. Thus the power struggle that occurred just after Charles V's death was not the source of the Orleanist-Burgundian feud. Libera refers, rather, to Philip's second seizure of power, that of 1392, as bringing on France's woes.

In part 2 of the *Advision*, Dame Opinion also begins to castigate the Burgundians. Just before the section draws to a close, the figure discusses those whom she has deceived. After reciting the stories of a long list of warriors whom she wrongfully convinced to attack, she turns to contemporary nobles who are unlawfully waging war: those who are not specifically defending their prince, their country, their land, the public good. We recall that the immediate context of the *Advision* was that in August 1405 Jean of Burgundy entered Paris with eight hundred armed men. Christine would in no way consider Jean's warmongering justified. Louis, by contrast, called his men to arms to protect the king and the dauphin, over whom Jean was preparing to seize guardianship. Listening to Dame Opinion's narrative, Christine expresses her anxiety that she, too, may be misled in her opinion of current events. But Opinion assures the poet of the clarity of her own vision.

And indeed, in part 3, Christine walks into the light of Philosophy. As she recounts the tale of her troubles, she repeats on a personal level the same woes that Libera has described. Once again, all goes well under Charles V. But when he dies, trouble breaks out: as we saw, Christine compares the situation that followed the demise of Alexander, and she mourns the treatment of her father at the hands of the *princes gouverneurs* (99). This discussion prepares the narrator for the consolation of Philosophy, who teaches that as long as one recognizes the worthlessness of earthly goods, which are only offerings of Fortune, being deprived of them is irrelevant. Many scholars, including Glenda McLeod in an insightful interpretive essay in her 2005 translation of the *Advision*, understand the consolation to be aimed at the princes of the blood, who, misled by false opinions, need to be transformed inwardly. However, such a message seems inadequate given Christine's investment in practical solutions to political problems. I suggest that although the poet's tutorial with Opinion is a necessary step that prepares her for the personal consolation that she receives, the point of the work as a whole is to deliver a much more pointed and material political message. In the 1405–6 political context, Christine's consolation is not aimed at France and its rulers. Rather, because she, like Boethius, is herself consoled, her vision unclouded by false opinion, she is in a position to act as the scold for the kingdom, its collective conscience. In this role she lays blame in each of the three sections of the work upon the parties responsible for the strife—the Burgundians—and her point is to rally support against them. She is not preaching to the leaders themselves but teaching her readers how to understand the relationships they see around them, and prompting them to engage. Opinion, like Purgatory, represents the best that one can hope for on earth.

Christine's Body Politic

In the *Livre du corps de policie*, of circa 1406, Christine employs the metaphor of the human body to discuss the interdependence of the different parts of society. The poet's vision of the relationships between the social levels of late medieval Paris as manifested in this work has been expertly treated by several scholars.[40] However, her unique configuration of the third part of the body politic has received insufficient emphasis.[41] The arrangement of the *peuple*, I suggest, holds the key to Christine's purpose in this work, and two points in particular demand consideration in this regard. The first is that Christine includes the university, or the *estat de clergié*, at the head of this third group, a significant downgrade from its higher position in similar works. Kate Langdon Forhan notes in the introduction to her translation of the *Corps de policie* that readers must have been shocked to discover that illustrious estate positioned so low in the body politic.[42] But the positioning is strategic. For Christine, the clergy, by which she means the University of Paris here, held a potentially decisive influence over the rest of the *peuple*, and for this reason she places the two in the same group. The second point is that the "merchants" of Paris, as Christine imagines them, consist of two separate categories. For her, the ruling burghers and the highly placed merchants follow just behind the clergy. Just behind this pair she places another group of merchants, and behind them artisans and laborers. This division of merchants into two groups is consistent with the social reality of early fifteenth-century Paris, where a powerful group of butchers shared characteristics with both the most highly placed merchants and the artisans and laborers. Through this configuration, I propose, Christine argues that if the university were to make common cause with the ruling burghers and well-placed merchants, they could control their more agitated brothers and sisters, the butchers and their thuggish followers, whom the Duke of Burgundy would finally persuade to rise up in 1413 in the Cabochian revolt.

Before focusing on Christine's arrangement of the third estate, it will be useful to discuss her conception of this part of the body politic more generally. Christine conceives of the diverse members of the body politic as bound together through a series of rights and, equally important, obligations. Good princes, Christine establishes in her first section of the *Corps de policie*, who correspond to the head of the body politic, owe their subjects love and care. This will prevent social unrest from occurring in the first place. The nobility, the arms and hands of the body politic, is bound to defend the *bien public* from exterior threat. As for the *peuple*, the common people, the stomach, legs, and feet of the body politic, their chief duty is to love and obey their prince.

But Christine does not simply call on the people to obey. She cultivates their sense of solidarity with the other members of the body politic by acknowledging their status as a crucial part of a magnificent whole:

> On our subject, I consider the people of France very happy. From its foundation by the descendants of the Trojans, it has been governed, not by foreign princes, but by its own from heir to heir, as the ancient chronicles and histories tell. This rule by noble French princes has become natural to the people. And for this reason and the grace of God, of all countries and kingdoms of the world, the people of France has the most natural and best love and obedience for their prince, which is a singular and very special virtue and praiseworthy of them and they deserve great merit. (3.2, 93; 92–93)[43]

Christine restates here the necessity of abandoning oneself to "natural" love that we have seen throughout her corpus. The French people had the best love and most natural obedience for their prince of any people in the world. This virtue is particular to the French, according to Christine. When she urges the people's obedience, then, she is asking them to follow their natural inclinations and behave according to their "French" nature.

For Christine, certain members of the people take their duty to support the king seriously. But as she argues for the fundamental cohesion between the people and the rest of the body politic, she also reveals that fissures divide the people. Occasionally, she proposes, some groups require guidance in order to understand their duties, and in these cases the more enlightened members of the third part of the body politic should aid their ignorant compatriots. Specifically, Christine assigns the wise burghers, *les saiges bourgois*, the job of keeping potential troublemakers calm. The wise burghers are not the only members of the body politic upon whom she calls upon to maintain the peace, however. Preceding them are the clergy (3.4–3.5, 96–100; 95–99), which she places at the very head of the *peuple*.

The clergy, as just noted, were generally accorded a loftier role than Christine gives them here. But her reasoning becomes clear when we examine the rest of the structure of this third part of the body politic. The clergy are followed by the burghers and the higher merchants (3.6, 100–101; 99–100). Between this group and the less important merchants (3.8, 104–6; 103–5), Christine appeals (3.7, lines 101–4; 100–103) to the former to keep the latter in line: "As we said before, the wise should teach the simple and the ignorant to keep quiet about those things which are not their domain and from which great danger can come and no benefit. And as testimony to this, it is written in chapter 22 of the book of Exodus that the law forbids complaints and says also 'you will not complain about great rulers nor curse the princes of the people'" (3.7, 101; 100). She separates the clergy and the city leaders, including the most important merchants, therefore, from the potentially troublesome lesser merchants.

In addition to placing the clergy in a class with the people, Christine makes one more transformation of the clergy in her discussion. The clergy were traditionally held to be an estate unto themselves, and they typically included members of the aristocracy who held important archbishoprics and bishoprics, along with priests of various social standing, as well as university clerics, masters, and students.[44] But Christine defines the clergy primarily as university students: "And because the clerical class is high, noble and worthy of honor among the others, I will address it first, that is, the students, whether at the University of Paris or elsewhere" (3.3, 96; 95).

Why this peculiar conception of the clergy? Christine targets students because control of them was key to the successful maintenance of the peace. Unruly, potentially seditious, and eager to arouse the lesser members of the people, university students created disturbances that caused the king to single them out for censure in royal ordinances of February and April 1407. In the ordinance of April 6, the king accused "some henchmen of our dear daughter, the University of Paris, and others incited by them of posting letters in churches that called the people to gatherings where 'many words highly prejudicial and damaging' to the king were pronounced." These gatherings were extremely dangerous, the ordinance continued, because they could lead the subjects of the realm to internal discord. The ordinance warned all the clergymen—people of the church—of Paris to forbid such assemblies in their churches. If "certain members of the said university wanted to gather or tried to gather such assemblies," they were to be turned over to the king's officers and the sergeants of the city of Paris.[45]

This ordinance helps us to imagine university students agitating to arouse the Parisians. The subgroup of the clergy directly responsible for the unrest, then, is the one that Christine explicitly targets in the *Corps de policie*: university students. When she includes students at the head of the third element of the body politic, her intention seems to be to persuade them to put aside the seditious behavior encouraged by the Duke of Burgundy and join with the burghers and well-placed merchants to act as a brake upon potential rioters. The university, of course, was not a monolithic body, and its members, starting with the chancellor, Gerson, did not uniformly follow the Duke of Burgundy, as we have seen. The members of the university are a privileged group, Christine writes, "disciples of the study of wisdom, who, by the grace of God and good fortune or nature apply yourselves to seek the heights of the clear rejoicing star, that is, knowledge" (3.3, 96; 95). But after capturing their good will through praise and enumerating the joys of knowledge, she reminds clerics that the ultimate goal of learning is to achieve an understanding of virtue; those who study do so because they "increase in goodness and virtue" (3.4, 98; 97). She then warns them about preaching wisdom to others without practicing it themselves. Those who do not practice what they preach "are more to blame when they are mistaken than others" (3.4, 98; 98).

Christine's next point of emphasis is the responsibility of the burghers and merchants to see that their less advantaged brothers and sisters not disturb the body politic. They are to guarantee that the *menu peuple* remain quiet and that they not conspire against the prince or council (3.6, 100; 99).[46] Most telling, however, is Christine's configuration of the merchants into two groups. The first merchants, as we have seen, are grouped with the burghers and thus associated with the city's ruling class. Christine appeals to this group to keep peace among the *menu peuple*. But in addition to these well-placed merchants, Christine acknowledges another type. Reminding this second group of merchants of their social obligation to be honest and hardworking, Christine seems to be targeting the butchers of Paris here.

Like her reduction of the clergy to university students, the poet's distribution of merchants across two groups follows a logic that corresponds precisely to a prevalent perception of her time. With the exception of the king and the princes and their entourages (the groups that Christine represents in the first two parts of the body politic), early fifteenth-century Parisians fell into two categories "whose aptitudes, political desires, differed in an obvious way, the *haute bourgeoisie*, that is, a major portion of the royal officers, and *certain groups of merchants*, gathered around the king in great numbers, on the one hand, and, on the other, the mass of workers, a fluid, open class."[47] A significant group belonging to the second category consisted of the butchers. Paris was home to several groups of butchers, the largest of which was that of the Châtelet, the *grande boucherie*. Although wealthy and respected, they were not part of the ruling burghers: they were merchants, but not of the same "quality" as the great merchants. Even the most important butcher families, the Saint-Yon, the Thibert, the Guérin, the Deux-Epées, and the Légois, were *gens de metier* and were therefore separated by a yawning gulf from Paris's ruling elite, in the eyes of that elite.[48] They were powerful and could muster followers, but these followers included many of doubtful character, in the eyes of the ruling burghers.[49] The butchers had led uprisings in Paris in 1382–84; they also led uprisings among the Parisians from 1408 to 1413. The *peuple* were not a cohesive body.

The third section of Christine's body politic, then, groups the university with the ruling members of Paris and urges them to stand up to the marauding elements of their estate to maintain order in the realm. She thus seeks to lure the university from the side of Jean of Burgundy and turn it against the *menu peuple*, destroying what Coville described as "the triple alliance which formed gradually between the university, the people of Paris and the duke of Burgundy." The alliance was not necessarily a natural one: Coville notes that the members were driven by different motives.[50] Members of the university were moved by a belief in the excellence of their own remedies for the evils facing the kingdom; the people of Paris, by their impatience; the Duke of Burgundy, by pure ambition. Still, Coville concludes, the three shared a common goal: a major role in the government for Jean.

The *Corps de policie* attempts to persuade the university that its real interest, the pursuit of knowledge for the enhancement of virtue, was not being served by its support for the Duke of Burgundy, and that the burghers and great merchants could only be harmed by social unrest. Christine presses both groups to protect themselves by listening carefully to the complaints of the *menu peuple* and presenting their problems to the Royal Council. Relations between the groups, as we have seen, were not always friendly, but Parisians of greatly varying social levels occupied the same physical space, which means that constant interaction was inevitable. As Bronislaw Geremek writes, it is not easy for historians of medieval Paris "to establish the respective locations of wealth and poverty, since they existed in close proximity to each other." Certain areas contained greater or lesser conglomerations of wealthy or poor, but in the *Cité*, for example, "wealth lived side by side with the greatest deprivation. This small island accommodated alike 'good' districts and the haunts of the very poor."[51] Thus people of high status were in a position to monitor the grumblings of their social inferiors. Christine's suggestion for riot control in the *Corps de policie* was entirely plausible. If the *cives* watched out for the *menu peuple*, intervening when murmuring began, assembling the wisest of the group, and taking them to the princes to let them make their case, they could prevent unrest.

Conclusion

In three different works, Christine attempts to warn her readers that Jean represented a genuine and increasingly dangerous threat and to move them to action. In the *Prodomie de l'homme*, she urges Louis to attend to his cousin's campaign of slander and to reestablish his image as a prince of great "prodomie," or prudence. In the mysterious *Advision*, she draws on her prophetic persona to warn readers what will happen if the Burgundians are not halted. Through the strange allegorical figure of Opinion, she grants that it is difficult to see through Jean's apparently reasonable claims, but as one who has suffered and survived harassment herself, she asks to serve as a mouthpiece for France, a consoled and clear-sighted advisor whose version of the situation merits the most serious consideration. Finally, in the *Corps de policie*, she maps the major groups of Parisian society onto the body politic, soliciting the most distinguished members of the bourgeoisie and merchant class to act as a counterweight against two groups among which Jean maintained a good deal of sway: the university, or at least its most dangerous elements, and the less prestigious merchants, specifically the butchers who would lead the Cabochian revolt of 1413. Jean of Burgundy was proving as dangerous to the stability of the kingdom as she had warned obliquely in the ballad deploring Philip of Burgundy's death and in the *Fais et bonnes meurs*. Christine depicts the period as a state of red alert, warning her readers as clearly as she can while remaining safe herself.

Emily Hutchison has analyzed the reasons for the success of the Burgundian propaganda machine. Whereas "John the Fearless's rhetorical campaign centered on contrasting his loyalty to the king and realm and his good government with the disloyalty, corruption, and tyranny of his rivals," Orleanist propaganda "did not have the same insight into what would excite the nonnobles of the realm." Louis and his followers "kept rehashing the injustice and dishonor they had endured at the hands of John the Fearless and their actions revolved around keeping him out of power."[52] Although, for the reasons I have stated, I do not believe that it is completely accurate to characterize Louis as "unpopular," as Hutchison does, her richly detailed analysis of the letter campaign waged between the two camps demonstrates convincingly why Christine would have worried that Louis's reputation required her intervention.

6

On November 20, 1407, the Duke of Berry brought the dukes of Orleans and Burgundy together to hear Mass. Immediately beforehand, the two had pledged to live in love and brotherhood. But, as Juvénal des Ursins notes ominously, "This did not last."[1] On November 23, the Duke of Orleans dined with the queen in her Hotel Barbette, located in what is today the third arrondissement on the corner of the rue des Francs-Bourgeois and the rue Vieille-du-Temple. Isabeau was still mourning her stillborn son, Philip, delivered on November 7. The loss of what would be her last baby, writes Pintoin, had touched the queen in her "innermost maternal being."[2] At about eight o'clock, the duke emerged from the Hotel Barbette, according to the report made by Nicolas de Baye, and, accompanied by three men on horseback and two on foot with torches, he headed in the direction of the Church of the Blancs-Manteaux. Suddenly, the small entourage was overtaken by a group of armed men, who proceeded to pummel Louis savagely, knocking him from his horse, splitting his head open, which caused his brains to fly across the pavement, and slicing his left hand from his arm. One of the duke's servants was killed interposing himself between his lord and the assassins, while one of the torchbearers was grievously injured.[3] Christine's warning to the Duke of Orleans in the *Prodomie de l'homme* about the dangers of cowardly defamers had been prescient.

The next day, during Louis's burial under the high altar at the Church of the Celestins, the inconsolable royal family bewailed the disgracefully slain illustrious duke, writes Pintoin, still unaware of the killer's identity.[4] Juvénal des Ursins reports that early rumors suggested that the murderer was a man with whose wife the duke had had a liaison. No one yet imagined that the Duke of Burgundy had committed the act, given the oaths, alliances, and other promises of friendship exchanged just days before. Indeed, Jean boldly appeared at the funeral, clad in black and mourning with the others.[5]

As for how his guilt was uncovered, accounts diverge slightly. Juvénal des Ursins reports that on Saturday Jean tried to attend a meeting of the royal relatives at the Duke of Berry's Hotel de Nesle, but that by this time an investigation led by Guillaume de Tignonville, *prévôt* of Paris, had turned up evidence pointing to Jean. Asked whether he knew anything about the murder, Jean abruptly confessed. The weeping Duke of Berry then advised his nephew to flee Paris. Jean heeded his uncle's advice.[6] According to Monstrelet's detailed account, during a meeting held on Friday, Tignonville announced that he needed to question the lords of the kingdom. At that point, Jean knew that he was caught and, calling his uncles aside, confessed. Even so, he reappeared on Saturday at a meeting of the Royal Council. Refused entry by his uncles, he decided to flee.[7] Pintoin's account claims that Jean confessed to his uncles on the Friday after the murder, not wanting an innocent man to pay for his crime. These words moved the men to trembling and horror. Refusing to listen to the duke's excuses, they met the next day in the Parlement de Paris. Jean appeared but was denied entry and decided to flee Paris for the north.[8]

In all of the accounts, the princes of the blood deplore the dreadful crime, especially because of its treasonous nature: Jean had publicly pretended to be Louis's friend and then had secretly had him killed. Why, then, did the princes fail to act? Although they consigned the Duke of Burgundy to eternal damnation, explains Pintoin, they did not wish to pursue the matter out of their regard for his position.[9] A more plausible explanation for this failure to act can be adduced: fear. Their first reaction was to pass in the Royal Council on December 26 an ordinance reinstating the ordinance of 1403 (the one that Louis had gotten revoked) abolishing regency altogether in favor of the immediate coronation of the new king, who would be assisted by the queen mother and a council of the princes of the blood.[10] Next, the king invited Jean to come to Paris to explain himself, requesting only that the duke turn over his accomplices. Jean refused. In response, the king sent the dukes of Berry and Anjou to Amiens to confer with Jean about his crime. (The Duke of Bourbon had declared himself not up to the task and headed home to his lands.) When the dukes of Berry and Anjou arrived in Amiens at the end of

January (dining with Jean on January 19), Pintoin remarks, they were helpless to prevent Jean's entering with armed guards.[11] After conferring, Jean agreed to present himself in Paris if he were guaranteed that no armed men would guard the gates to Paris. Thus he returned to Paris in March 1408, with university theologian Jean Petit, who in a four-hour declamation before the court asserted that Jean had acted in the interests of the kingdom.[12] As a tyrant, Louis had deserved to die. In addition, he had been greedy (trying to take over Normandy and helping himself to the taxes raised for the war). But chief among his crimes was that Louis had tried for years "to kill the king by some slow disorder that would not arouse suspicion of murder" for the purpose of becoming king himself.[13] As corroborating evidence, Petit detailed examples of Louis's alleged involvement with witchcraft dating from the early 1390s. Petit's claim that Louis had been involved with sorcery since the early 1390s suggests that the early accusations aimed at Valentina were in fact aimed at her husband, as I suggested in chapter 2.

Although the king missed the justification, having just lapsed into insanity, he recovered his senses the following day. After listening to a summary of the justification, he issued his cousin a full pardon, although, given that he had been out of his mind the previous day, his decision almost surely was not his own.[14] The queen, in turn, called the Duke of Brittany, husband of her daughter, Jeanne, to Paris with his army. Shortly thereafter, the king of Sicily and the Duke of Berry arrived with additional military support.[15] With political authority residing in physical possession of the dauphin when the king was mad, the boy was in danger of being kidnapped by Jean. Isabeau therefore fled with the royal children to the safety of the citadel at Melun, which she had fortified.[16]

Isabeau and the children remained in Melun that spring. In the summer, Jean departed Paris for Liège, where he helped to put down an uprising that summer, earning his nickname "sans peur." During his absence, Isabeau had his pardon revoked with the aid of the dukes of Guyenne, Berry, and Bavaria, the archbishop of Sens, and the bishop of Chartres, who met in Melun with the king on July 2. There the king rescinded the pardon in a document that demonstrates his befuddlement.[17] Jean had told Charles VI that Louis had labored every day for the death of the king and the "expulsion of us and our generation," trying by various means to steal the crown. But no one had mentioned Louis's death to him; he had heard only that Louis had been beaten up. Isabeau, not present at the meeting, seems to have begun to pass the torch to the twelve-year-old dauphin, although she remained active behind the scenes.[18] When she and the dauphin returned to Paris on August 26, Monstrelet recounts, the boy rode "a white horse led by four men on foot," with the queen following just behind. This position nicely staged her discreet rule.[19] On September 5, Juvénal des Ursins confirmed before the princes of the blood, prelates, and the people that the Royal Council had decided that, given the situation, the queen would continue to govern.[20] On September 11, buoyed by the king's revocation of Jean's pardon, Isabeau and Louis's widow, Valentina, had their vengeance on Jean Petit: his justification was refuted by Thomas de Bourg, abbot of Cérisy. This elicited a second justification by Jean Petit, refuted only in 1414. In the meantime, Valentina was silenced by her death, allegedly of sorrow, in December 1408.

Jean returned to Paris after defeating the Liegeois at Othea in November, probably not anticipating trouble in subduing the Orleanists, to discover that the royal family had foiled him by slipping off to Tours.[21] Without the king or dauphin, Jean had no claim to authority, and therefore he sent the Count of Hainaut-Holland, his own and the queen's kinsman, to Tours to negotiate their return.[22] This led to public reconciliation on March 9, 1409, between the Duke of Burgundy and the unwilling Charles of Orleans, son of the late duke, at Chartres Cathedral. Jean took his place as head of the government. Assuming that the young sons of the slain Duke of Orleans would seek to avenge their father's murder when they grew older, he worked in the meantime to keep other enemies under control. In the autumn he struck, disposing of one his most venerable detractors, Jean de Montaigu, whom he had executed on the pretext of corruption, on October 17, 1409. Other Orleanists were deprived of their offices and imprisoned.[23] Master of Paris, Jean next assumed the position of *tutelle* of the dauphin. A royal ordinance of December 27, 1409, promulgated in Vincennes, announced that because the dauphin was of an age to meet people from all estates of the realm, and because Isabeau had other heavy charges, Jean would become the boy's tutor.[24] Isabeau was in no position to resist. No complaints issued from the other princes of the blood: the Duke of Berry refused the joint *tutelle* of the dauphin that Jean proposed to him.

Why did the princes of the blood accept Jean's deeds so quietly? Besides being intimidated, they seemed not to believe that their interests would be served by energetic opposition to the Duke of Burgundy. I noted in chapter 1 that Timur Pollack-Lagushenko has shown that although the Orleanist and Burgundian factions had visible leaders, the other members cycled in and out, joining up with a faction when they needed the support of one of the leaders for their own purposes and remaining involved until they had achieved what they wanted.[25] The initial muted reaction of the princes of the blood to Jean's murder of Louis confirms this point. Only Louis's wife and young sons had anything to gain from vengeance.

The situation shifted in 1410. The Duke of Berry had never shared the Orleans sons' desire for revenge. However, he became furious with the Duke of Burgundy, who ignored his counsel and treated his men badly. Therefore, he teamed up with the Orleans sons against Jean.[26] At the same time, Bernard Count of Armagnac rejoined the Orleanists (having allied himself with Louis of Orleans in 1403) because he needed support in the Foix-Armagnac feud. Thus was formed the League of Gien on April 15, 1410, with supporters signaling their alliance in an open letter proclaiming their intention to liberate the king from his Burgundian oppressors.[27] On the day that the league was formed, Charles of Orleans contracted to marry the Count of Armagnac's daughter, Bonne.[28]

In August 1410 the Armagnacs marched on Paris to make good on their proclamation, but the factions did not come to arms. Summoned to mediate, Isabeau and others met with the dukes at Marcoussis. Her efforts failed, as Monstrelet notes, and the tension worsened throughout the fall.[29] Before open warfare broke out, the Peace of Bicêtre of November 2 brought respite. According to the terms of the treaty, the dukes were to return to their lands with their troops and not appear before the king unless summoned; they were not to commit aggression against one another until April 1412; the Royal Council was to be populated with nonpartisan advisors; and the dukes of Berry and Burgundy were to share *tutelle* of the dauphin.[30] Jean headed north to Lille, while the dukes of Berry and Orleans headed south to Bourges. Still, the peace was short-lived. Jean continued to control the government from afar, having managed to stack the Royal Council with his own men, despite the treaty signed at Bicêtre, because the Duke of Berry, ostensibly on the side of Charles of Orleans, had allowed the Duke of Burgundy to populate the Royal Council with Burgundians. To assure his own influence in the government, the Duke of Berry had signed an alliance with Jean on November 7.[31] When the Duke of Berry pulled back, Charles took matters into his own hands, seizing an ambassador, Jean de Croy, sent by the Duke of Burgundy from Paris in January 1411.[32] Believing that he was complicit in the assassination of Louis of Orleans, Charles had Jean de Croy imprisoned and tortured. Both sides prepared for war. In response to ambassadors from the king demanding that he disperse his men, Jean of Burgundy replied that he was happy to obey the king and waited for the Armagnacs to break the peace. He did not have to wait long. Throughout the spring and summer of 1411, the Duke of Orleans sent letters to the king and the cities of the realm denouncing Jean's assassination of his father. On July 18, the sons of the slain Duke of Orleans openly challenged their father's assassin. Jean responded on August 13, officially beginning the war.[33]

During the first months, Jean prevailed in terms of both military superiority and public relations. He cast the Armagnacs as traitors plotting to remove the king from the throne and extravagant imposers of taxes.[34] But in 1412 the dauphin Louis of Guyenne began to assert himself. Monstrelet dramatizes the young man confronting a stunned Jean with the news that it was time to make peace with the Armagnacs, among whom he, the dauphin, counted many relatives. Although Jean humbled himself before the dauphin, he was not happy.[35] R. C. Famiglietti argues that the dauphin conceived and carried out a strategy intended to build enough support to force a reconciliation.[36] His desire to bring the dukes to an accord manifested itself first in the Treaty of Auxerre of August 22, 1412.[37] Unfortunately, the peace that he brokered between the factions was unenforceable. It also brought to the fore long-term tensions among the different strata of Parisian society. The Armagnac view of power as court-focused had long coexisted uneasily with the more populist Burgundian vision, Michael Sizer writes, and the tension was played out in various ways, including the disdain of the ruling burghers for the wealthy corporation of butcher families, the Saint-Yon, the Thibert, the Guérin, the Deux-Epées, and the Légois.[38] The Parisian elite viewed these butcher families, although wealthy and powerful, as hoodlums. Alfred Coville explains that many of their followers were eager for bloodshed, forming a small army unafraid of violence.[39] Certainly, this is the impression created by contemporary chronicles. In an entry for 1411, Juvénal des Ursins explains that the butchers were followed by "people of several trades of Paris" but that "poor people and bad ones wanting to pillage and steal" were also among the group.[40] Sizer has critiqued assumptions, based on contemporary chronicles, of a division between the Parisian "rabble" and their political philosophy, which was supported by the Burgundians and the University of Paris.[41] Although the university dropped its support during the summer of the revolt, it originally supported the reforms demanded by the Cabochians, as did the Burgundians.

Revolt broke out in April 1413. Leading up to the violence, the Estates General of northern France had been summoned in January. The treasury empty, new funds were required to pay off the debts accumulated during the recent hostilities and to guard the borders in anticipation of further fighting with the English, who had landed in France in August 1412.[42] The meeting, however, quickly turned to loud verbal assault on the government, putting Jean, head of the government, in an awkward position.[43] After a mass demonstration on April 28, violence erupted as crowds led by Simon Caboche broke into the court and arrested several members. They then broke the doors and windows at the Duke of Berry's Hotel de Nesle, forced the *prévôt des marchands* and many of his circle to leave the city, and burst into the hotel of the dauphin.[44] They threatened clerics and officers close to the king and queen with imprisonment and even execution. Further fighting took place on May 22. On May 26, Charles VI issued the ordinance for administrative reform known as the Ordonnance cabochienne. Still, the initial success was limited, for the violence horrified the ruling burghers and the university.[45] The dauphin called in the Armagnacs to crush the revolt. Lucid as of May, the king now threw his support behind the Armagnacs. On August 4, the Cabochians fell. The articles of the Peace of Pontoise were published, the Ordonnance cabochienne revoked, and the Duke of Burgundy forced to flee.[46]

Once again, Christine's words were prescient. This was precisely the uprising that she had warned against in the *Livre du corps de policie*. She must have been cheered that the dauphin and Isabeau had returned visibly to the Orleanists. And yet the Orleanist ascendance that she had so long awaited turned disastrous. The dauphin, emerging from the crisis with new strength, resented the condescension of the Orleanist leaders, who were unwilling to accord the young man the respect he demanded.[47] Moreover, they had no interest in restoring relations with the Burgundians. On the contrary, they sought above all to monopolize power.[48] The Bourgeois de Paris complained that the dauphin was held a virtual prisoner and was not allowed to see anyone but the Armagnacs.[49] To loosen their unwelcome grip, the dauphin summoned Jean sans Peur back to Paris.[50]

Thus the factionalism continued. The royal family marched with the Armagnacs against Jean of Burgundy in 1414, besieging Arras. When their efforts led to impasse, they signed the Treaty of Arras on September 4, 1414.[51] External conflict exacerbated the problem when the English under Henry V invaded the kingdom in 1415.[52] The first of many catastrophes resulting from this invasion was the Battle of Agincourt on October 25, which deprived the kingdom of its greatest knights, including Charles of Orleans, who spent twenty-five years in English captivity. The situation would have been less dire had dauphin

Louis of Guyenne not succumbed to a sudden illness on December 15, 1415.[53] His brother, Jean of Touraine, succeeded him; Jean had been raised in Hainaut by the parents of his wife, Jacqueline, William Count of Hainaut-Holland and Marguerite, sister of Jean sans Peur. Given his family relationship, it appeared likely that the dauphin would be inclined toward the Burgundians. A Burgundian-controlled dauphin would menace the Armagnacs, all the more so if he fell under the control of the queen, whom they no longer trusted. Arriving in Paris days after the death of Louis of Guyenne, Bernard of Armagnac was appointed *connétable* and governor of all finances. Pintoin reports that throughout 1416, Isabeau actively tried to mediate between the warring parties.[54] The result, however, was that she was regarded with suspicion by both the Armagnacs and the Burgundians.

The Armagnac control of Paris gave the bishop of Paris the opportunity to condemn Jean Petit's second justification in February 1414, although Petit himself had died in 1411.[55] In March, Jean sans Peur appealed the condemnation to Rome, and in September, Pope Jean XXIII appointed three cardinals to examine it.[56] A delegation headed by Jean Gerson, now a public enemy of the Duke of Burgundy, attempted to get Petit's justification condemned at the Council of Constance (1414–18). However, he was countered by a Burgundian embassy that was more "focused, methodical, political and perfidiously political," as Coville put it.[57] The result was that although the council pronounced against tyrannicide in general, it refused to name names. Moreover, on January 15, 1416, the cardinals annulled the condemnation by the bishop of Paris.[58] In response, on September 16, 1416, the Parlement de Paris made publication in favor of tyrannicide or its justification illegal.[59]

On April 4, 1417, the new dauphin died. One son, Charles, remained, married to the daughter of Louis and Yolande of Anjou, devoted Armagnacs. There was no chance that the new dauphin would be left in the possession of the queen. Isabeau was imprisoned, watched over, as Monstrelet reports, by guardians appointed by the Armagnac government that controlled her husband and son, who would not even allow her to write a letter. The powerless queen thus teamed up with Jean of Burgundy, who delivered her to freedom on November 2.

The Armagnacs countered with a royal ordinance of November 6, 1417, announcing that Charles was the true regent.[60] Isabeau in turn sent out missives to the "good cities in the kingdom of France," exhorting them not to listen to anything issued by the Armagnacs, "people of low degree" who had seized control of the king.[61] To that the dauphin replied by claiming that the queen was a prisoner of Jean of Burgundy.[62]

In a letter of January 10, 1418, Isabeau ceded her regency powers to Jean.[63] Nonetheless, she soon resumed her attempts to reconcile the factions, endeavoring to make contact with the dauphin. With Henry V colonizing France, unity was more necessary than ever. Although the Count of Armagnac opposed any effort at reconciliation, other members of the faction recognized that coming to terms with the Burgundians was the only chance of heading off the English king. Peace suddenly appeared to be a possibility when an assembly in Paris convened on April 18, 1418, and arrived at a resolution on May 26, requiring just the signatures of the faction leaders. However, as we saw in chapter 1, the Count of Armagnac opposed this settlement, instigating the Burgundian massacre of May 1418.[64] In March 1419, with Jean back in power in Paris after the infamous massacre, the Parlement de Paris revoked all condemnations of Jean Petit's doctrines.[65] But it mattered little by this time, because Jean of Burgundy was himself assassinated by men of the dauphin Charles, later Charles VII, in October of that year.

Christine on Jean of Burgundy's Return

The Bourgeois de Paris reported that Parisians felt that they had entered into a reign of terror in October 1409: on October 7, Christine's friend Jean de Montaigu was seized from the hotel of the king, at which news the people rose up in protest as intense as if Paris were filled with "Sarrazins," and the new prévôt of Paris, Jean's man Pierre des Essarts, ordered that torches burn all night and that guards circulate.[66] On October 17, Jean de Montaigu was beheaded. Juvénal des Ursins describes the distress, the "grands murmures et divisions," of the Parisians, including the princes, at the execution.[67] Some Orleanists took the path of least resistance: stripped of the prévôté, Guillaume de Tignonville remained active in city life. As we have seen, Isabeau held out against Jean until 1409, but eventually ceded tutelle of the dauphin to him.

Scholars have offered divergent hypotheses about Christine's reaction to the news of Louis of Orleans's murder and Jean of Burgundy's subsequent rise. Pointing to her horror of civil unrest, many have concluded that although she could not have supported Jean of Burgundy, she prudently lay low during his tenure. Others have imagined her as a Burgundian propagandist, as we saw in the prologue. It is true that the Duke of Burgundy's accounts show a payment to the poet in October 1412 "for several notable books that she had presented to my lord without receiving payment."[68] However, the positive response to a request for a work by the Duke of Burgundy cannot be seen as serving Burgundian propaganda. With Jean de Montaigu's head displayed on a pike nearby, and Jean distributing tokens representing his ominous emblem, the *rabot*, Christine is unlikely to have refused any request from the powerful duke.[69]

Nonetheless, she managed to express her sentiments, discreetly, in her first work after the assassination, the *Sept psaumes allégorisés*, extant in three manuscripts and commissioned by Charles III of Navarre, son of the pretender to Charles V's throne.[70] Because the work mentions Pope Alexander in its call for prayers, it can be dated to sometime between June 26, 1409, and May 3, 1410, the dates of his reign. As for Christine's sentiments, the call for prayers for the souls of the departed members of the royal family in the oldest of the three manuscripts, in a private collection, contains the name of Louis of Orleans.[71] In contrast, one of the two manuscripts of the work available to the public, BnF, nouvelles acquisitions françaises 4792, original owner unknown, does not mention Louis, referring only to the good-doers ("bien faiteurs") "King Charles Quint" and "Philippe de Bourgongne" (fol. 55v). The manuscript must have been prepared for a Burgundian reader. However, Louis's name has been added in the margin of manuscript 10987 of the KBR, which resided in the chapel of Jean himself.[72] Ouy et al. note that all three of the manuscripts (and the insertion) are written in Christine's hand. It looks as if she accommodated one Burgundian owner but added Louis's name to the litany of the KBR manuscript as a defiant gesture.

Charles III of Navarre had promised to aid Jean of Burgundy against Charles of Orleans in a treaty signed on July 7, 1409, but even he was so disgusted with Jean's execution of Jean de Montaigu, writes Juvénal des Ursins, that he left Paris and allied himself with the Duke of Berry, although his distaste apparently passed quickly.[73] In the remainder of this chapter I examine four works in their immediate contexts to trace the development of Christine's political thought during this troubled period. In the *Lamentacions sur les maux de la guerre civile* of August 1410, she lends support to Isabeau's efforts to make peace between the Armagnacs and Burgundians and calls on the Duke of Berry to negotiate with his nephew Jean of Burgundy. However, with the *Livre des fais d'armes et de chevalerie*, written shortly afterward, she changes tactics, recognizing the futility of peace negotiations and justifying Charles of Orleans's challenges to the Duke of Burgundy as she offers him practical military advice. Her hopes rise in 1412, when the dauphin negotiates the Treaty of Auxerre, which she describes in the *Livre de paix*. However, this work straddles the Cabochian revolt, an uprising that sends her into despair. Still, in the same work, she records the aftermath of the revolt, lauding the dauphin's arbitration efforts and proclaiming him a new Charles V, while deploring Jean's tyranny. With the Queen's Manuscript, Harley 4431, she shows her approval of the queen's decision to rejoin forces with the Armagnacs, who take Paris, ejecting the Duke of Burgundy and his men from the city, but makes no new attempt to promote Isabeau as a central figure in the government. Christine's hopes for lasting concord are dashed once again by the brutal reality of Armagnac government in Paris, and after the disastrous Battle of Agincourt, she describes her sorrow in the *Epistre de la prison de vie humaine*.

Lamentacions sur les maux de la guerre civile

Christine's open letter, the *Lamentacions*, must be considered in the context that gave rise to it. As we saw, the Duke of Berry initially reacted to Jean of Burgundy's murder of Louis of Orleans with hesitation and dread. However, Monstrelet records the duke's mounting anger as Jean settled into government in Paris: "Berry, because his access to and influence with the king and the Duke of Guyenne were limited, became angry, and returned to his land, not at all pleased with those who controlled the government, and especially with his nephew and godson, the Duke of Burgundy. And immediately afterward, he went to Angers, where he assembled with the Dukes of Orleans and Bourbon and the other great lords of this alliance, who all together in the cathedral swore and promised solemnly with oaths, to maintain from that point on the honor and profit of each other."[74] As we have seen, the result was the League of Gien, formed on April 15, 1410. Jean responded in Paris by calling his own men to arms. The anxious Parisians waited as the Armagnacs remained in the Poitou during much of the summer, while the troops called up by Jean of Burgundy mingled in Paris. In the third week of August, the king sent messengers to the Armagnacs, then in Poitiers, to inform them that anyone who joined up with them would be considered guilty of rebellion. But if Jean of Berry would come unaccompanied to Paris, the king would mediate between him and Jean of Burgundy and give him an important place in the government. Sensing a trap set by the Duke of Burgundy, who was in control of the king and his troops, the Duke of Berry refused.[75] Instead, the Armagnac armies began the march toward Paris.

Christine intervened in the crisis on August 23, 1410. The weeping narrator, "seulette," "alone, and suppressing with great difficulty the tears which blur my sight and pour down my face like a fountain" (85),[76] tries to ward off disaster by soliciting the help of the Parisian elite: the princes of the blood, the knights of France, the ladies of France, the queen, the wise men of the kingdom, the pious women of Paris, and finally Jean Duke of Berry—Jean of Burgundy, master of Paris, is strikingly absent from the appeal. There is a good reason for this absence. One of Christine's goals is to bolster the authority of Isabeau to mediate between the factions, a task that the queen would soon assume. As we have seen, the poet had successfully employed a similar strategy in October 1405. Although, like the *Epistre a la reine*, this short apostrophe to Isabeau has created the impression that Christine was critical of the queen, in its exaggeration of the queen's influence at that moment it more plausibly represents an attempt to create authority for her. But equally important, and the reason why Christine does not appeal to Jean of Burgundy, is that she means to convince the queen to join forces with the Duke of Berry and the Armagnacs.

Christine had reason to hope that Isabeau would be amenable. As we have seen, the queen had allied herself with Louis of Orleans around the time of Jean's succession as Duke of Burgundy, and although she had acquiesced to Jean after Louis's assassination, nothing suggests that she was happy about the situation. Isabeau was in Melun when Christine composed the letter, and in an entry for September 24, 1410, a month later than Christine's *Lamentacions*, Monstrelet writes that common knowledge ("commune renommee") held the queen to be much inclined toward the Orleanists ("fort affectée à ladicte parti d'Orléans").[77] Isabeau's position in 1410 was weaker than it had been in 1405. And yet, if she and the Duke of Berry were to make common cause, they might be able to force Jean from power, especially with the support of the group to which Christine addressed her lament. Christine summons Isabeau to action, asking that she mediate peace: "Oh, crowned Queen of France, are you still sleeping? Who prevents you from restraining now this side of your kin and putting an end to this deadly enterprise? Do you not see the heritage of your noble children at stake? You, the mother of the noble heirs of France, Revered Princess, who but you can do anything, and who will disobey your sovereignty and authority, if you rightly want to mediate a peace?" (89). Christine's plea is particularly forceful, recalling Psalm 43:23–24, which asks

God to awaken and remember his people: "Exsurge quare dormis Domine exsurge et; ne repellas in finem; quare faciem tuam avertis oblivisceris inopiae nostrae et tribulationis nostrae" (Arise, why are you sleeping, O Lord? Arise, and do not cast us off to the end. Why do you turn your face away? Have you forgotten our troubles and tribulations?). Isabeau does not at the moment possess the authority to gather the French around her: Christine's call to a sleeping queen is thus performative, defining the subject it summons. In announcing that the queen need only arise and assume the authority that the public is ready to accord her, Christine creates the conditions for Isabeau's intervention.

As for the Duke of Berry, mounted and ready on August 23 to lead men against the Burgundians from somewhere south of Paris, he is the addressee of the *Lamentacions* most capable of preventing violence. Indeed, he is the "remedy" to the danger (91). Adding her voice to those of the messengers from the king, who, as we saw above, tried to persuade the duke to come to Paris alone to negotiate with Jean, she urges him: "So, come, come, Noble Duke of Berry, Prince of High Excellence, and follow the divine law which orders peace!" And yet, even as she pleads for calm, it is important to notice that she does not exclude battle, if, in the worst-case scenario, negotiations prove futile: "Take a strong hold of the bridle, and stop this dishonorable army," she urges the Duke of Berry, "*at least until you have talked to the parties*" (91–93, emphasis added). Once he arrives in Paris, the duke should go among the Parisians—many of whom support Jean—to calm them, correcting them if necessary: "Come quickly to comfort this suffering city, and come to your children with correcting words if you see them err, like a good father, and pacify them while correcting them as you must appropriately do, teaching them the reasons on one side and the other that, whatever their disagreement may be, they, who should be the pillars, defenders, and supports of the noble crown, and the shields of the kingdom which never harmed them, must weigh what they ask from each other, must not destroy it" (93). Christine plays at neutrality here, but she is urging the Duke of Berry to persuade the followers of the Duke of Burgundy to turn away from him. This is clear in that only the Burgundian Parisians are in a position to apply useful pressure: the Duke of Burgundy is in Paris with his armies and presumably is susceptible to the demands of his supporters. The Armagnac Parisians, by contrast, had no influence with the Duke of Burgundy.

Christine structures the *Lamentacions* to begin and end with appeals to leaders who possess some power to lead France away from a destructive course of action: the princes of the blood and Jean of Berry. Between these book-ends, apostrophes to the mournful knights, ladies of France, Isabeau, the wise men of the kingdom, and the pious ladies suggest that significant influence could be brought to bear if the community united to work for peace. The knights of France, Christine's first addressees, once defended the Crown and the public good; now they are involved in a battle pitting father against son and brother against brother (87). They need to return to their defense of the king, abandoning the evil causes of the Armagnacs and Burgundians, which only divide the kingdom. They could stop the war by refusing to fight. Indeed, it would please God if they were too cowardly to proceed to battle ("it would indeed please God, had not [men], on either side, the courage to bear arms") (87). Christine also calls upon the women of France to weep and beat their hands, as sad Argia and the ladies of Argos did, along with the wise men of France, to aid their queen with their reason. What have they been doing; why have they not been offering counsel to the king, as they used to do? You used to concern yourselves with matters of little consequence, the poet continues, but now what will France have to pride herself on if her wise men find no means of guaranteeing her safety (89)?

The *Lamentacions* with its apostrophes suggests that although each group may be helpless alone, together they represent a significant force. A strong queen would give the French a rallying point. Detached from the Duke of Burgundy and returned to the Armagnac cause, in the scenario that Christine lays out, Isabeau represents a powerful symbol for peace. Joined to the Duke of Berry and his Armagnacs, she could form part of a coalition sufficient to intimidate the Duke of Burgundy.

This letter had little effect. Far from seeking peace, the Orleans princes wrote the king from Tours on September 2, declaring their intent to rescue him from the Burgundians.[78] Nor was the queen able to achieve an accord, although she tried throughout September, eventually abandoning the cause and returning to Paris on September 23. The Orleanists would not back down. When Isabeau announced this to the king, he was enraged and called for war against the intransigents. But cooler heads prevailed. The rector of the university reported that the institution would leave Paris because life was no longer tenable there, resulting in a special meeting of the Royal Council, at which Charles III of Navarre persuaded the king to give negotiations another try. The queen attempted again to negotiate peace, again without success.[79] The Armagnacs, having surrounded Paris, were in a strong position, able to replenish provisions, while the Burgundians inside the city were not. But, according to Monstrelet, the king proclaimed that the goods of the Armagnacs would be confiscated, which sent the Duke of Berry hurrying to negotiate. On November 2, 1410, the dukes signed the Peace of Bicêtre, which stipulated that the leaders of both factions leave Paris. On November 9, Jean left Paris for his territories, not to return until late October 1411.[80] Of the goals of the *Lamentacions*, only the queen's cooperation with the Duke of Berry was achieved. In July 1411 they were at Melun, at the king's request, to work together on the conflict.[81]

The *Livre des fais d'armes et de chevalerie*

Given the context, a guide for conducting a just and effective war seems highly relevant. Still, when the *Fais d'armes* has been discussed (it has attracted relatively little scholarly attention), it has often been read as an argument in favor of crusading. As we saw in chapter 3, Christine alludes to crusading in the *Chemin de longue étude*. Also, near contemporaries like Geoffroy de Charny promote Holy War in their treatises on chivalry, and Christine's work has been read in a similar light. Liliane Dulac and E. Jeffrey Richards have focused recently on the poet's use of Minerva, arguing persuasively that the poet's motivation is not to argue for a crusade. On the contrary, they suggest, by evoking "Italianate" context through the figure of Minerva, Christine quietly signals her alliance with Italian legal humanists who refused to approve crusades uncritically but judged each example on its merits.[82]

But this work, like her others, contains multiple levels of meaning. In what follows, I consider one of these, taking as my point of departure the question of why Christine shifted from urging peace in the *Lamentacions* to advising on the effective conduct of warfare in the *Fais d'armes*. To begin, we must imagine the intended recipients of the *Fais d'armes*. The slightly more recent of the two original manuscripts, BnF, fonds français 603, was prepared for an Armagnac reader, because it carries none of the references to Jean sans Peur found in the older one. Manuscript 10476 in the Royal Library of Belgium was modified for Jean sans Peur, evoking his recent victory over the Liegeois in 1408.[83] This praise is an insertion. Did Jean sans Peur discover that Christine was writing such a work and ask for a copy, prompting her to alter her work? In any case, Christine takes advantage of the occasion, as she did in the case of the *Fais et bonnes meurs*, to turn out a work that quietly promotes the Orleanist cause. For reasons that I will outline, I believe that Christine composed the work to justify the intractable position of the Armagnacs when she became convinced that peace would not be forthcoming. Scholars believe that the *Fais d'armes* was written around 1410. The date that I propose, based on events, of very late 1410 or early 1411 fits with this hypothesis.

Christine opens the *Fais d'armes* by considering who could engage legitimately in warfare. Medieval theoreticians of just war typically did not question the right to private warfare but promoted moral justifications for resorting to arms among those who enjoyed the right, drawing upon a body of theories based on Augustinian theology and later refined by Thomas Aquinas, Roman law, commentaries on Gratian, the Old Testament, and chivalric codes.[84] James T. Johnson has written that such theoreticians generally believed that only "those with no earthly superior" could legitimately wage war.[85] Although scholars often assume that Christine believed that only the king could raise an army, she too asserts that "those with no earthly superior" hold this right.[86] It is important to be clear about this. Christine claims that those who hold their territories on the basis of no higher authority (which means the dukes for some but not all of their territories) have the right to raise an army. Her words are unambiguous: included are "sovereign princes, like emperors, kings, dukes [ducx] and other landed seigneurs, who are the principal heads of their jurisdictions" (fol. 3r; 15).[87] Why does she include dukes? Charity Cannon Willard claims that Christine intended to please the Duke of Burgundy with her reference to dukes as sovereign lords, but this seems unlikely. Even from a distance, the Duke of Burgundy controlled the French government and the king's army. He had no need of reassurance that his cause for war was just. The young Duke of Orleans, however, needed just such support, if not for himself then for potential supporters. The Peace of Bicêtre had not removed his own motivation for war: the need to avenge his father's assassination. The alliance signed at Gien in 1410 united the Orleanists, writes Monstrelet, to settle "how and by what manner to proceed against the Duke of Burgundy to wreak vengeance on his person."[88]

As we have seen, fighting broke out between the Armagnacs and Burgundians on August 12, when a royal ordinance authorized the Burgundians and their men to take arms, and in this context Christine works to justify Armagnac belligerence.[89] She gives five reasons why war can be waged justly, three that she identifies as causes dependent on law and two dependent on will. The first cause is to preserve the church, which is not pertinent to either of the dukes (fols. 3v–4r; 16–18). The last cause, to conquer foreign lands, is also irrelevant. However, the remaining three all describe very precisely the situation of the Duke of Orleans and his followers. The second, for example, specifies that a prince may justly go to war to give aid to a vassal who has been harmed by an evildoer. Surely, the vassals of the assassinated Duke of Orleans had been harmed by an evildoer. The third, which seems calculated to sway any lord hesitating to join the cause of the Duke of Orleans, is to lend aid to widows, orphans, and anyone oppressed by an unjust power. The Duchess of Orleans had been a widow; the Duke of Orleans was an orphan. The fourth cause is vengeance. Christine initially questions the validity of this cause but quickly moves to reassert it, pointing out the fallacy of rejecting this cause on moral grounds. In fact, she argues, divine law demands that a prince seek justice and retribution. The reference can only be to the Duke of Orleans— the Duke of Burgundy was not looking for vengeance, having perpetrated the initial act of violence himself.

The Duke of Burgundy's slaying of the Duke of Orleans and his seizure of power were injustices that demanded action. It is true that in other works Christine writes eloquently on peace and addresses the terrible effects of the feud upon the body politic, with its brother eating brother and the plight of the people.[90] As Berenice Carroll explains, Christine saw the problem of maintaining the peace in an innovative way, revealing an "expanded consciousness of emerging classes in society and attention to their needs and roles." Furthermore, her writings suggest that she envisioned "a reduction of the role and authority of the church and of theological explanation," with the effect of placing responsibility for war in the hands of those waging it.[91] James T. Johnson explains that Christine represents a point of convergence between what previously had been two distinct traditions of peace theory: religious and chivalric. Her near contemporary, Honoré Bovet, on whose *Arbre des batailles* (1387) Christine drew heavily in the *Fais d'armes* and who believed that feuding between nobles was inevitable and sanctioned by God, offers a point of comparison.[92] Bovet writes:

> Thus we must understand that war comes from God, and not merely that He permits war, but that He has ordained it; for God commanded a man called Joshua that he should do battle against his enemies, and advised him how he should set an ambush for the discomfiture of his enemies. Further, we say that our Lord God Himself is lord and governor of battles. And for this reason we must accept and grant that war comes from divine law, that is the law of God: for the aim of war is to wrest peace, tranquility and reasonableness from him who refuses

to acknowledge his wrongdoing. And if, in the waging of war, the good have to suffer for the bad, it cannot be otherwise, for, indeed, war is to be compared to a medicine.[93]

For Christine, by contrast, violence was the result of selfish human ambition, not the will of God; she assigns it no medicinal value.

The remaining three books of the *Fais d'armes* offer advice that would have been practical for a young man creating an army. Book 2, drawing heavily on Vegetius, discusses qualities to be sought in a leader; books 3 and 4, indebted to Frontinus and Honoré Bovet, discuss military strategies. As she had done in the *Epistre d'Othea a Hector*, Christine compiles a work of counsel for a knight filtered through the consciousness of a woman devoted to practical reality, one who knows how to marshal the best sources of her age and put them together in such a way as to be useful to a young man and create authority for his actions.

I began this section by observing that Christine's works served multiple purposes. That they were often dedicated to more than one person suggests that she envisioned different readings for them, as do her own interpretive guides, like that attached to the ex-Phillips manuscript of the *Advision*. Nothing in the work proclaims its purpose as a vehicle for supporting the cause of Charles of Orleans. However, given the social climate of the time, it seems clear that this would have been one of Christine's motives.

The *Livre de paix*

The Cabochian revolt interrupted Christine's composition of the *Livre de paix*. Part 1 of the three-part work, which "exhorts my lord of Guyenne to preserve the peace, and speaks of the virtue of prudence and its application in princely government" (58), was begun just after the Treaty of Auxerre, which the dauphin had negotiated between the dukes on August 22, 1412, and completed on the last day of November of that year.[94] However, a hiatus of nearly a year separates this date and the composition of parts 2 and 3. Christine explains that the rest "was put aside because of the failure of the peace" (58). As Karen Green has noted, the timing is odd, because the Cabochian revolt intervened only in the spring of 1413, which suggests that Christine's anxiety may have been the result of the Burgundian refusal to restore goods confiscated from the Armagnacs, as promised in the Treaty of Auxerre.[95] Certainly, bad blood persisted after the treaty. Although the Armagnacs and Burgundi-ans had pledged to work together in peace, Parisian Burgundians suspected that the Armagnacs sought only the destruction of the king and city, as the Bourgeois de Paris remarks bitterly.[96] Despite his domination of the Royal Council, the Duke of Burgundy found himself surrounded by intrigue.[97] Tensions ran high in the streets of Paris as well. Monstrelet reports that an encounter between a Bourbon prince and a butcher, Denisot de Chaumont, nearly led to an uprising in October.[98] Moreover, the English, having invaded France in August, were pillaging their way toward Paris; despite the Treaty of Auxerre, Charles of Orleans had signed a secret alliance with Thomas of Clar-ence on November 13.[99] For these reasons, Christine may have felt too disil-lusioned to continue her book of peace. But the Cabochian revolt erupted and passed, and the second part of the *Livre de paix*, begun on September 3, 1413, when the Peace of Pontoise had restored calm to Paris, "speaks once again of the benefits of peace," giving the example of Charles V (58). Part 3 "speaks of governing the people and the polity well" (58).

Despite the rupture written into the *Livre de paix*, the work as a whole is hopeful, for Christine now fixes on the fifteen-year-old dauphin as capable of bringing an end to the strife. One of her purposes is to bolster the authority of the young man in his new task as mediator, because he, like his mother, the queen, would face difficulties in bringing the dukes to heel. Thus Christine evokes the dauphin's connection to the divine and his relationship to Charles V. Inspired by God to restore the peace, she writes, the dauphin rightly com-mands the obedience of the princes as well as the love and confidence of his people. Still, she is realistic, counseling the young man in practical terms on how to nourish the fragile peace that he has helped to bring about. Berenice Carroll has described the *Livre de paix* as Christine's "first attempt at a system-atic analysis of the requirements of peace and the practical policies necessary to achieve it in the monarchical nation-state."[100] The virtues that Christine advises Louis to embrace, the most important of which is prudence, represent what Kate Langdon Forhan describes as "procedural," that is, "applied" virtues.[101]

In part 1, Christine praises God for the present peace (59). Calm returned to a France mired in civil war, Christine writes, when God saw fit to speak through the mouth of a child, inspiring the fifteen-year-old dauphin to "staunch the fearsome, unremitting bloodshed from which your catholic kingdom of France was dying" (60). "How unlike a light unstable youth," Christine marvels (59). Already in this characterization, she alludes to the dauphin's lineage. We have seen her praise the early maturity of Charles V and Louis of Orleans: Louis of Guyenne follows in the family footsteps.

During the reading of the Gospel of Saint Jean, Christine reports, Louis had suddenly turned joyfully to his confessor and announced that this would be a wonderful day to establish peace between the two enemy Jeans, of Berry and Burgundy. She depicts the young man as a mediator, a vassal of God, "the restorer and comforter of all France" (62). But the question is how to maintain the peace. Prudence is required (64). In chapter 4 of part 1, Christine describes Louis crowned with virtue. Although he is not yet king, she reminds her readers of the sacred nature that he will one day acquire, and points out that in the meantime he is royally crowned with prudence and the practical virtues to which it gives flower (65). In this way, she links the dauphin yet more tightly to his grandfather. In chapter 5, she dissects prudence, which has to do with "choses ouvrales" (208–9), that is, "things one wants to achieve" (68). She makes Louis's relationship to Charles V explicit in chapter 6, where she begins to depict the wise king as a role model.

Christine advises the dauphin to regulate his own life in this chapter: his "prudence and the good order of his life can benefit all his subjects, as much by good example as by their being well governed" (71). She then turns to the example of Charles V. The passage gains its full relevance in the context of Christine's belief that the king links earthly with divine order. A brief examination of how Christine lays out this connection in the *Fais et bonnes meurs* will show how she applies it in the *Livre de paix*. Throughout the former work, Christine interweaves ritualistic, symbolically laden acts, like changing clothes, to the application of practical virtue. The wise king reflected "higher things" in his habits, his attire, and his virtue, and this personal order exerted a positive regulating effect upon society (1:31). When Charles V matured, Christine explains, he had laid aside "pretty, whimsical and curious clothing" to reveal his sacred kingly nature through his "royal and pontifical vestments, wise and imperial, as appropriate to such dignity" (1:37). The titles of the early chapters of book 1 of the *Fais et bonnes meurs* reveal the importance that Christine accorded order (1:2–3). Chapter 15 is titled, "Here is told how the King Charles established lovely order in his own living"; this is followed by the slightly broader chapter 16, "Here are given examples of virtuous princes living beautifully ordered lives, recalling the theme of how Charles was well ordered in all things." In chapter 19, Christine reveals how the same principle of order that Charles demonstrates in his personal behavior becomes a public virtue: "Here is described the order in which Charles maintained revenues and distributions of payments in his kingdom."

To return to the *Livre de paix*, Christine sees the successful king as a crucial link between microcosm and macrocosm, reflecting divine order in the order of his person and household and thereby transmitting it throughout the kingdom. The dauphin's authority ("auctorité") (71, 210) should issue not only from his "dignity," that is, his royalty, but from his virtue and his prudence. He should follow in the footsteps of his grandfather, who was also youthful when responsibility devolved upon him: "O, who was more prudent than he, or more cultivated and in all good things more perfect? For, by God's grace, even in the flower of youth, realizing with his great prudence that it is noble and necessary for a prince, no matter how young, to have a mature heart and to understand what should be pursued and abandoned, he gave up all youthful habits, and behaved in every way as wisdom teaches" (71).

Christine continues to place Louis in his royal familial context, the details of which I can only suggest here. But one point in particular from book 1 of the *Livre de paix* is important for my reading because it reflects the principle of regency and kingship that Christine has consistently promoted: that of choosing counselors carefully, to which she devotes chapters 9 through 12 of part 1. In chapter 9, she explains that the ideal counselor is a wise old man, someone who has seen everything. Age alone is not enough—foolish old men abound. Beyond this, she insists that counselors should represent a broad swath of the body politic. Two kinds of nobles should be present: knights with knowledge of arms and older, sensible knights "of good life and well-ordered estate" who live near the prince and can advise him on running the royal estate (80–81). Members of the clergy and jurists, whether religious or lay, and wealthy burghers should also be part of the king's council (81–82). As before, she strongly supports the preeminence of men like the marmousets.

After the break in her narrative, Christine takes up her pen again on September 3, 1413 (93). Books 2 and 3 offer advice for the ruling prince, but they also contain angry expositions on evildoers and bad lords who have power and authority. With Jean of Burgundy safely distanced from Paris after the revolt, Christine gives vent to her anger at his disruptive acts. Chapter 4 of book 3 begins: "Since the wickedness of corrupt men can express itself more fully in powerful men than in others, by causing many evils, there is nothing worse than when a bad man—full of venom, cruelty, and belligerence—is powerful" (129). Because of the faults of the evil prince, "countless evils will spring up and overrun him and his country" (130). However, he will be too obstinate to back down. It is interesting to note that only one of the two extant manuscripts available to the public, Royal Library of Belgium, MS 10366, contains this sharply critical passage targeting Jean personally, as an insertion.[102] Tania van Hemelryck describes the effect of the insertion as a "bitter criticism of a cruel and untrustworthy tyrant," in contrast with the "universal condemnation of evil princes" that emerges from the other manuscript, BnF, fonds français 1182.[103]

The great question, as always, is how to keep unruly bad lords in line. Christine does not provide a straightforward answer. The rest of book 3 is concerned with many of the virtues attributed to Charles V in the *Fais et bonnes meurs* and recommends them to Louis. The only hope that Louis will "exercise his rule without discord among his subjects" seems to lie in imitating his grandfather (133), who created a public persona that inspired great loyalty, thus enabling him to rule over a divided kingdom. In highlighting the relationship between Charles V and the Duke of Guyenne, Christine tries to create authority for the young man, rallying readers to back him, by imbuing him with his grandfather's mystique.

The Queen's Manuscript

Christine had reinforced the authority of Louis of Orleans, Isabeau, and finally the dauphin, celebrating the young man's assertion of power in her *Livre de paix*. The sumptuous Queen's Manuscript, today British Library, Harley 4431, reflects Christine's recognition that by 1414 the queen had retreated from political life. The manuscript, commissioned by Isabeau, manifests either the poet's vision of the queen in semiretirement, or perhaps the queen's taste for courtly poetry and didactic literature.[104] Whatever the case, the manuscript's contents suggest that the queen finally has time to devote to her books and her entourage, having passed the business of royal politics on to her son.

Copied by Christine's scribes and illustrated with 132 miniatures, this luxury volume must have been created early in 1414, just after the Cabochian revolt. James Laidlaw bases this date on the inclusion of a *balade* celebrating a victory over the English in Aquitaine by Jean of Bourbon, a member of the League of Gien, in November 1413.[105] The manuscript is a diverse anthology of many of the pieces collected in the *Livre de Christine* and the Duke's Manuscript, but with some key omissions and one important addition.

As for the omissions, that of the *Epistre a la reine*, a response to a political crisis, is striking, all the more so because the last three columns of it were stricken from the manuscript, leaving legible traces.[106] Also missing is the *Mutacion de fortune*, with its theme of the transformation from passive female to active male when necessity calls. In fact, none of the works generally deemed overtly "political" (*Advision, Corps de policie, Lamentacions, Fais d'armes, Livre de paix*) is included. Another telling absence is that of the *Dit de la rose*, which I have proposed should be read as Christine's rejoinder on behalf of Louis of Orleans to the insult perpetrated by Philip of Burgundy and the queen through the fabrication of the *cour amoureuse*. As for the new addition, this manuscript, like the *Livre de Christine* and its analogues, opens with the *Cent balades* and other courtly lyrics. But it ends with a long cycle of love poems, which appear only in this manuscript, called the *Cent balades d'aman et de dame*, composed for someone sweet and affable ("doulce et debonnaire") (Harley 4431, fol. 376r) to whom Christine claims to owe recompense ("amende"). It seems reasonable to imagine that the queen herself requested this conclusion for her manuscript. Last among the pessimistic mininarratives in the *Cent balades* and the *Autres balades*, the pathetic story recounted in the *Cent balades d'aman et de dame* achieves its full meaning in the context of Charles VI's court. It seems a tragic end to the collection, and yet it captures something fundamental about the life of the queen: the terrible uncertainty that had dogged her career, interspersed with rare bursts of happiness and love.

This dialogue between the cycle's two lovers, with interventions from Amour and a narrator, consists of one hundred *balades*, along with a final lay that brings the total to 101. The cycle dramatizes a sad love story. A young man declares his love to a woman who at first is distant and does not reciprocate until she receives a visit from Amour, the god of love. Once again, the absence at the center of things pervades Christine's work. Amour, convinced of the lover's sincerity, obliges the lady to respond. "Your arrogance is overweening" (Trop est folle ta vantise), he chastises her (fol. 378r). Prey to a power greater than herself, the lady surrenders. She enjoys long stretches of happiness. But *médisans* appear, as they always do; the lover seems to grow less interested; the lady dies dramatically. As always, the lady can never know for sure whether her lover is loyal, and the opportunity for betrayal, coupled with the impossibility of knowing whether it has taken place, kills her. These *balades*, like Christine's others, recount the terrible suffering of those who cannot penetrate the ceiling of earthly knowledge.

The lady has the final word in the "lay mortel" that ends the cycle, describing herself, as she has done in some of the preceding *balades*, as small and lonely ("seullecte à part") (fol. 398r). As we have seen, this is one of Christine's personal narrator's guises for herself in the *Cent balades* and the *Lamentacions*.[107] The manuscript comes to an end with the lady describing her lifeless body floating on a barge down the river, like the Lady of Astolat of Arthurian legend.

We know that Isabeau appreciated poetry; as we have seen, in 1399 she ordered a copy of Jean le Seneschal's *Cent ballades*. The *Livre de Christine*, as we have seen, was created for her. The commission of a gorgeous manuscript containing examples of a beloved genre seems an apt gesture on the eve of the queen's retirement.

The *Epistre de la prison de vie humaine*

The peace that Christine describes with such hope in the *Livre de paix*, and that must have sustained her as she supervised production of the Queen's Manuscript, did not endure. Not only did the ruling Armagnacs make themselves despised by the Parisians, but the conflict continued, allowing Henry V of England to invade France and deliver a crushing defeat in the Battle of Agincourt, on October 25, 1415. In the *Epistre de la prison de vie humaine*, completed in Paris on January 20, 1418, more than two years after that terrible day, Christine attempts to comfort the bereaved family members of the battle's victims, including the ostensible addressee, Marie of Berry and Auvergne. Marie was the daughter of the Duke of Berry and the wife of the Armagnac Jean of Bourbon, whose victory over the English gives us the date for the Queen's Manuscript. But Jean had been taken prisoner at Agincourt and would die in captivity in London in 1434. Christine apologizes at the close of the letter for writing so tardily and copiously, pleading "great worries and troubles of courage which because of many displeasures that, since the moment I started it, and it was long ago, have kept my poor understanding in such check with all these sad thoughts and ideas" (67–69).[108]

As she composed her sorrowful letter, Christine must have been mindful of the unhappy anniversary of the assassination of the Duke of Orleans ten years earlier, in November 1407. Jean de Montreuil's correspondence suggests that the date was marked by Louis's followers. In a letter to Martin Talayero, master at the University of Paris from 1407 to 1417, Jean discusses the act of treachery that was the remote cause of the English invasion and the debacle of Agincourt. After some philosophical musing about why fortune fails to compensate men who devote their lives to the common good, Jean turns to the brother of the king, slaughtered while the perpetrators remained free. The "greatest and most powerful prince of his kingdom and the only brother of the king" had been murdered by "vile traitorous accomplices, 6 in number," who afterward remained in Paris, coming and going as they pleased with impunity.[109] Jean's letter suggests not only that the anniversary was observed but that some of Louis's former friends, beyond those committed militarily to Charles of Orleans, still deplored the brutal slaying.

To return to the *Prison de vie humaine*, Christine, too, seems to have been thinking about Louis of Orleans, because the opening lines of her letter excoriate treachery. Although she evokes the necessity of patience in the face of Fortune, a reasonable way to begin a letter of comfort, she shifts abruptly to condemning traitors. Christine attributes Alexander's abrupt downfall to Fortune, but she hastens to condemn the treacherous servants who poisoned him. Caesar, too, was a victim of Fortune, but also of the stab wounds of his "privé conseil" and citizens. Judas, the arch-traitor, is evoked next, and then Scipio, exiled by his political enemies. Christine continues in this vein, writing of "evil men, full of venom and false ambition, persecutors and destroyers of humankind, avid to shed blood and do any evil" (11). Why this emphasis on ambition, intrigue, and treachery? The context provides the answer. The Orleanists were victims of Fortune, but also of treachery. Louis's murder on the orders of Jean of Burgundy had caused the current disarray, the feud without end that enabled the invasion of Henry V and resulted in the disaster at Agincourt. The addressee of the *Prison de vie humaine*, given her Armagnac milieu, would have been receptive to angry words about treachery and ready to link the defeat at Agincourt to the assassination of Louis of Orleans.

Christine then moves to examples of men who committed evil and were later themselves hit by acts of divine vengeance, first offering comfort to the grieving with her assertion that God is just and will treat traitors harshly (11). Cain, Absalom, and others prove the point: the end of "wicked men is miserable" (13). Once again, Christine is prescient: the death of Jean of Burgundy in 1419 at the hands of the Armagnacs, under the eyes of the dauphin, was still to come. Well before that event, Christine has envisioned it, for "whoever doubts God's vengeance is a fool!" (15).

Finally, the letter shifts to its primary purpose, consoling Marie and other grieving women for their recent losses. As Louise D'Arcens has observed, in this work the poet identifies the misfortune of France with her own widow-hood, creating "the French polity in the feminized image of a weeping widow." Widowhood in this case "reflects the reality of France stripped of its noblemen and soldiers," an entity whose healing will come from "reading the comforting words of the *auctores*."[110] But, as D'Arcens notes, Christine does not present the grieving widow as a healing mediatrix, as she had done earlier. This work offers no figure around whom to rally: the new dauphin Charles, promoted through the deaths of his two older brothers, Louis in 1415 and Jean in 1417, had not yet emerged as a leader, Charles of Orleans had been taken prisoner at Agincourt, and Isabeau had recently been delivered by Jean of Burgundy, which must have eliminated her from Christine's vision of pos-sible saviors.

Christine dates this letter January 20; on January 10, Isabeau had ceded her regency to Jean of Burgundy. This collaboration must have been a blow to the poet. For the moment, there was no visible way forward. The letter verges on despair.

Conclusion

The winter of 1418 returns us to chapter 1 and to the buildup to the Burgun-dian massacre. Christine had predicted just such a showdown for more than a decade. The bruised and bleeding Libera of the *Advision* plants herself between the armies of her children, personifying the destruction that the poet warned her compatriots against. In the *Livre de paix*, Christine optimistically describes the seizure of power by the Armagnacs after the Cabochian revolt in 1413, hoping for peace. And yet her hopes for lasting concord were dashed again, when the new government, far from attempting to create good will, further stoked hatred between the Armagnacs and Burgundians by implementing a series of unpopular policies: strict surveillance to minimize any possibility of revolt; onerous taxes to fund the defense of the country against the Eng-lish; harassment of Burgundian sympathizers. As we have just seen, Christine describes her dismay at this turn in a letter consoling Marie of Bourbon, wid-owed during the Battle of Agincourt, for her losses.

Scholars writing on Christine's political ideas have stressed the poet's love of peace and impartiality and her dread of the violence that she predicted. Certainly, she promoted reconciliation between the factions through her writings. But those who lived through the Armagnac-Burgundian conflict were not peace-loving or impartial. Juvénal des Ursins describes Burgundian treatment of Armagnacs in different cities of the kingdom well before the Burgundian massacre of the Armagnacs in Paris: "they chopped off their heads, pillaged them, and robbed them of their goods"; to get a man killed, it was enough to call him an Armagnac. The Armagnacs retaliated. Supporters of the Duke of Burgundy "were penalized and their goods taken."[111] As Michel Pintoin, the monk of Saint Denis, observed, the people of Paris were filled with an implacable hatred.[112]

From 1410 on, Christine's writing becomes less encouraging of peace and more openly partisan. In the *Lamentacions*, she attempts to bolster the authority of the Duke of Berry and the queen to force Jean of Burgundy to lay down arms, although she urges a peaceful solution. In the *Fais d'armes*, she supports the Orleanist right to conduct war. In the *Livre de paix*, dedicated to the Armagnac duke Jean of Berry, she identifies with the Armagnacs, reporting the joy of the Parisians in September 1413, just after Jean of Burgundy had been forced to flee to Flanders because of his role in the Cabochian uprising. She does the same in 1413 when she presents the deluxe manuscript known today as Harley 4431 to the queen, who was at the moment still working with the Armagnacs. She writes the *Prison de vie humaine* for Marie of Bourbon, daughter and wife of committed Armagnacs, the Duke of Berry and Jean of Bourbon, respectively, comforting her with assurances of divine vengeance.

Christine fled Paris either during the Burgundian massacre or soon afterward, taking refuge in a convent, possibly the Dominican priory at Poissy, home of her beloved daughter, though no one knows for sure.[1] Although she lived for another thirteen years or so, she composed only two more known works. The first was the *Heures de contemplacion sur la passion de notre Seigneur*, completed sometime after 1420, the year in which the Treaty of Troyes was signed, making the English king Henry V regent and heir to the French throne. Devotion to Christ's Passion, observes Maureen Boulton, "was a source of comfort and consolation in times of trial."[2] But even in a work aiming to offer solace during what Christine would have considered one of the blackest moments of history, her erudition is remarkable. Possibly composed for the nuns at Poissy, the *Heures de contemplacion* "is consistent with Dominican practice as recommended by Thomas Aquinas in the *Summa*," and it reflects Gerson's intellectualized "'mystic theology' of the 1420s," in the words of E. Jeffrey Richards and Liliane Dulac.[3]

But when the poet emerges in 1429 to compose her last known work, the *Ditié de Jehanne d'Arc*, the situation in France has suddenly brightened: victory for the Armagnacs has become possible after a long period of English occupation. The narrator of this work is a committed Armagnac, fiercely devoted to Charles VII, whose succession she attributes to a new female mediator, Joan of Arc. Christine's tone is anything but peaceful. She demands to know whether Burgundy will bar Charles VII's entrance to Paris, hastening to assure Parisian readers that the king is their friend. Joan is leading him to

Paris, and although many will lose their lives when the two arrive, the king does his best to avoid killing and wounding people. But if Parisians refuse to cede to him what is rightfully his, he will recover it by force and bloodshed.[4]

No one disputes the poet's Armagnac allegiance at this point. However, I have tried to show that Christine's commitment to the Orleanist or Armagnac cause dates to the very beginning of her career and that her earliest works are already partisan, intended to alert her public to the danger of Burgundian pretensions to regency power. This point, I believe, is essential for understanding Christine as a political writer interested in contemporary issues, that is, for understanding her approach to the overwhelming problem that the kingdom faced from the first episode of Charles VI's madness, in 1392, until his death in 1422. How could the Valois kingship be maintained during the king's periods of madness and proper governance of the kingdom be assured? Had the dauphin been of an age to govern when the king's malady first struck him, or had a formal and undisputed procedure for regency existed, accompanied by an enforcement mechanism sufficient to dissuade different claimants from contesting the regent, the problem would not have arisen. In theory, Charles VI's insanity, although certainly an inconvenience, need not have been catastrophic for the kingdom. Even with the dauphin a child, Charles VI had a brother, Louis of Orleans, able in mind and body, who was the obvious choice to govern during the minority of the royal heir. Both Charles V and Charles VI had created ordinances naming a brother regent in the event that they died leaving a minor heir, and from these ordinances it could have been inferred that regency during Charles VI's episodes of madness should go to his brother.

However, Philip of Burgundy (and later his son and successor, Jean) disregarded these ordinances and claimed regency for himself; more specifically, because Philip had no clear basis for such a claim, given Louis's presence, he propagated the view that regency should be invested in a council headed by himself, basing authority in a vague principle of popular approval. As Bernard Guenée writes, the question was, "in the absence of the king, would power be individual or collective, returning to the closest relatives of the king, in a corporation?"[5] Although it was never formally articulated, the Burgundian claim can be gleaned from the Burgundians' letters and from chronicle accounts of their activity. As we have seen, the Burgundian chronicle of Pierre Cochon associates Jean of Burgundy's regency claim with a fictitious ancient principle of governance through the Three Estates.[6] In fact, the Burgundian claim was based on force and the capacity to rally popular support, or, to use the contemporary terms, deeds ("faits"), rather than words ("dits") or any coherent narrative of authority.

Against this hazily formulated claim, which Christine views as rebellion, the poet offers an opposing view, and thus gives shape and authority to Louis's claim to regency. In addition to loathing social disorder, she manifests in numerous places her allegiance to the principles set out in writing by Charles V and then Charles VI—that is, to a single ruling figure, one who retains a council but rules unencumbered by the chaos of a group. On this score, she proclaims herself in agreement with Aristotle, writing that governance by a number of people "is never a very profitable thing, and we never see it last long." She sees nothing positive in "a diversity of opinions and wills."[7] Influenced by her father's relationship with Charles V, and by Charles's attempts to strengthen the monarchy with a strict vertical lineage that would prevent his brothers from seizing power if he died prematurely, leaving a minor heir, Christine was the natural ally of Louis of Orleans.

I have also tried to show that a second, equally important element of Christine's writing on regency has been overlooked: her support for a central government role for Queen Isabeau of Bavaria. The feminist aspect of Christine's work has attracted enormous attention, occasioning the resurgence of interest in her corpus beginning in the 1970s. But Christine's defense of women did not emerge out of the blue; it was motivated, I submit, by her interest in the regency problem and can be correlated very precisely with Isabeau's mediation between the dukes, outlined in royal ordinances, suggesting an effort to bolster the queen's authority. As the struggle between Louis and Philip (and Jean after Philip's death) sharpened, Christine began to envision a weightier role for the queen, who, if allied with Louis, would create a formidable defense against the Burgundian challenge.

Burgundian chroniclers, who are the most widely read sources for the reign of Charles VI, make the still common view that Christine regarded Philip as the natural leader of the kingdom during the king's episodes of insanity seem plausible. But another factor was Louis of Orleans's failure to promote himself in terms that were apt to appeal to Parisians and therefore get recorded in contemporary chronicles. As Françoise Autrand explains, "the Duke of Orleans, like his cousin, sent letters to the cities of the kingdom, but, secure in his position of first among the Princes of the Blood next to the sick king, he did not concern himself about popularity." Rather, he focused on his program, "constructing an efficient and strong state without worrying too much about dialogue with the subjects. . . . Moreover, Louis did not need to grab power, he had only to exercise it."[8]

In conclusion, I would like to strengthen this point by revisiting a debate over Christine's literary heritage that, although waged nearly thirty years ago, raises an issue still relevant to criticism on the poet's political vision. The debate began when Sheila Delany posed the question of whether Christine constituted a worthy literary model for women, a "mother to think back through," as Virginia Woolf put it. For Delany, Christine was a reactionary, both politically and regarding women, and therefore an unsuitable icon. In Delany's view, Christine tried "to beat back the tide of social change, of protest and nascent democracy, with her little broom of pious anecdotes and exhortations from the Bible and other ancient authorities. In a time when even courtiers and clerics wanted change, Christine continued in her quiet little neo-Platonic hierarchies and her feudal nostalgia."[9] Christine Reno responded to Delany's "charges" that Christine, viewed in context, was in fact a worthy literary forebear. Reno demonstrated the many ways in which the poet had responded compassionately to the world around her and to women in her texts.[10] Delany, countering Reno, pointed out that her original piece on Christine's reactionary politics had not been a "charge": there are "no 'charges' because having reactionary opinions is not a crime or a sin."[11]

This debate over whether Christine was reactionary or progressive is a fitting stopping point for this study. Delany's assertion that Christine clung to her "feudal nostalgia" is another example of the way in which her politics has been approached, that is, without careful consideration of the political society within which she lived and wrote. If we want to describe a political view as "feudal nostalgia," it can only reasonably be applied to the Burgundians. As we have seen, they cast their populist position as a return to the good old days. Their insistence on rule by council hearkened back to the mythological period before the Valois kings, to the Capetians. The revolts of the Jacquerie and the Cabochians, to which Delany refers as early democratic movements, were anything but progressive; the rebels were demanding a return to the golden era of Saint Louis, the period before corrupt officials were free to rob the people blind. In cleaving to what she saw as Charles V's centralizing tendency, his vesting of power in his immediate family and his careful co-opting of his brothers, Christine promoted a type of kingship in which modern historians see the origins of the absolutist state, although that concept itself has been heavily challenged and qualified in recent years. Still, in the fight between the Armagnacs and the Burgundians, it was the Armagnacs who must be imagined as "progressive," if we want to think in those terms. The Armagnacs were protoabsolutists, as Michael Sizer writes.[12] In her devotion to the king, Christine was in the forefront, politically speaking.

$\mathcal{N}otes$

PROLOGUE

1. The "maladie qui ainsi court parmi [l]a terre," in the words of the doleful Libera, figure of France in the *Livre de l'advision Cristine*, 32. Throughout this study, I use the terms "feud" and "conflict" interchangeably. In chapter 1, I justify my designation of the Armagnac-Burgundian conflict as a feud and lay out its implications for Christine's political writings. All translations are my own unless otherwise noted.

2. To quote Nichols's review of Cerquiglini-Toulet's *New History of Medieval French Literature*.

3. Gauvard, "Christine de Pizan et ses contemporains," 106.

4. Important exceptions include the work of Karen Green, esp. her introduction to the *Livre de paix*; Richards, esp. "Political Thought as Improvisation"; Laidlaw, esp. "Christine de Pizan: The Making of the Queen's Manuscript"; and Hindman, *Christine de Pizan's "Epistre Othéa,"* all of which look beyond the traditional construction of Christine's political loyalties.

5. Krynen, *Empire du roi*, 200.

6. Monstrelet, *Chronique*, 2:102, describes how the Orleanists came to be called the Armagnacs.

7. Gauvard, "Christine de Pisan," 423–24.

8. Wheeler, "Christine de Pizan's *Livre des fais d'armes*," 155.

9. Willard, *Christine de Pizan*, 196. On Jean de Castel, notary for Charles VII, see Thomas, "Jean Castel," 273.

10. See Autrand, *Christine de Pizan*, 271–73; and Gonzalez, *Prince en son hôtel*, 13–14. Other factors have increased the distortion, as Gonzalez explains, including the source materials. For the Burgundians, these are abundant and are located primarily in Paris, Lille, and Dijon. For the dukes of Orleans, sources are fragmented and widely dispersed.

11. Kéralio, *Crimes des reines de France*, 132–33, 142.

12. See Michelet, *Histoire de France*, 5:93–158; Guizot, *Histoire de France*, 2:209–84; Martin, *Histoire de France populaire*, vol. 1; Coville, *Cabochiens et l'ordonnance de 1413*; and Thibault, *Isabeau de Bavière*. For a nineteenth-century monarchist historian's narrative, see Jarry, *Vie politique de Louis de France*.

13. Thomassy, *Essai sur les écrits politiques*, xv. See also Fletcher, "Crisis and *Luxuria* in England and France," 30; and Cazelles, "Exigence de l'opinion depuis saint Louis," 95.

14. Thomassy, *Essai sur les écrits politiques*, lix.

15. Pintoin, *Chronique du religieux*, 3:228–32, 266–70, 288–90, 330. The much cited *Songe véritable* cannot be included because it was written as a piece of Burgundian political propaganda, and thus is not indicative of any widespread dislike. See also Adams, *Life and Afterlife of Isabeau*, chaps. 2 and 4.

16. Forhan, *Political Theory of Christine de Pizan*, 86.

17. Willard, "Christine de Pizan: From Poet to Political Commentator," 23.

18. Delogu, *Theorizing the Ideal Sovereign*, 154.

19. Forhan, *Political Theory of Christine de Pizan*, 16.

20. Willard, *Christine de Pizan*, 150.

21. In this, my argument differs slightly from that of Gauvard in her important study "Christine de Pizan et ses contemporains," 115, although my study reinforces much of what she writes.

22. Heckmann, *Stellvertreter, Mit- und Ersatzherrscher*, 1:324. As Heckmann explains, the regent's ruling in the name of the king is a bit of a fiction, but it is a useful one, less likely to result in usurpation than the regent's ruling in his own name.

23. Scanlon, "King's Two Voices," 217.

24. These include Small, *Late Medieval France*; Sizer, "Making Revolution Medieval"; Pollack-Lagushenko, "Armagnac Faction"; Schnerb, *Armagnacs et les Bourguignons*; Allmand, *Hundred Years War*; Autrand, *Charles VI*; and Famiglietti, *Royal Intrigue*. I also rely on the older but essential studies Lehoux, *Jean de France*, and Nordberg, *Ducs et la royauté*.

25. See van Hemelryck's insightful discussion in "Christine de Pizan et la paix," especially 685–89.

26. Tarnowski, "Perspectives on the *Advision*," 110.

27. See Autrand, *Christine de Pizan*; and Roux, *Christine de Pizan*.

28. Margolis, *Introduction to Christine de Pizan*, 93. See also Willard, *Christine de Pizan*.

29. See Le Ninan, *Sage roi et la clergesse*; Nederman, "Expanding Body Politic: Christine de Pizan" and "Expanding Body Politic: The Diversification," along with the other articles in Green and Mews, *Healing the Body Politic*; Forhan, *Political Theory of Christine de Pizan*; Gauvard, "Christine de Pizan et ses contemporains"; Carroll, "Christine de Pizan and the Origins" and "On the Causes of War"; and Krynen, *Empire du roi* and *Idéal du prince*.

30. Spiegel, *Past as Text*, 22.

CHAPTER 1

1. The following account is based on the story of the massacre as recounted in Monstrelet, *Chronique*, 3:260–74; Bourgeois de Paris, *Journal d'un bourgeois de Paris*, 107–29; Pintoin, *Chronique du religieux*, 6:228–68; Fenin, *Mémoires de Pierre de Fenin*, 292–301; and Le Fèvre, *Chronique de Jean Le Fèvre*, 1:326–34.

2. The Porte Saint Germain, also known as the Porte de Buci, was located on the present-day rue Saint André, a few steps past the Church of Saint Germain des Près, at the time part of a fortified abbey lying just outside the city walls. The Burgundians entered there because Perrinet Leclerc, a Burgundian sympathizer, was able to steal the keys from his father, keeper of that gate. Monstrelet describes Perrinet Leclerc as one of a group of young men "of middle estate and easily moved who had earlier been chastised for their wrongdoings [by the governing Armagnacs]," explaining that despite the heavy surveillance by Armagnac guards, the young men had managed to speak secretly to the Seigneur de L'Isle-Adam in his garrison in Pontoise. With Isle-Adam they had arranged to let an army of about eight hundred Burgundians into Paris. See Monstrelet, *Chronique*, 3:260–62.

3. Juvénal des Ursins, *Histoire de Charles VI*, 540.

4. Ibid., 541.

5. Monstrelet, *Chronique*, 3:263–64.

6. Bourgeois de Paris, *Journal d'un bourgeois de Paris*, 115–17.

7. Beaune, *Jeanne d'Arc*, 257–77.

8. On this question, see Netterstrøm and Poulsen, *Feud in Medieval and Early Modern Europe*; Kalyvas, *Logic of Violence in Civil War*; Carroll, *Blood and Violence*; Kaminsky, "Noble Feud"; and Halsall, *Violence and Society*. Anthropological work on feuding is useful as well; see Boehm, *Blood Revenge*.

9. Otterbein, *Anthropology of War*, 43.

10. Kalyvas, *Logic of Violence in Civil War*, 71.

11. Sizer, "Making Revolution Medieval," 766–68.

12. Monstrelet, *Chronique*, 3:255–58. Pintoin, *Chronique du religieux*, 6:208–22, gives the details of the negotiations.

13. Sizer, "Calamity of Violence," 34. See also the discussions in Schnerb, *Armagnacs et les Bourguignons*, 11–13; and Autrand, *Charles VI*, 189–213.

14. See Netterstrøm's introduction in Netterstrøm and Poulsen, *Feud in Medieval and Early Modern Europe*, esp. 54–56.

15. Hutchison, "Partisan Identity in the French Civil War," 274.

16. Famiglietti, "French Monarchy Crisis," 329–402.

17. "This would recognize the existence of a structure, a leader, and organized ways of popularization that did not exist around the king." Gauvard, "Christine de Pizan et ses contemporains," 115.

18. Pollack-Lagushenko, "Armagnac Faction," 235–39.

19. Ibid., 242–43, 252–63.

20. On contemporary court writers, see Gauvard, "Christine de Pizan et ses contemporains"; Autrand, *Jean de Berry*, 465–72; Cadden, "Charles V, Nicole Oresme, and Christine de Pizan"; and Monfrin, "Humanisme et traductions au Moyen Age," esp. 173–81.

21. Gauvard, "Christine de Pizan et ses contemporains," 115.

22. Pintoin, *Chronique du religieux*, 4:372–76.

23. On the dissemination of news in Paris, see Novák, "Source du savoir"; and Offenstadt, "Crieurs publics." On the Hotel Saint Pol, in the *Fais et bonnes meurs*, 1:44–45, Christine gives an impression of freedom of movement—the king was solicited by "all manner of ambassadors from foreign countries, and diverse lords, foreign princes, knights from different regions, so that often there was such a throng of lords and knights, both foreign and native, that in the chambers and great and magnificent halls, one could barely turn around." The influence of the *Grandes chroniques* is particularly obvious in the *Fais et bonnes meurs*; see Solente's introduction, 1:xli–lxiv.

24. *Ordonnances des rois de France*, 6:26–32, 28, 45–46, 50.

25. Autrand, *Charles V*, 649.

26. Guenée, "Roi, ses parents et son royaume," 456.

27. Spiegel, *Chronicle Tradition*, 11; and Jones, *Eclipse of Empire*, 86–90. Other important works on the history of the *Grandes chroniques* are Guyot-Bachy and Moeglin, "Comment ont été continuées les *Grandes chroniques de France*"; Hedeman, *Royal Image*; and Guenée, "*Grandes chroniques de France*." For the description of the regency ordinances, see *Grandes chroniques: Chronique des règnes de Jean II*, 2:177–78.

28. *Grandes chroniques: Chronique des règnes de Jean II*, 2:236–37, 249–51. See *Fais et bonnes meurs*, 1:39–48.

29. *Grandes chroniques: Chronique des règnes de Jean II*, 2:177–78.

30. Potin, "Coup d'état 'révélé,'" 184.

31. *Grandes chroniques: Chronique des règnes de Jean II*, 2:383–85.

32. Pintoin, *Chronique du religieux*, 1:10. The debate is recorded in ibid., 1:7–15; and Juvénal des Ursins, *Histoire de Charles VI*, 339–41.

33. Pintoin, *Chronique du religieux*, 1:12. Pierre, Charles V's chancellor, is generally believed to have composed Charles V's section of the *Grandes chroniques*.

34. Potin, "Coup d'état 'révélé,'" 196. Lehoux believes that Louis of Anjou, having lost the regency thanks to Pierre, was responsible. *Jean de France*, 2:13n4.

35. *Ordonnances des rois de France*, 6:47, 50, 52.

36. Ibid., 6:51–52. The name, common among historians, comes from Froissart's reference in *Œuvres de Froissart*, 15:2–3.

37. See Henneman, "Who Were the Marmousets," 22, 40–43; and Autrand, *Charles VI*, 21. See also Vaughan, *Philip the Bold*, which explains that Philip had earlier tried to co-opt both Bureau de La Rivière and Jean Le Mercier, but that both declined his offer of allowances in return for homage.

38. Lehoux, *Jean de France*, 2:15.

39. Potin, "Coup d'état 'révélé,'" 194.

40. Pintoin, *Chronique du religieux*, 1:16. See also the *Grandes chroniques de France*, 2:385–86.

41. Lehoux, *Jean de France*, 2:21.

42. Ibid., 2:292–93.

43. Guenée, "Roi, ses parents et son royaume," 457.

44. Juvénal des Ursins, *Histoire de Charles VI*, 421. See also Pintoin, *Chronique du religieux*, 3:12.

45. Cazelles, *Société politique et la crise* and *Société politique, noblesse et couronne*. See Gauvard, *"De grace especial,"* 948–52 (on the nostalgia, see 950).

46. Vallet de Viriville, *Chronique de la pucelle*, 373.

47. For the episode, see Pintoin, *Chronique du religieux*, 4:372–76.

48. Autrand, *Charles V*, 452–53.

49. The author was named Pèlerin de Prusse and the title of the work was *Traité des elections universelles des douze maisons*. Cited in ibid., 745.

50. Cazelles, *Société politique et la crise*, esp. 427–36.

51. Giesey, "Juristic Basis of the Dynastic Right," 11. The fundamental work on the event is Viollet, "Comment les femmes ont été exclues." See also Potter, "Development and Significance of the Salic Law"; and Taylor, "Salic Law and the Valois Succession," "Salic Law, French Queenship," and *Debating the Hundred Years War*, in which Taylor describes Jean de Montreuil's hesitation at the use of the *lex Salica* as the source of female exclusion. Viennot's *France, les femmes et le pouvoir* also describes the development of the Salic law. See also Green, "Christine de Pizan," 237–40.

52. Giesey, "Juristic Basis of the Dynastic Right," 11.

53. Eudes of Burgundy, Jeanne's maternal uncle, had led the Burgundians against King Louis X as part of the confederation of regional leagues that had first risen up under Philip the Fair.

54. See Norbye, "Genealogies and Dynastic Awareness," 311–17, for manuscript evidence of different attitudes toward female exclusion.

55. Autrand, *Charles V*, 100–113.

56. Ibid., 114–35.

57. Ibid., 150–73; Sumption, *Trial by Fire*, 199–200.

58. Autrand, *Charles V*, 174, 182.

59. Small, *Late Medieval France*, 73–75.

60. Autrand, "Force de l'âge," 206.

61. Autrand, *Charles V*, 452.

62. Small, *Late Medieval France*, 121.

63. Henneman, "Military Class and the French Monarchy," 946.

64. Allmand, *Hundred Years War*, 22.

65. Small, *Late Medieval France*, 127–31; Autrand, *Charles V*, 523–28, 661–68.

66. Autrand, *Charles V*, 693–712, 641–46.

67. See Delisle, *Recherches sur la librairie de Charles V*; Sherman, *Portraits of Charles V*, chap. 1, 7–16; and Quillet, *Charles V le roi lettré*, 96–114, for an overview of the literary activity at Charles V's court.

68. Dodu, "Idées de Charles V," 24.

69. Contamine, Guyotjeannin, and Le Jan, *Moyen Âge*, 364.

70. See Sherman, "Representations of Charles V."

71. Babbitt, *Oresme's "Livre de Politiques,"* 129–31.

72. Hedeman, *Royal Image,* 124.

73. Salet, "Mécénat royal et princier," 627. On the sculpture, see also Girault, "Portraits et images du prince vers 1400," 155–56; and Sherman, *Portraits of Charles V,* 60–63.

74. Wandruzka, "Familial Traditions of the *de Piçano,*" 895 (quotation), 899–901, 892n11.

75. *Livre de l'advision Cristine,* 96.

76. See Solente's introduction to the *Fais et bonnes meurs,* 1:ivn2.

77. Autrand, *Christine de Pizan,* 22–25.

78. *Livre de l'advision Cristine,* 98–99.

79. Ibid., 97.

80. *Fais et bonnes meurs,* 1:iv.

81. *Livre de l'advision Cristine,* 97.

82. Christine describes her husband as "ung jeune escolier gradué," a young university graduate (ibid., 97), and recounts that he died in an epidemic while accompanying the king in Beauvais (100).

83. Bonnardot, *Dissertations archéologiques,* 74.

84. *Livre de l'advision Cristine,* 99.

85. *Fais et bonnes meurs,* 1:179, 101.

86. *Livre de l'advision Cristine,* 99.

87. Quoted in Solente's introduction to *Fais et bonnes meurs,* 1:x. Original in BnF, Collection de Bourgogne 26, fol. 196.

88. Ibid., 1:xi. Original in BnF, pièces originales 452, doss. 10196, p. 5.

89. Thorndike, *History of Magic,* 2:820, 3:611–27. See also Holmyard, *Alchemy,* 255–58.

90. Thorndike, *History of Magic,* 2:802. The story is recounted in BnF, fonds latin 7737.

91. Thorndike, *History of Magic,* 3:615. The letter can be read in BnF, fonds latin 11201, fols. 1–13.

92. See Solente's introduction to *Fais et bonnes meurs,* 1:xiin4. Original in BnF, fonds latin 11201, fols. 12, 6.

93. Thorndike, *History of Magic,* 3:617–20.

94. *Livre de l'advision Cristine,* 83.

95. Pinet, *Christine de Pisan,* 96–98.

96. On the details of the events and the dates, see Laidlaw, "Christine de Pizan, the Earl of Salisbury."

97. See *balade* 20 of the *Autres balades,* in *Oeuvres poétiques,* 1:232–33. The refusal is described in the *Livre de l'advision Cristine,* 113.

98. Christine offers her son to the service of the Duke of Orleans: "Qu'il vous plaise le prendre a vo servise." *Balade* 20, line 16, in *Oeuvres poétiques,* 1:233.

99. *Livre de l'advision Cristine,* 113–14.

100. Douët-d'Arcq, *Choix de pièces inédites,* 1:204–7.

101. Ouy and Reno, "Où mène *Le chemin de long estude?*"

102. Barret, "Pratique, normalisation, codification," 34.

103. Desjardins, "Savoirs des notaires et secrétaires du roi," 88.

104. On Guillaume Fillastre, Jean Lebègue, and Pierre l'Orfèvre, see the first section of Heribert Müller's chapter "Der französische Frühhumanismus um 1400: Patriotismus, Propaganda und Historigraphie," in his *Frankreich, Burgund und das Reich,* 156–73. Jean de Montreuil worked as Louis's secretary in 1389–91 (see Montreuil, *Opera,* 4:305–7); see also Ornato, *Jean Muret et ses amis,* 97. On Gontier Col, see Coville, *Gontier et Pierre Col,* 10–98; on Jacques de Nouvion, see Coville, "Ami de Nicolas Clamanges."

105. Ouy, "Humanisme et propagande politique," 15.

106. *Fais et bonnes meurs*, 1:174.

107. *Livre de la mutacion de fortune*, 1:x–xi.

108. Jarry, *Vie politique de Louis de France*, 274.

109. Hicks, "Excerpts and Originality."

110. Autrand, *Charles VI*, 204–13; Gauvard, *"De grace especial,"* 950.

CHAPTER 2

1. Pintoin, *Chronique du religieux*, 3:12.

2. Bartlett, "Mortal Enmities," 197–200.

3. Nordberg, *Ducs et la royauté*, 95. See also Vaughan, *Philip the Bold*, 44. For similar assessments, see Schnerb, *Armagnacs et les Bourguignons*; Famiglietti, *Royal Intrigue*; Autrand, *Charles VI*.

4. See the self-serving letter read before the Parlement de Paris, in which Philip explains that he has heard bad things about the way the kingdom was being governed: "It was a great pity to hear what he had heard, and he could hardly believe that things were in the state that they were in." Douët-d'Arcq, *Choix de pièces inédites*, 1:213.

5. See Valois, *France et le grand schisme*, 1:305–29, for a discussion of Charles V's view and motivation regarding the Schism. Valois sees two French policies, that of Charles V, whose support of Clement VII, Valois believes, was motivated by genuine belief in that pope's legitimacy, and that of Louis of Anjou, who was motivated by his need for Clement VII's support to claim the kingdom in Naples, according to Valois.

6. On the tendency to abolish taxes, see Brown, "Taxation and Morality"; and on Charles V's abolition of the *fouage*, Radding, "Estates of Normandy."

7. *Chronique des quatre premiers Valois*, 287–88.

8. Miskimin, however, makes the case that Charles V was motivated not by piety but by the desire to curtail the political ambitions of the dukes of Anjou and Burgundy. "Last Act of Charles V," 441.

9. Lehoux, *Jean de France*, 2:22; *Chronique des quatre premiers Valois*, 291–92.

10. *Chronique des quatre premiers Valois*, 292.

11. Radding, "Estates of Normandy," 80–82.

12. On the revolts, see Leguai, "Revoltes rurales dans le royaume de France," and "Troubles urbains dans le nord"; Radding, "Estates of Normandy"; and Mirot, *Insurrections urbaines*.

13. Pintoin, *Chronique du religieux*, 1:30–32.

14. Quoted in Lehoux, *Jean de France*, 2:20n1.

15. See Mirot, *Insurrections urbaines*, 70.

16. On the disastrous expedition, see Valois, *France et le grand schisme*, 2:7–89. Valois gives the adventure a partially positive spin. See also Bueno de Mesquita, *Giangaleazzo Visconti*, 87–88.

17. Lehoux, *Jean de France*, 2:56n2, 57.

18. See Boffa, *Warfare in Medieval Brabant*, 30–35; and Palmer, *England, France, and Christendom*, 55.

19. Indeed, Olivier told an emissary from the Duke of Lancaster that he had made Charles VI "king and lord in his [own] kingdom and removed him from the government and hands of his uncles." Henneman, *Olivier de Clisson and Political Society*, 131.

20. Ibid., 129.

21. Demurger, *Temps de crises*, 88. On the marmousets' agenda, see Autrand, *Charles VI*, 205–13. For a less positive view, see Sizer, "Making Revolution Medieval," 368–74.

22. See Lehoux, *Jean de France*, 2:255–59.

23. See Bryant, *King and the City*, 81.

24. Collas, *Valentine de Milan*, 2.

25. Kipling, *Enter the King*, 294.

26. See Bryant, *King and the City*, 81. See also Kipling, *Enter the King*, 78–85, for a detailed description of the pageants relating Isabeau to the Virgin Mary.

27. Bryant, *King and the City*, 142.

28. Lehoux, *Jean de France*, 2:259.

29. Ibid., 2:257; Jean le Seneschal, *Cent ballades*, 1; see Louis's poem on 205–6, and Jean's on 213–14. See also Cayley, *Debate and Dialogue*, 40–44.

30. Jarry, *Vie politique de Louis de France*, 47–49.

31. For the details, see Camus, *Venue en France*.

32. "Louis, with the strength of France behind him, could safeguard the Milanese state, and by the natural development of his own ambitions would keep the Piedmontese princes fully occupied. He would be the instrument of Visconti policy in Piedmont, holding the important Genoese passes open for Giangaleazzo." Bueno de Mesquita, *Giangaleazzo Visconti*, 67.

33. Jarry, *Vie politique de Louis de France*, 8.

34. Jarry, "'Voie de fait,'" 215. For more detail, see Jarry, *Vie politique de Louis de France*, 4–16.

35. Jarry, "'Voie de fait,'" 215.

36. Dale, "Contra damnationis filios," 25.

37. Cited in Jarry, "'Voie de fait,'" 231.

38. Bueno de Mesquita, *Giangaleazzo Visconti*, 125, 155.

39. Nordberg, *Ducs et la royauté*, 83–84.

40. Bueno de Mesquita, *Giangaleazzo Visconti*, 155.

41. Dale, "Contra damnationis filios," 28.

42. Kovacs, *Âge d'or de l'orfèvrerie Parisienne*, 350–401.

43. Froissart gives a detailed description, although Lehoux notes that the account is subject to caution because the chronicler incorrectly reports that the Duke of Berry accompanied the group to Brittany. Froissart, *Œuvres de Froissart*, 15:35–43; Lehoux, *Jean de France*, 2:292n1.

44. See Jarry, *Vie politique de Louis de France*, 98–100, for a description of what happened immediately following the king's attack.

45. Froissart recounts the story of Philip's coup in *Œuvres de Froissart*, 3:164; see also Pintoin, *Chronique du religieux*, 2:26–28.

46. Nordberg, *Ducs et la royauté*, 232.

47. Pintoin, *Chronique du religieux*, 2:24.

48. See the first chapter of Famiglietti, *Royal Intrigue*, for information on the probable cause of Charles VI's episodes, which Famiglietti argues was schizophrenia.

49. *Ordonnances des rois de France*, 7:535–38.

50. Pintoin, *Chronique du religieux*, 2:88, 90.

51. Froissart, *Œuvres de Froissart*, 15:352–55. See also the chronicle of Monstrelet, which reports that Jean Petit made the same accusation during his justification of Jean of Burgundy's assassination of Louis. Monstrelet, *Chronique*, 1:228–29.

52. Bührer-Thierry, "Reine adultère," and Stafford, *Queens, Concubines, and Dowagers*, have documented the symbolic reciprocal relationship in the early Middle Ages between order in a queen's or princess's personal life and order in the kingdom, showing that to question her virtue was to challenge her spouse's authority.

53. See Monstrelet, *Chronique*, 1:224–34, for accusations of sorcery; see 239 for the accusation of trying to kill the dauphin with a poisoned apple.

54. Pintoin, *Chronique du religieux*, 2:406. For more on the accusations against Valentina of poisoning the king, see Collard, *Crime de poison*, especially 120, 222–23.

55. Froissart, *Œuvres de Froissart*, 15:355.

56. Pintoin, *Chronique du religieux*, 2:544, 542.

57. Juvénal des Ursins, *Histoire de Charles VI*, 415.

58. See Boudet, "Condamnations de la magie."

59. Gerson, *Oeuvres complètes*, 7.2:572.

60. For the sermon, see ibid., 7.2:938–40; on the circumstances, see Bourret, *Sermons français de Gerson*, 40.

61. Gerson, *Oeuvres complètes*, 7.2:946.

62. Ibid., 7.2:541, 548, 549.

63. See McGuire, *Companion to Jean Gerson*, 11.

64. Gerson, *Opera Omnia*, vol. 4, col. 727.

65. Walters, "Figure of the *Seulette*." See also Richards, "Christine de Pizan and Jean Gerson," and "Gerson's Writings to His Sisters."

66. *Fais et bonnes meurs*, 1:74–75.

67. No historian today believes in the story of an affair between Louis and the queen. The myth has been treated in many places; see, for example, Famiglietti, *Royal Intrigue*, 43.

68. Jean fathered several children out of wedlock. See Vaughan, *John the Fearless*, 236. On Burgundian mistresses, see Cartellieri, *Court of Burgundy*, 55–56.

69. Pintoin, *Chronique du religieux*, 3:739. In addition, in 1398 Jehan de Charentes, lieutenant governor of Orleans, accused Jehan de Baigneux, standing in as king's procurer, of having five years earlier discussed the king's insanity, adding that the Duke of Orleans was "young and enjoyed playing dice games and liked prostitutes." However, Jehan de Baigneux was found not guilty, and Jehan de Charentes was fined for the false accusation. See the description of the incident in Carbonnières, *Procédure devant la chambre criminelle*, 813–24.

70. Pintoin, *Chronique du religieux*, 3:36.

71. Douët-d'Arcq, *Choix de pièces inédites*, 1:143.

72. Paravicini, "Paris, capitale des ducs de Bourgogne," 477.

73. Alexandre, "'Que le roi le puisse toujours avoir,'" 386.

74. Jameson, *Political Unconscious*, 5.

75. Elliott, *Remembering Boethius*, 45.

76. Ouy et al., *Album Christine de Pizan*, 190. On the *Livre de Christine*, see also Laidlaw, "Christine de Pizan: A Publisher's Progress," 42–49; for a table of the contents of Chantilly 492–493, see 68–69.

77. See Autrand, *Charles V*, 751–78; Leri and Jacob, *Vie et histoire du IVe arrondissement*; Mirot, "Formation et le démembrement."

78. Faure, *Marais*; Leri and Jacob, *Vie et histoire du IVe arrondissement*; and Pleybert, *Paris et Charles V*.

79. Desmond and Sheingorn, *Myth, Montage, and Visuality*, 8. See also McGrady, "Reading for Authority," esp. 171–72; Cayley, *Debate and Dialogue*; Swift, *Gender, Writing, and Performance*, 103–9; and Taylor, "Courtly Gatherings and Poetic Games."

80. Cayley, "Collaborative Communities," 228.

81. See Laidlaw, "*Cent balades*," 67. See also Reid, "Piety, Poetry, and Politics," 152–53; Boulton, *Knights of the Crown*, 26.

82. On the incident, see Ricci, "Cronologia dell'ultimo 'certamen' petrarchesco"; Wilkins, *Petrarch's Later Years*, 233–40; and Ouy, "Paris, l'un des principaux foyers de l'humanisme," 83. Choquart's speech is printed in Du Boulay, *Historia Universitatis Parisiensis*, 4:396–412.

83. Furr, "Quarrel of the *Roman de la Rose*," 335.

84. See Furr's analysis of the debate, ibid., 245–88.

85. See Coville, *Gontier et Pierre Col*, for excerpts in French. Furr, "Quarrel of the *Roman de la Rose*," 294–307, analyzes the meaning of this part of the exchange.

86. Furr, "Quarrel of the *Roman de la Rose*," 354–55.

87. Cayley, *Debate and Dialogue*, 13.

88. Bozzolo and Ornato, "Princes, prélats, barons," 161–62.

89. References to the *Cent balades* are to the *Oeuvres poétiques*, vol. 1, hereafter cited parenthetically in the text by poem number and page number.

90. Léglu and Milner, "Introduction," in Léglu and Milner, *Erotics of Consolation*, 2–3.

91. Kay, "Touching Singularity," 29, 27.

92. Holderness, "Fiction and Truth in Ballad 15," 424–29, and "Christine, Boèce et saint Augustin," 280–81. For William's schema, see Guillaume de Conches, *Guillelmi de Conchis*, 19–21.

93. Holderness, "Fiction and Truth in Ballad 15," 427–28.

94. Walters, "Boethius and the Triple Ending," 129–32.

95. Roy identifies the damoiselle de Montpensier as Marie de Berry in the *Oeuvres poétiques*, 1:229; Green, in "Christine de Pizan," argues that she is Anne de Montpensier (233).

96. *Autres balades*, 29, 30, 31, in *Oeuvres poétiques*, 1:240–44.

97. See Given-Wilson, " 'Quarrels of Old Women,' " 38.

98. References to *Le livre du debat de deux amans* are to Altmann's edition, hereafter cited parenthetically in the text by page and line numbers.

99. See Altmann's introduction to the *Love Debate Poems*, 27.

100. References to the *Epistre au dieu d'amours* are from Fenster and Erler's translation in their edition *Poems of Cupid, God of Love*, hereafter cited parenthetically in the text by page and line numbers.

101. Bozzolo and Loyau, *Cour amoureuse*, 1:36.

102. Some evidence suggests that it met as well, or at least that it may have been intended to produce poetic competition from time to time when the charter was created. See Piaget, "Manuscrit de la cour amoureuse," which notes an item from the accounts of the Hotel de Ville of Amiens in which a herald was paid for delivering an announcement from the Prince d'amour that a feast and meeting of the *cour amoureuse* was to take place in Paris on April 15, 1410. The coincidence of this date and that of the signing and sealing of the Treaty of Gien by the Armagnac faction, united to avenge the assassination of Louis of Orleans and chase Jean sans Peur from power, suggests that the purpose of the Burgundian *cour amoureuse* was not merely literary, but that it represented Burgundian power. Another sign that the *cour amoureuse* actually met can be found in the description of the city of Paris, supposedly written for 1407, where Guillebert de Metz recounts the wonders of the city, among them artists like the diamond carver; Herman, the goldsmith; Willelm, the brass worker; Andry and other illuminators; and scribes like Flamel. He goes on to mention women in trade: female salt sellers, butchers, carpenters, and other ladies. He then remarks upon Christine de Pizan. Finally, he acknowledges the Prince d'amour, who was surrounded by musicians and gallants who knew how to sing all manner of songs, ballads, rounds, *virelais*, and other love ditties. Finally, a poem composed between 1408 and 1413 by Amé Malingre, member of the *cour amoureuse*, describes a scenario wherein the narrator comes across a lady lamenting her vilification. She asks him to see that the complaint she has turned into a poem be presented before Pierre de Hauteville and the other members of the *cour amoureuse*. See Piaget, "Cour amoureuse dite de Charles VI," 450–54.

103. The charter is printed in Bozzolo and Loyau, *Cour amoureuse*, 1:35–45.

104. A number of references in the charter specify that the date in question is February 14. This date correlates with what Kelly has shown, that although earlier celebrated on May 3, Valentine's Day came to be celebrated on February 14 in the late fourteenth century. See his *Chaucer and the Cult of Saint Valentine*.

105. Bozzolo and Loyau, *Cour amoureuse*, 1:45, 36.

106. Straub, "Grundung des Pariser Minnehofs," 7–8.

107. Ernest Petit's *Itinéraires de Philippe Le Hardi* shows that on Monday and Tuesday, January 5 and 6, Philip was in Neauphle, just eighteen miles from Mantes. He often traveled far greater distances in one day. On January 6 he supped and slept at Neauphle but dined at

Dangu, nearly forty-two miles from Neauphle. The road from Dangu to Neauphle passes directly through Mantes, where he may have stopped.

108. Grandeau, "Itinéraire d'Isabeau de Bavière," 582.

109. Wenceslas was deposed only in August 1400, replaced by Robert, but the movement against him was already fully in motion by 1399. Isabeau's brother, Louis of Bavaria, was a central member of the opposition to Wenceslas. See Jarry, *Vie politique de Louis de France*, 234–36.

110. The members of the circle of Louis of Orleans were not entirely absent. Orleanists Bureau de Danmartin, patron of Laurent de Premierfait, humanists Gontier and Pierre Col, Jean de Montreuil, Charles d'Albret, Guillaume Cousinot, and Guillaume de Tignonville were included. On Louis as a patron of humanists, see Schultz, "Artistic and Literary Patronage," 368–94; and Ouy, "Paris, l'un des principaux foyers de l'humanisme." The Burgundian presence was much larger, manifest in the many members from the towns of Burgundy. On the Burgundian presence, see Small, "Centre, the Periphery, and the Problem"; and Bozzolo and Ornato, "Princes, prélats, barons," 167–68. For a description of the manuscripts, see Bozzolo and Loyau, *Cour amoureuse*, 1:18; for the influx, 1:7–34. That a large influx of new members joined when Philip the Good succeeded his father, Jean sans Peur, who was assassinated by followers of the dauphin Charles in 1419, reinforces the impression of Burgundian dominance, in addition to demonstrating the longevity of the institution.

111. Bozzolo and Loyau, *Cour amoureuse*, 1:37. Autrand describes Louis II of Bourbon as an ideal prince, loyal throughout his life to the Crown (*Charles VI*, 194–98). He later took sides with the Orleanists against Jean sans Peur.

112. Bozzolo and Loyau, *Cour amoureuse*, 1:39.

113. See Jean le Seneschal, *Cent ballades*, xx–xxi. The editor Gaston Raynaud explains that no work by Grandson called the *Cent ballades* exists; however, one manuscript of the *Cent ballades* by Jean le Seneschal contains many poems by Grandson. Raynaud concludes that the librarian mistook Grandson for the author of all the poems in the inventory.

114. Ibid., 205–60.

115. Bozzolo and Loyau, *Cour amoureuse*, 1:40.

116. Kelly draws a similar conclusion about the relationship between the *cour amoureuse* and the *Dit de la rose*. See *Chaucer and the Cult of Saint Valentine*, 35, 38.

117. Bozzolo and Loyau, *Cour amoureuse*, 1:35. On Pierre de Hauteville, see 1:59.

118. Ibid., 1:35.

119. The others are BnF, MSS français 606, 836, and 605. On the excision, see Ouy et al., *Album Christine de Pizan*, 231. For the contents of 835 see Laidlaw, "Christine de Pizan: A Publisher's Progress," 71–72.

120. See Chattaway, *Order of the Golden Tree*, 21.

121. References to the *Livre des trois jugemens* (and to the *Livre du dit de Poissy*, discussed below) are to Altmann's edition, the *Love Debate Poems*, hereafter cited parenthetically in the text by page and line numbers.

122. Nuttall, *Creation of Lancastrian Kingship*, 5–6.

123. Poirion, *Poète et le prince*, 514.

124. Jameson, *Political Unconscious*, 62.

CHAPTER 3

1. See Guenée, *Meurtre, une société*, 153–75.

2. On Anglo-French relations during this period, see Given-Wilson, "'Quarrels of Old Women'"; Phillpotts, "Fate of the Truce of Paris"; Tuck, "Richard II and the Hundred Years'

War." On Richard's death and how the French were informed of it, see Mortimer, *Fears of Henry IV*, 213–17.

3. Phillpotts, "Fate of the Truce of Paris," 68.

4. Ibid., 71. See also Ford, "Piracy or Policy."

5. See Given-Wilson, "'Quarrels of Old Women.'"

6. Pintoin, *Chronique du religieux*, 3:33.

7. On these years, see McGuire, *Jean Gerson and the Last Medieval Reformation*; and Morall, *Gerson and the Great Schism*, 44–75.

8. McGuire, *Jean Gerson and the Last Medieval Reformation*, 35.

9. Kaminsky, "Politics of France's Subtraction of Obedience," 366.

10. Valois writes, "'The *aides* are running out,' observed the Duke of Burgundy. 'And if the *aides* ran out, we would not be able to continue with great acts of war in this kingdom,' which the Duke of Berry repeated in almost the same terms, 'The *aides* are failing, and if they drop once, they will never rise again.'" Valois, *France et le grand schisme*, 3:164–67.

11. Autrand, "France Under Charles V and Charles VI," 429.

12. See Gerson, *Oeuvres complètes*, 6:22–24, for the treatise. See also Meyjes, *Jean Gerson, Apostle of Unity*, 51–52. Gerson always mistrusted the zealous attitudes of some members of the university toward Benedict. See Valois, *France et le grand schisme*, 3:71–74.

13. Douët-d'Arcq, *Choix de pièces inédites*, 1:143.

14. Nordberg, *Ducs et la royauté*, 152.

15. Jarry, *Vie politique de Louis de France*, 198–99.

16. Ibid., 253.

17. In addition to the letters cited below, see Weizsäcker, *Deutsche Reichstagsakten*, letters 290, 289, 5:391–94.

18. Ibid., letter 298, 4:354–55.

19. Lehoux, *Jean de France*, 2:451.

20. Jarry, *Vie politique de Louis de France*, 253. See Weizsäcker, *Deutsche Reichstagsakten*, letter 296, 4:350–51; Lehoux, *Jean de France*, 2:445.

21. Lehoux, *Jean de France*, 2:451.

22. See Douët-d'Arcq, *Comptes de l'Hôtel des rois*, 145–47, for accounts of payment for delivery of these letters.

23. See the record of the event in ibid., 170–71.

24. Jarry, *Vie politique de Louis de France*, 250–52; Lehoux, *Jean de France*, 2:445n7.

25. Autrand, *Charles VI*, 145–49.

26. Lehoux, *Jean de France*, 2:452–53.

27. Weizsäcker, *Deutsche Reichstagsakten*, letter 298, 4:354–55.

28. Lehoux, *Jean de France*, 2:453. For the letters exchanged between Robert and Philip, see Weizsäcker, *Deutsche Reichstagsakten*, letters 153–57, 5:194–200.

29. Lehoux, *Jean de France*, 2:454–55.

30. Jarry, *Vie politique de Louis de France*, 261. Pot served as Philip's messenger to Robert; see Weizsäcker, *Deutsche Reichstagsakten*, letters 154 and 156, 5:195–98.

31. Lehoux, *Jean de France*, 2:460.

32. Ibid., 2:458; and Valois, *France et le grand schisme*, 3:249ff.

33. Lehoux, *Jean de France*, 2:458–59. Lehoux explains that although the Duke of Orleans's excuse was perfectly valid, it was not the only reason for his decision. That Philip of Burgundy was making a special trip to Senlis would have been sufficient to explain the absence of Louis, who would never have agreed to sit next to his uncle.

34. See the letter in Douët-d'Arcq, *Choix de pièces inédites*, 1:213.

35. Lehoux, *Jean de France*, 2:463. See also Schnerb, *Armagnacs et les Bourguignons*, 52.

36. See Douët-d'Arcq, *Choix de pièces inédites*, 1:220–26, esp. 225.

37. Pintoin, *Chronique du religieux*, 3:116–18, 12.

38. For an enumeration of the reasons for restoring obedience, see Bellitto, *Nicolas de Clamanges*, 19–24.

39. Valois, *France et le grand schisme*, 3:257. See also Lehoux, *Jean de France*, 2:468–69, 477–78.

40. Valois, *France et le grand schisme*, 3:478.

41. Douët-d'Arcq, *Choix des pièces inédites*, 1:227–39.

42. Ibid., 1:231.

43. Ibid., 1:234–35.

44. Lehoux, *Jean de France*, 2:516–25; Jarry, *Vie politique de Louis de France*, 285.

45. Jarry, *Vie politique de Louis de France*, 265.

46. See Schnerb, *Armagnacs et les Bourguignons*, 53.

47. Baye, *Journal de Nicolas de Baye*, 1:36–37n1. See also Schnerb, *Armagnacs et les Bourguignons*, 52–53; and Jarry, *Vie politique de Louis de France*, 265–66.

48. Baye, *Journal de Nicolas de Baye*, 1:37n2.

49. Douët-d'Arcq, *Choix de pièces inédites*, 1:241.

50. *Ordonnances des rois de France*, 8:582.

51. For the letter patent, see Isambert, *Recueil général des anciennes lois françaises*, 7:59.

52. Creighton, *History of the Papacy*, 176–78.

53. Ouy, "Humanisme et propagande politique," 33. The letter is edited in Weizsäcker, *Deutsche Reichstagsakten*, letter 293, 5:398.

54. Jarry, *Vie politique de Louis de France*, 297.

55. See ibid., 304–6; Pintoin, *Chronique du religieux*, 3:138–40.

56. Schnerb, *Armagnacs et les Bourguignons*, 56.

57. Demurger, *Temps de crises*, 87; Vaughan, *Philip the Bold*, 104.

58. See Nordberg, *Ducs et la royauté*, 12–23.

59. Lehoux, *Jean de France*, 2:443.

60. BnF, fonds italien 1682, fol. 29r–v (June 23, 1389).

61. That spouses assumed the quarrels of each other's families was taken for granted. In this regard, see Weizsäcker, *Deutsche Reichstagsakten*, letter 116, 5:163–64, recounting a scene where Charles VI explains to his brother that the king's own loyalty must be first to his wife's kin, just as Louis's must also be to his wife's kin.

62. Hindman, *Christine de Pizan's "Epistre Othéa,"* 138–39.

63. Akbari, "Movement from Verse to Prose," 137.

64. All citations of the *Epistre d'Othea a Hector* are my translations from Parussa's edition, hereafter cited parenthetically in the text by page and line numbers.

65. Scanlon, *Narrative, Authority, and Power*, 237.

66. Christine borrows the formulation from *Le chapelet des vertus*. This work has not been edited, but a manuscript version of it, BnF, fonds français 1892, can be consulted in digitized form through Gallica.

67. Le Ninan, *Sage roi et la clergesse*, 14–15.

68. Wheeler, "Christine de Pizan's *Livre des fais d'armes*," 150–51.

69. The six illustrations of the *Epistre d'Othea a Hector* in the *Livre de Christine*, although they are in color and more skillfully executed, closely reproduce the six illustrations of the first example and thus do not require separate commentary here. See Laidlaw, "Christine de Pizan: A Publisher's Progress," 47.

70. Hindman, *Christine de Pizan's "Epistre Othéa,"* 43.

71. Ibid., 46–47.

72. See Laidlaw, "Christine de Pizan: The Making of the Queen's Manuscript."

73. See Ornato, *Jean Muret et ses amis*, 187.

74. McGrady, "Reading for Authority," esp. 157–63.

75. Cayley, *Debate and Dialogue*, 72–73.

76. McGrady, "Reading for Authority," 155–57.

77. Ibid., 69–71.

78. See Furr's discussion of *eloquentia* versus *sapientia* in "Quarrel of the *Roman de la Rose*," 270–88.

79. Quoted in ibid., 286.

80. On Christine's style and use of prose in the debate, see Fenster's illuminating essay, "Perdre son Latin."

81. Citations are from Hult's edition, *Debate of the "Romance of the Rose,"* hereafter cited parenthetically in the text with page citations for the French followed by page numbers for Hult's translation.

82. See ibid., lii, for timeline.

83. Cayley, *Debate and Dialogue*, 84.

84. Citations of *Le chemin de longue étude* are from Tarnowski's edition and translation into modern French, with my translations into English, hereafter cited parenthetically in the text by page and line numbers.

85. Armstrong and Kay, *Knowing Poetry*, 18.

86. Ouy, "Humanisme et propagande politique"; Ouy and Reno, "Où mène *Le chemin de long estude?*"

87. See Ouy, "Humanisme et propagande politique," 25.

88. "In that same year, he will obtain a double crown [imperial added to the royal]. Afterward, crossing the sea with a great army, he will enter Greece and be named the King of Greece. He will subjugate the Chaldeans, Turks, Ypsicos, Barbares, Jurgios, and Palsticos and make them submit to his reign, making an edict that whoever does not adore the crucifix will die. And there will be no one who is able to resist him, because the holy arm of God will be with him and he will possess dominion over the whole earth." Chaumé, "Prophétie relative à Charles VI," 29.

89. Quoted in Reeves, *Influence of Prophecy*, 320. See also Dubois, *De recuperatione Terre Sancte*, 98n1.

90. On Pierre, see Dubois, *De recuperatione Terre Sancte*, v–xxiv. See also Reeves, *Influence of Prophecy*, 320.

91. Dubois, *De recuperatione Terre Sancte*, 88.

92. See Zeller, "Rois de France."

93. For details of Louis's acquisitions, see Nordberg, *Ducs et la royauté*, 152–84.

94. Ouy, "Humanisme et propagande politique," 23.

95. See Jones, "Understanding Political Conceptions," 84.

96. See Le Ninan, "Idée de croisade."

97. See Laennec, "Prophétie, interprétation et écriture"; Reeves, *Influence of Prophecy*; Chaumé, "Prophétie relative à Charles VI." See also Mézières, *Songe du vieil pelerin*, esp. 2:382, where the queen encourages Beau Filz to make peace with England and then to lead a crusade with the English.

98. Ouy, "Humanisme et propagande politique," 33.

99. Ibid., 22. This is Ouy's translation into French of the Latin, which he appends to the article (38–39), and which I have translated into English.

100. Ibid., 24.

101. Ouy and Reno, "Où mène *Le chemin de long estude?*" 193.

102. Brownlee, "Image of History," 49–50.

103. *Ordonnances des rois de France*, 8:577.

104. References are to Solente's edition of *Le livre de la mutacion de fortune*, hereafter cited parenthetically in the text by volume, page, and line numbers.

105. Mézières, *Songe du vieil pelerin*, esp. 2:218.

106. *Livre de l'advision Cristine*, 111.

107. Kelly, *Christine de Pizan's Changing Opinion*, 141.

108. *Le dit de la pastoure*, in *Oeuvres poétiques*, 2:223–94, 24–32.

109. *Fais et bonnes meurs*, 2:176–77.

110. With certain fascinating and well-studied exceptions, like the prose section on Jewish history in the *Mutacion de fortune*.

111. *Débat sur le "Roman de la rose,"* 8.

CHAPTER 4

1. Schnerb, *Armagnacs et les Bourguignons*, 56; Vaughan, *Philip the Bold*, 101.

2. All citations of this *balade* are from the *Cent balades* in Christine's *Oeuvres poétiques*, vol. 1, hereafter cited parenthetically in the text by page and line numbers.

3. Coville, *Jean Petit*, 242.

4. Margolis, "Fortunes of a Text," 260–62.

5. Margolis dismisses the possibility, insisting on Christine's sincerity. Ibid., 261.

6. See, for example, Thonon, "Métiers sur l'échiquier"; and Mehl, "Roi de l'échiquier."

7. "France, plourez, d'un pillier es déserte, / Dont tu reçoys eschec a descouverte, / Gar toy du mat quant mort par son oultrage / Tel chevalier t'a toulu, c'est dommaige" (256, lines 26–29).

8. See Vaughan, *John the Fearless*, 4; see also the itinerary of the dukes of Burgundy, which shows that Jean spent a good deal of time with his father in Paris. Petit, *Itinéraires de Philippe Le Hardi*.

9. See Given-Wilson, "'Quarrels of Old Women,'" 32; and Lehoux, *Jean de France*, 2:517.

10. Lehoux, *Jean de France*, 2:520.

11. "The troops headed in good order toward their enemies, but these had been alerted, and they began to shoot arrows so that the French could not resist. In a short time, the majority of the Flemish and the foot soldiers began to panic and take flight for fear of the arrows." Monstrelet, *Chronique*, 1:102–3.

12. Coville, *Cabochiens et l'ordonnance de 1413*, 2.

13. Pintoin, *Chronique du religieux*, 3:139–41.

14. Petit, *Itinéraires de Philippe Le Hardi*, 342.

15. Vaughan, *John the Fearless*, 30.

16. Ibid., 31. See also Jarry, *Vie politique de Louis de France*, 319; and Monstrelet, *Chronique*, 1:97.

17. Pintoin, *Chronique du religieux*, 3:230.

18. Ibid., 3:228, 230.

19. Vaughan, *John the Fearless*, 31.

20. Ibid., 32; see also Valois, *France et le grand schisme*, 3:419–26.

21. See Plancher, *Histoire générale et particulière*, 3:234.

22. Pintoin, *Chronique du religieux*, 3:266.

23. See Phillpotts, *Fate of the Truce of Paris*.

24. Pintoin, *Chronique du religieux*, 3:272.

25. See Adams, *Life and Afterlife of Isabeau*, 136–37.

26. See Vaughan, *John the Fearless*, 41; Schnerb, *Jean sans Peur*, 156–58.

27. Vaughan reports that Philippe received 188,600 francs in gifts and pensions from the royal treasury, as compared to the 37,000 francs that Jean was assigned (although not paid in full) during the first year of his reign and the 2,000 francs he received in the second year. *John the Fearless*, 42.

28. See Chousat's letter describing the affair, in Mirot, "Enlèvement du dauphin," 395–96. See Schnerb, *Jean sans Peur*, 157, on Jean's nonpayment; on Louis's annual income from the treasury, see Vaughan, *John the Fearless*, 42–43.

29. Monstrelet, *Chronique*, 1:98.

30. See his justificatory letter, published in Mirot, "Enlèvement du dauphin," 396.

31. See Nordberg, *Ducs et la royauté*, 193. Jean's written request for reforms, which was presented at the Louvre by Jean Nielles, makes no mention of the dauphin, who presided over the presentation, referring instead to Charles, who was mad at the time (the king's latest lapse had taken place on August 16 or 17).

32. Guenée, *Folie de Charles VI*, 295.

33. Mirot, "Enlèvement du dauphin," 396.

34. Baye, *Journal de Nicolas de Baye*, 1:139.

35. See Douët-d'Arcq, *Choix des pièces inédites*, 1:270. "And it was forbidden to Monsieur of Burgundy, and cried everywhere in Paris on behalf of the king, that he assemble or keep any soldiers for any reason. And also, my mighty Lord, I would like you to know that Monsieur of Bourbon and the others of the Royal Council went to Melun to Monsieur of Orleans to forbid him to do the same."

36. See Nordberg, *Ducs et la royauté*, 201. The Chambre des comptes document is preserved in BnF, fonds français 10237, fol. 53r–v.

37. Nordberg, *Ducs et la royauté*, 195.

38. Douët-d'Arcq, *Choix des pièces inédites*, 1:273, 274, 276, 282.

39. Printed in Mirot, "Enlèvement du dauphin," 405–13.

40. Ibid., 398.

41. Autrand, *Christine de Pizan*, 271–73.

42. On Jean's populist propaganda, see Hutchison, "Winning Hearts and Minds," 12–16.

43. See Vallet de Viriville, *Chronique de la pucelle*, 109. For more on the Burgundian propaganda machine, see Nordberg, "Sources Bourguignonnes"; and Willard, "Manuscripts of Jean Petit's Justification."

44. Pintoin, *Chronique du religieux*, 3:330.

45. The discourse is printed in Mirot, "Enlèvement du dauphin," 399–403.

46. Rey, *Domaine du roi et les finances extraordinaires*, 338–39.

47. See Tournier, "Jean sans Peur et l'Université de Paris," 300–301; Tuilier, *Histoire de l'Université de Paris*; and Gross, "Political Influence of the University of Paris."

48. Vallet de Viriville, *Chronique de la pucelle*, 111.

49. Pintoin, *Chronique du religieux*, 3:340.

50. Juvénal des Ursins, *Histoire de Charles VI*, 437.

51. Nordberg, *Ducs et la royauté*, 201–2.

52. Lehoux, *Jean de France*, 3:58–59; see also 59n1.

53. Pintoin, *Chronique du religieux*, 3:340.

54. Juvénal des Ursins, *Histoire de Charles VI*, 433.

55. *Ordonnances des rois de France*, 12:222–23.

56. Pintoin, *Chronique du religieux*, 3:344.

57. Lehoux, *Jean de France*, 3:63n1.

58. Pintoin, *Chronique du religieux*, 3:344.

59. Richards, "Poems of Water," 210–11.

60. Armstrong and Kay, *Knowing Poetry*, 178.

61. Akbari, "Movement from Verse to Prose," 136.

62. Richards, "Poems of Water," 224–25.

63. That the *Fais et bonnes meurs* served as a mirror for princes is a common perspective among scholars. See Solente's introduction to *Fais et bonnes meurs*, xxvii–xxviii, for example,

and Krueger, "Christine's Anxious Lessons." "Christine's overtly didactic objectives link her *Livre des fais* to the tradition of the *miroir du prince*, works intended to guide the intellectual, moral, and spiritual development of rulers by presenting a princely ideal." Delogu, *Theorizing the Ideal Sovereign*, 155.

64. Delogu, *Theorizing the Ideal Sovereign*, 154.

65. All citations are to Solente's edition of the *Livre des fais et bonnes meurs*, hereafter cited parenthetically in the text by volume and page numbers.

66. Delachenal, *Histoire de Charles V*, 1:110. In particular, attempts to trace rumors that the king had fathered an illegitimate child (possibly Jean de Montaigu) to his own time have yielded nothing.

67. Autrand, *Christine de Pizan*, 250–51.

68. See Autrand, *Charles VI*, 20–21.

69. On the entire incident, see Given-Wilson, "'Quarrels of Old Women.'"

70. Rey, *Domaine du roi et les finances*, 338–39.

71. The incident is described in Pintoin, *Chronique du religieux*, 3:140–42.

72. Ibid., 3:230.

73. Gauvard, "Christine de Pisan," 423, 429.

74. Citations of *Cité des dames* are to Caraffi and Richards's edition *La città delle dame*, which gives the edited version of the French text with facing translations in Italian. I give the page number of the French (hereafter cited parenthetically in the text).

75. Beaune, "Mauvaise reine des origines," 41.

76. Ibid., 32.

77. *Ordonnances des rois de France*, 6:28–29.

78. Richards sees this group of women as an ideal Royal Council. "Political Thought as Improvisation," 12–13.

79. Thanks to Jeff Richards for pointing out the similarities between Isabeau's entry into Paris and the Virgin's entry into the Cité des dames.

80. Allen, *Concept of Women*, 641. Depending on the numbering system, Masoretic or Septuagint, the number of the psalm may be 86. Allen makes the connection to Justice, who, upon welcoming the Virgin into the city, proclaims that holy ladies may now live in the city of ladies, about which it may be said, "Gloriosa dicta sunt de te, civitas Dei"—this the third line of Psalm 87 (496).

81. This association can be seen most clearly in sculpture. See Rickard, "Iconography of the Virgin Portal," 153; Ostoia, "Two Riddles of the Queen of Sheba," 78–79; and Watson, "Queen of Sheba in Christian Tradition."

82. Watson, "Queen of Sheba in Christian Tradition," 117.

83. *Ordonnances des rois de France*, 12:222–23.

84. *Grandes chroniques de France*, 7:38–39.

85. Citations of the *Epistre a la reine* are to Wisman's edition, with page references to Wisman's translation, hereafter cited parenthetically in the text.

86. Guenée, *Folie de Charles VI*, 206–8.

87. Juvénal des Ursins, *Histoire de Charles VI*, 432.

88. Citations of the *Livre des trois vertus* are to Willard and Hicks's edition, hereafter cited parenthetically in the text by page number.

89. Citations of the *Livre du duc des vrais amans* are to Fenster's edition, hereafter cited parenthetically in the text by page and line numbers.

90. Sebille's letter is at pp. 171–80. Sebille's last name is more mysterious. It has been suggested that it might allude, as a warning, to the legend of the Tour de Nesle, loosely based on the alleged adultery of Philip IV's daughters-in-law, but this seems unlikely. Although Villon

first refers to the legend, only Brantôme calls it the affair of the Tour de Nesle. See Krappe, "Legend of Buridan," 217.

CHAPTER 5

1. Schnerb, *Jean sans Peur*, 179.
2. Ibid.
3. Juvénal des Ursins, *Histoire de Charles VI*, 433.
4. Hobbins, "Schoolman as Public Intellectual," 1310.
5. Nordberg, *Ducs et la royauté*, 205. Autrand refers to the "veiled reproaches that [Gerson] addresses to Louis of Orleans and the queen." *Charles VI*, 413.
6. Gerson, "Vivat Rex," in *Oeuvres complètes*, 7.2:1138, hereafter cited parenthetically in the text by page number.
7. Pintoin, *Chronique du religieux*, 3:346.
8. Gerson continued to deplore popular uprising, preaching against it all his life. See, for example, a sermon of January 5, 1415, in which he blames the woes of the kingdom on the fact that the king and the "bonne bourgeoisie" are in the servitude of the rabble ("gens de petit état"). Gerson, *Opéra omnia*, 4:658.
9. Juvénal des Ursins, *Histoire de Charles VI*, 433.
10. Baye, *Journal de Nicolas de Baye*, 1:143–44.
11. Douët-d'Arcq, *Choix des pièces inédites*, 1:284–85.
12. Vaughan, *John the Fearless*, 36.
13. Ibid., 37.
14. Petit, *Itinéraires de Philippe Le Hardi*, 352, Guenée, *Folie de Charles VI*, 295.
15. See Plancher, *Histoire générale et particulière*, 3:243; see also *preuves*, no. 244, in which the king names Jean one of the guardians of the royal children should the king die while they are still minors. Famiglietti describes the contents of this second ordinance as shocking. It revised the regency ordinance of 1393, which had created a council of guardians for the royal children that included Jean in place of his father; but this ordinance, along with the 1393 ordinance granting Louis regency, had been superseded by the 1403 ordinance creating a ruling council, which itself arguably had been invalidated by a letter patent from the confused king reiterating, as we have seen, that nothing would be done to the prejudice of Louis. Jean had effectively pushed Louis out of the regency council, because the 1393 ordinance presumably remained invalid. Famiglietti hypothesizes that Louis never saw this second ordinance. *Royal Intrigue*, 52–53.
16. Baye, *Journal de Nicolas de Baye*, 1:150–53.
17. Douët-d'Arcq, *Choix de pièces inédites*, 1:288–98.
18. Famiglietti, *Royal Intrigue*, 57.
19. Baye, *Journal de Nicolas de Baye*, 1:168.
20. Famiglietti, *Royal Intrigue*, 60–61.
21. Petit, *Itinéraires de Philippe Le Hardi*, 354; Schnerb, *Jean sans Peur*, 181. In retrospect, the gift seems ominouseas; Louis's device was a knotty baton; Jean chose his, the plane, to smooth the knots.
22. Schnerb, *Jean sans Peur*, 187–91, 193–202.
23. Rey, *Finances royales sous Charles VI*, 39–40.
24. Vallet de Viriville, *Chronique de la pucelle*, 112.
25. Schnerb, *Jean sans Peur*, 193–99.
26. References to the *Songe véritable* are to Moranvillé's edition, hereafter cited parenthetically in the text by page and line numbers.

27. See Coville, "Recherches sur Jean Courtecuisse," 476; and Picherit, "*Livre de la prod'hommie.*"

28. In "Date de deux ouvrages," Solente refers to her previous review of Pinet, in which she dates *Prudence.*

29. See Ouy et al., *Album Christine de Pizan*, 625–29.

30. Ibid., 281.

31. All citations of the *Livre de prodomie de l'homme* are to BnF, fonds français 5037, hereafter cited parenthetically in the text by folio number.

32. Citations of the *Livre de l'advision Cristine* are from Reno and Dulac's edition, hereafter cited parenthetically in the text by page number.

33. Cockshaw, "Mentions d'auteurs," 137–38.

34. Dulac and Reno, "Traduction et adaptation," 122, 124, 128–29.

35. See http://dhspriory.org/thomas/Metaphysics.htm.

36. All citations are to Cropp's edition, *Le livre de Boece de consolacion*, hereafter cited parenthetically in the text.

37. References to the prologue of Aquinas's commentary on the *Metaphysics* are from http://dhspriory.org/thomas/Metaphysics.htm.

38. See Cropp, "Philosophy, the Liberal Arts, and Theology"; and Semple, "Critique of Knowledge as Power."

39. Laennec, "Prophétie, interprétation et écriture," 131.

40. See Dudash, "Christine de Pizan and the 'Menu Peuple'"; and Blumenfeld-Kosinski, "'Enemies within/enemies without.'"

41. See Kennedy's introduction to his edition of the *Corps de policie.*

42. See Langdon's edition, *Book of the Body Politic*, xxii–xxiii.

43. I have used Forhan's translation for quotations from the *Livre du corps de policie.* Citations are to Kennedy's edition of the work, hereafter cited parenthetically in the text by book, section, and (where applicable) page numbers, followed by the page numbers in Forhan's translation. Thus (3.2, 93; 92–93) refers to Kennedy's edition, book 3, section 2, p. 93; pp. 92–93 in Forhan's translation.

44. On the three estates, see Lot and Fawtier, *Histoire des institutions françaises*; and Major, *Representative Institutions in Renaissance France.*

45. *Ordonnances des rois de France*, 12:224–25.

46. Ibid., 98.

47. Coville, *Cabochiens et l'ordonnance de 1413*, 92 (emphasis added).

48. Ibid., 103.

49. Juvénal des Ursins, *Histoire de Charles VI*, 467.

50. Coville, *Cabochiens et l'ordonnance de 1413*, 143.

51. Geremek, *Margins of Society*, 77.

52. Hutchison, "Winning Hearts and Minds," 4, 5.

CHAPTER 6

1. Juvénal des Ursins, *Histoire de Charles VI*, 444.

2. Pintoin, *Chronique du religieux*, 3:739.

3. Baye, *Journal de Nicolas de Baye*, 1:206.

4. Pintoin, *Chronique du religieux*, 3:738.

5. Juvénal des Ursins, *Histoire de Charles VI*, 445.

6. Ibid.

7. Monstrelet, *Chronique*, 1:161–64.

8. Pintoin, *Chronique du religieux*, 3:740.

9. Ibid., 3:742.

10. *Ordonnances des rois de France*, 9:267–69.

11. Pintoin, *Chronique du religieux*, 3:742. For the date, see Petit, *Itinéraires de Philippe Le Hardi*, 363.

12. See Petit's declamation in Monstrelet, *Chronique*, 1:217–21, 224–34.

13. Vaughan offers a summary of Petit's main charges in *John the Fearless*, 70–72.

14. Printed in Plancher, *Histoire générale et particulière*, vol. 3, *preuves*, no. 256.

15. Famiglietti, *Royal Intrigue*, 67.

16. Pintoin, *Chronique du religieux*, 3:766.

17. Printed in Bernier, *Histoire de Blois*, *preuves*, xxxii.

18. Ibid., xxxiii. Her name is missing from the list of attendees at the bottom of the document.

19. Monstrelet, *Chronique*, 1:267.

20. Juvénal des Ursins, *Histoire de Charles VI*, 447. Pintoin seems to consider the powers granted to the queen—and to the dauphin, jointly—more far-reaching. *Chronique du religieux*, 4:90.

21. Juvénal des Ursins, *Histoire de Charles VI*, 449.

22. Vaughan, *John the Fearless*, 74–75.

23. See Pintoin, *Chronique du religieux*, 4:272–73.

24. The document awarding the *tutelle* to the Duke of Burgundy is reprinted in Plancher, *Histoire générale et particulière*, vol. 3, *preuves*, no. 261.

25. Pollack-Lagushenko, "Armagnac Faction," 235–39.

26. Schnerb, *Argmagnacs et les Bourguignons*, 103–7.

27. Pollack-Lagushenko, "Armagnac Faction," 242–43, 252–63.

28. See Vaughan, *John the Fearless*, 82–83; Famiglietti, *Royal Intrigue*, 88–89.

29. Monstrelet, *Chronique*, 2:91–92.

30. Terms reprinted in Vaughan, *John the Fearless*, 84–85.

31. Burgundians remained predominant on the Royal Council. See Lehoux, *Jean de France*, 3:205–6. For the agreement between the dukes, see Famiglietti, *Royal Intrigue*, 92–93. Lehoux, *Jean de France*, 3:203–4, doubts the authenticity of the agreement, of which the original is not extant. The agreement is reprinted in Plancher, *Histoire générale et particulière*, vol. 3, *preuves*, no. 268.

32. Famiglietti, *Royal Intrigue*, 93; Schnerb, *Jean sans Peur*, 220–23.

33. Schnerb, *Jean sans Peur*, 527–30.

34. For the first accusation, see Juvénal des Ursins, *Histoire de Charles VI*, 467. For the second, see Monstrelet, *Chronique*, 2:241–42.

35. Monstrelet, *Chronique*, 2:282–83.

36. See Famiglietti's convincing arguments in *Royal Intrigue*, 133–52, and in his dissertation, "French Monarchy Crisis," 329–402.

37. For the treaty, see Plancher, *Histoire générale et particulière*, vol. 3, *preuves*, no. 287.

38. Sizer, "Making Revolution Medieval," 620–21; see also Coville, *Cabochiens et l'ordonnance de 1413*, 103.

39. See Coville, *Cabochiens et l'ordonnance de 1413*, 105.

40. Juvénal des Ursins, *Histoire de Charles VI*, 467.

41. Sizer, "Making Revolution Medieval," 621.

42. Vaughan, *John the Fearless*, 97.

43. See Sizer, "Making Revolution Medieval," 632–36.

44. Pintoin, *Chronique du religieux*, 5:130.

45. McGuire, *Jean Gerson and the Last Medieval Reformation*, 201.

46. Pintoin, *Chronique du religieux*, 5:130.

47. Mirot, "Autour de la paix d'Arras."

48. Famiglietti, *Royal Intrigue*, 137.

49. Bourgeois de Paris, *Journal d'un bourgeois de Paris*, 71.

50. Famiglietti, *Royal Intrigue*, 138.

51. Schnerb, *Armangacs et les Bourguignons*, 149–54; Famiglietti, *Royal Intrigue*, 149–51.

52. Vaughan, *John the Fearless*, 205.

53. Pintoin, *Chronique du religieux*, 5:586–90.

54. Ibid., 6:50.

55. Denifle, *Chartularium Universitatis Parisiensis*, 4:283, no. 2015. See Guenée, *Meurtre, une société*, 232–64; and Leveleux-Teixeira's illuminating article on the doctrinal debate, "Du crime atroce."

56. Coville, *Jean Petit*, 504.

57. Ibid., 511.

58. Valois, *France et le grand schisme*, 4:324, 330.

59. Baye, *Journal de Nicolas de Baye*, 2:270–71.

60. *Ordonnances des rois de France*, 10:424–26.

61. Monstrelet, *Chronique*, 3:231.

62. *Ordonnances des rois de France*, 10:427–29.

63. Plancher, *Histoire générale et particulière*, vol. 3, *preuves*, no. 302.

64. Fresne de Beaucourt, *Histoire de Charles VII*, 1:76, 85.

65. Guenée, *Between Church and State*, 244–45.

66. Bourgeois de Paris, *Journal d'un bourgeois de Paris*, 33–34. See also *Fais et bonnes meurs*, 1:179.

67. Juvénal des Ursins, *Histoire de Charles VI*, 451.

68. Cockshaw, "Mentions d'auteurs," 142.

69. See Lehoux, *Jean de France*, 3:163.

70. Willard notes that the commentary on Psalm 102 mentions the commission. "Christine de Pizan's Allegorized Psalms," 320. See also Vaughan, *John the Fearless*, 79.

71. Ouy et al., *Album Christine de Pizan*, 671n4.

72. Ibid., 675–79. Willard, "Christine de Pizan's Allegorized Psalms," 322, argues that the manuscript had come into the Burgundian library only at the time of Jean's son, Philip the Good. However, Ouy et al. show that it belonged to Jean. *Album Christine de Pizan*, 665–66.

73. Juvénal des Ursins, *Histoire de Charles VI*, 451. Charles III of Navarre was back speaking for Jean of Burgundy a year later. Pintoin, *Chronique du religieux*, 3:372–74.

74. Monstrelet, *Chronique*, 2:77.

75. Lehoux, *Jean de France*, 3:171, 178, 179.

76. All references to the *Lamentacions sur les maux de la guerre civile* are to Wisman's translation, hereafter cited parenthetically in the text by page number.

77. Grandeau, "Itinéraire d'Isabeau de Bavière," 632; Monstrelet, *Chronique*, 2:94.

78. Lehoux, *Jean de France*, 3:188.

79. Monstrelet, *Chronique*, 2:92–94.

80. See Petit, *Itinéraires de Philippe Le Hardi*, 376, 384.

81. Lehoux, *Jean de France*, 3:225; Monstrelet, *Chronique*, 2:168.

82. Dulac and Richard, "Affective and Cognitive Contemplation."

83. Ouy et al., *Album Christine de Pizan*, 688.

84. On medieval theories of peace and just war, see Johnson, *Just War Tradition* and *Ideology, Reason, and the Limitation of War*; and Russell, *Just War in the Middle Ages*.

85. Johnson, *Just War Tradition*, 151.

86. Keen explains that because sovereignty was a flexible term, referring to "anything from the possession of high and low justice to possession of final secular jurisdiction," Christine's definition was designed to include the dukes. *Laws of War*, 78.

87. All citations of the *Livre des fais d'armes et de chevalerie* are from BnF, fonds français 603, hereafter cited parenthetically in the text by folio number, followed by the page number of Sumner Willard's translation in *The Book of Deeds of Arms and of Chivalry*.

88. Monstrelet, *Chronique*, 2:65.

89. See Plancher, *Histoire générale et particulière*, vol. 3, *preuves*, no. 272.

90. See Blumenfeld-Kosinski, "'Enemies within/enemies without'"; and Dudash, "Christine de Pizan and the 'Menu Peuple.'"

91. Carroll, "Christine de Pizan and the Origins," 31.

92. Johnson, *Ideology, Reason, and the Limitation of War*, 66–75.

93. Bonet [Bovet], *Tree of Battle*, 125.

94. All citations of the *Livre de paix* are to Green, Mews, Pindar, and van Hemelryck's edition, translation, and commentary, *The Book of Peace*, hereafter cited parenthetically in the text by page number of the translation.

95. See Green's introduction, *Book of Peace*, 15. Monstrelet describes the bad blood in *Chronique*, 2:306–7.

96. Bourgeois de Paris, *Journal d'un bourgeois de Paris*, 55. The author bitterly opposed the Treaty of Auxerre, complaining that the king was still sick, that the dauphin acted according more to his will than to reason, and that the Armagnacs could do as they pleased (54).

97. Schnerb, *Jean sans Peur*, 550–52.

98. Monstrelet, *Chronique*, 2:305.

99. Ibid., 2:307; Vaughan, *John the Fearless*, 98.

100. Carroll, "On the Causes of War," 344.

101. Forhan, *Political Theory of Christine de Pizan*. In chapter 5, Forhan distinguishes between substantive and procedural justice, that is, between normative justice and justice that arises from the application of "just" processes.

102. For the insertion, see the *Book of Peace*, 43–47; see also Ouy et al., *Album Christine de Pizan*, 691–94.

103. Van Hemelryck, introduction to the *Book of Peace*, 47.

104. See the dedication: "As soon as I received your commission for it" (Dès que vo command en recue). BL, Harley 4431, fol. 3v.

105. Laidlaw, "Christine de Pizan: The Making of the Queen's Manuscript," 302.

106. For a description of the manuscript, see Ouy et al., *Album Christine de Pizan*, 317–43.

107. For the best-known example, see *balade* 11 in Christine's *Oeuvres poétiques*, 1:11.

108. All citations of the *Epistre de la prison de vie humaine* are from Wisman's translation, hereafter cited parenthetically in the text by page number.

109. Quotations are from Montreuil, *Opera*, vol. 2, letter 202.

110. D'Arcens, *"Petit estat vesval*," 222, 223.

111. Juvénal des Ursins, *Histoire de Charles VI*, 533.

112. Pintoin, *Chronique du religieux*, 6:62.

EPILOGUE

1. See Green, "Was Christine de Pizan at Poissy?"

2. Boulton, "Christine's *Heures de contemplacion*," 100.

3. Dulac and Richards, "Affective and Cognitive Contemplation," 71.

4. *Ditié de Jehanne d'Arc*, 39, 457–64.

5. Guenée, "Roi, ses parents et son royaume," 464.

6. Vallet de Viriville, *Chronique de la pucelle*, 373.

7. *Livre du corps de policie*, 93.

8. Autrand, *Christine de Pizan*, 273.

9. Delany, "'Mothers to Think Back Through,'" 96.

10. See Reno, "Christine de Pizan."

11. Delany, "History, Politics, and Christine Studies," 196.

12. Sizer, "Making Revolution Medieval," 620.

Bibliography

PRIMARY SOURCES

Manuscripts

Bibliothèque nationale de France (BnF)
    Collection de Bourgogne 26
    Fonds français 603
    Fonds français 1892
    Fonds français 5037
    Fonds français 10237
    Fonds italien 1682
    Fonds latin 7737
    Fonds latin 11201
    Nouvelles acquisitions françaises 4792
    Pièces originales 452
British Library (BL)
    Harley 4431
Koninklijke Bibliotheek van België (KBR)
    10476

Printed Sources

Aquinas, Thomas. *Commentary on the Metaphysics.* Trans. John P. Rowan. http://dhspriory.org/thomas/Metaphysics.htm.

Baye, Nicolas de. *Journal de Nicolas de Baye, Greffier de Paris, 1400–1417.* Ed. Alexandre Tuetey. 2 vols. Paris: Renouard, 1885.

Boethius. *Le livre de Boece de consolacion.* Ed. Glynnis Cropp. Geneva: Droz, 2006.

Bonet [Bovet], Honoré. *The Tree of Battle.* Trans. G. W. Coopland. Cambridge: Harvard University Press, 1949.

Bourgeois de Paris. *Journal d'un bourgeois de Paris.* Ed. Colette Beaune. Paris: Librairie Générale Française, 1990.

Chronique des quatre premiers Valois (1327–1393). Ed. Siméon Luce. Paris: Renouard, 1862.

Denifle, Heinrich, ed. *Chartularium Universitatis Parisiensis.* 4 vols. Paris: Delalain, 1889–97.

Douët-d'Arcq, Louis Claude. *Choix de pièces inédites relatives au règne de Charles VI.* 2 vols. Paris: Renouard, 1863.

———. *Comptes de l'Hôtel des rois de France aux XIVe et XVe siècles.* Paris: Renouard, 1865.

Dubois, Pierre. *De recuperatione Terre Sancte: Traité de politique générale.* Ed. Charles-Victor Langlois. Paris: Picard, 1891.

du Boulay, César Egasse. *Historia Universitatis Parisiensis.* 6 vols. Paris: F. Noel-P. de Bresche, 1665–73.

Fenin, Pierre de. *Mémoires de Pierre de Fenin, escuyer et panetier de Charles VI, roy de France, contenans l'histoire de ce prince, depuis l'an 1407 jusques l'an 1422.* Ed. Pierre Petitot. Vol. 7 of *Collection complète des mémoires relatifs à l'histoire de France, depuis le règne de Philippe-Auguste jusqu'au commencement du XVIIᵉ siècle, avec des notices sur chaque auteur,* series 1, 52 vols. Paris: Foucault, 1819–26.

Froissart, Jean. *Œuvres de Froissart: Chroniques.* Ed. Joseph-Marie-Bruno-Constantin Kervyn de Lettenhove. 26 vols. Osnabrück: Biblio Verlag, 1967.

Gerson, Jean. *Oeuvres complètes.* Ed. Palémon Glorieux. 10 vols. Paris: Desclée et Cie, 1960–71.

———. *Opera omnia.* 5 vols. Ed. Louis E. Dupin. Antwerp: Sumptibus Societatis, 1706.

Les grandes chroniques de France. Ed. Jules Viard. 10 vols. Paris: Champion, 1920–53.

Les grandes chroniques de France: Chronique des règnes de Jean II et de Charles V. Ed. Roland Delachenal. 4 vols. Paris: Renouard, 1916–20.

Guillaume de Conches. *Guillemli de Conchis: Glosae super Boetium, Opera omnia II.* Ed. Lodi Nauta. Corpus Christianorum Continuatio Mediaevalis 158. Turnhout: Brepols, 1999.

Isambert, François André. *Recueil général des anciennes lois françaises, depuis l'an 420 jusqu'à la Révolution de 1789.* 29 vols. Paris: Belin-Le Prieur, Plon, 1824–57.

Jean de Montreuil. *Opera.* Ed. Nicole Grévy-Pons, Ezio Ornato, and Gilbert Ouy. 4 vols. Turin: Giappichelli, 1963–86.

Jean le Seneschal. *Les cent ballades: Poème du XIVᵉ siècle.* Ed. Gaston Raynaud. Paris: Firmin-Didot, 1905.

Juvénal des Ursins, Jean. *Histoire de Charles VI, roy de France, et des choses mémorables advenues durant quarante-deux années de son règne: Depuis 1380 jusqu'à 1422; Nouvelle collection des mémoires pour servir à l'histoire de France.* Ed. Joseph-François Michaud and Jean-Joseph-François Poujoulat. 3 series, 34 vols. 1st series, vol. 2. Paris, 1836–39.

Kéralio, Louise de. *Les crimes des reines de France depuis le commencement de la monarchie jusqu'à Marie-Antoinette.* Paris: Prudhomme, 1791.

Le Fèvre de Saint Rémy, Jean. *Chronique de Jean Le Fèvre, seigneur de Saint-Rémy.* Ed. François Morand. 2 vols. Paris: Renouard, 1876, 1881.

Mézières, Philippe de. *Le songe du vieil pelerin.* Ed. G. W. Coopland. 2 vols. Cambridge: Cambridge University Press, 1969.

Monstrelet, Enguerran de. *La chronique d'Enguerran de Monstrelet, 1400–1444.* Ed. Louis Claude Douët-d'Arcq. 6 vols. Paris: Renouard, 1857–62.

Les ordonnances des rois de France de la troisième race. Ed. Denis-Francois Secousse et al. 21 vols. Paris: L'Imprimerie Nationale, 1723–1849.

Pintoin, Michel. *Chronique du religieux de Saint-Denys contenant le règne de Charles VI, de 1380–1422.* 1844. Ed. and trans. Louis Bellaguet. 6 vols. Paris: Éditions du Comité des Travaux Historiques et Scientifiques, 1994.

Plancher, Urbain. *Histoire générale et particulière de Bourgogne.* 4 vols. Dijon: Imprimerie de A. de Fay, 1739–81.

Le songe véritable. Ed. Henri Moranvillé. *Mémoires de la Société de l'Histoire de Paris et de l'Ile de France* 17 (1890): 217–438.

Vallet de Viriville, Auguste, ed. *Chronique de la pucelle ou chronique de Cousinot, suivie de la chronique Normande de P. Cochon, relatives aux règnes de Charles VI et de Charles VII, restituées à leurs auteurs et publiées pour la première fois intégralement à partir de l'an 1403, d'après les manuscrits, avec notices, notes, et développements.* Paris: Adolphe Delahays, 1859. Reprint, Elibron Classics, 2002.

Weizsäcker, Julius. *Deutsche Reichstagsakten.* 5 vols. Gotha: Friedrich Andreas Perthes, 1885.

Works of Christine de Pizan

The Book of Deeds of Arms and of Chivalry. Trans. Sumner Willard. Ed. Charity Cannon Willard. University Park: Pennsylvania State University Press, 1999.
The Book of Peace by Christine de Pizan. Trans. and ed. Karen Green, Constant J. Mews, Janice Pindar, and Tania van Hemelryck. University Park: Pennsylvania State University Press, 2007.
The Book of the Body Politic. Ed. and trans. Kate Langdon Forhan. Cambridge: Cambridge University Press, 1994.
Le chemin de longue étude. Trans. and ed. Andrea Tarnowski. Paris: Librairie Générale Française, 2000.
La città delle dame. Ed. and trans. Patrizia Caraffi and E. J. Richards. Milan: Luni Editrice, 1997.
Debate of the "Romance of the Rose." Ed. and trans. David F. Hult. Chicago: University of Chicago Press, 2010.
Le débat sur le "Roman de la rose." Ed. Eric Hicks. Paris: Champion, 1977.
Ditié de Jehanne d'Arc. Ed. Angus J. Kennedy and Kenneth Varty. Oxford: Medium Aevum Monographs, 1977.
"The Epistle of the Prison of Human Life" with "An Epistle to the Queen of France" and "Lament on the Evils of the Civil War." Ed. and trans. Josette Wisman. New York: Garland, 1984.
Epistre d'Othea. Ed. Gabriella Parussa. Geneva: Droz, 1999.
Le livre de l'advision Cristine. Ed. Christine Reno and Liliane Dulac. Paris: Champion, 2001.
Le livre de la mutacion de fortune. Ed. Suzanne Solente. 4 vols. Paris: Picard, 1959–66.
Le livre des fais et bonnes meurs du sage roy Charles V par Christine de Pisan. Ed. Suzanne Solente. 2 vols. Paris: Champion, 1936.
Le livre des trois vertus. Ed. Charity C. Willard and Eric Hicks. Paris: Champion, 1989.
Le livre du corps de policie. Ed. Angus J. Kennedy. Paris: Champion, 1998.
Le livre du duc des vrais amans. Ed. Thelma S. Fenster. Binghamton, N.Y.: Medieval and Renaissance Texts and Studies, 1995.
The Love Debate Poems of Christine de Pizan: Le livre du debat de deux amans, Le livre des trois jugemens, Le livre du dit de Poissy. Ed. Barbara K. Altmann. Gainesville: University Press of Florida, 1998.
Oeuvres poétiques de Christine de Pisan. Ed. Maurice Roy. 3 vols. Paris: Librairie de Firmin Didot et Cie, 1884–96.
Poems of Cupid, God of Love: Christine de Pizan's "Epistre au dieu d'amours" and "Dit de la rose," Thomas Hoccleve's "Letter of Cupid," with George Sewell's "The Proclamation of Cupid." Ed. and trans. Thelma S. Fenster and Mary C. Erler. Leiden: Brill, 1990.
Les sept psaumes allégorisés de Christine de Pisan. Ed. Ruth Ringland Rains. Washington, D.C.: Catholic University of America Press, 1965.
The Vision of Christine de Pizan. Trans. Glenda K. McLeod and Charity Cannon Willard. Cambridge: D. S. Brewer, 2005.

SECONDARY SOURCES

Adams, Tracy. *The Life and Afterlife of Isabeau of Bavaria.* Baltimore: Johns Hopkins University Press, 2010.
Akbari, Suzanne Conklin. "The Movement from Verse to Prose in the Allegories of Christine de Pizan." In *Poetry, Knowledge, and Community in Late Medieval France,* ed. Rebecca Dixon and Finn E. Sinclair, 136–50. Cambridge: D. S. Brewer, 2008.

Alexandre, Arnaud. "'Que le roi le puisse toujours avoir près de lui': Présence de Louis d'Orléans à Paris, résidences et chapelles privées." In *Paris, capitale des ducs de Bourgogne,* ed. Werner Paravicini and Bertrand Schnerb, 373–88. Ostfildern: Jan Thorbecke Verlag, 2007.

Allen, Prudence. *The Concept of Women: The Early Humanist Reformation (1250–1500).* Grand Rapids: W. B. Eerdmans, 1997.

Allmand, Christopher T. *The Hundred Years War: England and France at War, c. 1300–c. 1450.* Cambridge: Cambridge University Press, 1989.

Armstrong, Adrian, and Sarah Kay. *Knowing Poetry: Verse in Medieval France from the Rose to the Rhétoriqueurs.* Ithaca: Cornell University Press, 2011.

Autrand, Françoise. *Charles V.* Paris: Fayard, 1994.

———. *Charles VI: La folie du roi.* Paris: Fayard, 1986.

———. *Christine de Pizan: Une femme en politique.* Paris: Fayard, 2009.

———. "La force de l'âge: Jeunesse et vieillesse au service de l'état en France aux XIVᵉ et XVᵉ siècles." *Comptes-rendus des Séances de l'Académie des Inscriptions et Belles-Lettres* 129 (1985): 206–23.

———. "France Under Charles V and Charles VI." In *The New Cambridge Medieval History,* vol. 6, *c. 1300–c. 1415,* ed. Michael Jones, 422–41. Cambridge: Cambridge University Press, 2000.

———. *Jean de Berry: L'art et le pouvoir.* Paris: Fayard, 2000.

Babbitt, Susan M. *Oresme's "Livre de Politiques" and the France of Charles V.* Philadelphia: American Philosophical Society, 1986.

Barret, Sébastian. "Pratique, normalisation, codification: La rédaction des actes à la chancellerie royale française de la fin du Moyen Âge." In *La codification: Perspectives transdisciplinaires,* ed. Gernot Kamecke and Jacques Le Rider, 33–42. Paris: Collège Doctoral Européen, 2007.

Bartlett, Robert. "Mortal Enmities: The Legal Aspects of Hostility in the Middle Ages." In *Feud, Violence, and Practice: Essays in Medieval Studies in Honor of Stephen D. White,* ed. Belle S. Tuten and Tracey L. Billado, 197–212. Burlington, Vt.: Ashgate, 2010.

Beaune, Colette. *Jeanne d'Arc.* Paris: Perrin, 2004.

———. "La mauvaise reine des origines: Frédégonde aux XIVᵉ et XVᵉ siècles." *Mélanges de l'École Française de Rome Italie et Méditerranée* 113 (2001): 29–44.

Bellitto, Christopher M. *Nicolas de Clamanges: Spirituality, Personal Reform, and Pastoral Renewal on the Eve of the Reformation.* Washington, D.C.: Catholic University of America Press, 2001.

Bernier, Jean. *Histoire de Blois contenant les antiquitez et singularitez du comté de Blois, les éloges de ses comtes et les vies des hommes illustres qui sont nez au païs blésois, avec les noms et les armoiries des familles nobles du mesme païs.* Paris: Imprimerie de F. Muguet, 1682.

Blumenfeld-Kosinski, Renate. "'Enemies within/enemies without': Threats to the Body Politic in Christine de Pizan." *Medievalia et Humanistica* 26 (1999): 1–15.

Boehm, Christopher. *Blood Revenge: The Anthropology of Feuding in Montenegro and Other Tribal Societies.* Lawrence: University Press of Kansas, 1984.

Boffa, Sergio. *Warfare in Medieval Brabant.* Woodbridge, UK: Boydell and Brewer, 2004.

Bonnardot, Alfred. *Dissertations archéologiques sur les anciennes enceintes de Paris.* Paris: Dumoulin, 1852.

Boudet, Jean-Patrice. "Les condamnations de la magie à Paris en 1398." *Revue Mabillon* 12 (2001): 121–57.

Boulton, D'Arcy Jonathan. *The Knights of the Crown: The Monarchical Orders of Knighthood in Later Medieval Europe, 1325–1520.* Woodbridge, UK: Boydell Press, 1987.

Boulton, Maureen. "Christine's *Heures de contemplacion de la Passion* in the Context of Late-Medieval Passion Devotion." In *Contexts and Continuities: Proceedings of the IVth International Colloquium on Christine de Pizan,* ed. Angus J. Kennedy, Rosalind Brown-Grant, James C. Laidlaw, and Catherine M. Müller, 99–113. Glasgow: University of Glasgow Press, 2002.

Bourret, Joseph-Christian Ernest. *Essai historique et critique sur les sermons français de Gerson.* Paris: Charles Douniol, 1858.

Bozzolo, Carla, and Hélène Loyau. *La cour amoureuse, dite de Charles VI.* 2 vols. Paris: Léopard d'Or, 1982, 1992.

Bozzolo, Carla, and Monique Ornato. "Princes, prélats, barons et autres gens notables à propos de la cour amoureuse dite de Charles VI." In *Prosopographie et genèse de l'état moderne,* ed. Françoise Autrand, 159–70. Paris: École Normale Supérieure de Jeunes Filles, 1986.

Brown, Elizabeth A. R. "Taxation and Morality in the Thirteenth and Fourteenth Centuries: Conscience and Political Power and the Kings of France." *French Historical Studies* 8 (1973): 1–28.

Brownlee, Kevin. "The Image of History in Christine de Pizan's *Livre de la Mutacion de Fortune.*" In *Contexts: Style and Its Values in Medieval Art and Literature,* ed. Daniel Poirion and Nancy Regalado, 44–56. New Haven: Yale University Press, 1991.

Bryant, Lawrence M. *The King and the City in the Parisian Royal Entry Ceremony: Politics, Ritual, and Art in the Renaissance.* Geneva: Droz, 1986.

Bueno de Mesquita, David M. *Giangaleazzo Visconti: Duke of Milan (1351–1402).* Cambridge: Cambridge University Press, 1941.

Bührer-Thierry, Geneviève. "La reine adultère." *Cahiers de Civilisation Médiévale* 35 (1992): 299–312.

Byock, Jesse L. "Defining Feud: Talking Points and Iceland's Saga Women." In *Feud in Medieval and Early Modern Europe,* ed. Jeppe Büchert Netterstrøm and Bjørn Poulsen, 95–112. Aarhus: Aarhus University Press, 2007.

Cadden, Joan. "Charles V, Nicole Oresme, and Christine de Pizan: Unities and Uses of Knowledge in Fourteenth-Century France." In *Texts and Contexts in Ancient and Medieval Science: Studies on the Occasion of John E. Murdoch's Seventieth Birthday,* ed. Edith Sylla and Michael McVaugh, 208–44. Leiden: Brill, 1997.

Camus, Jules. *La venue en France de Valentine Visconti Duchesse d'Orléans.* Turin: F. Casanova, 1898.

Carbonnières, Louis de. *La procédure devant la chambre criminelle du Parlement de Paris au XIVe siècle.* Paris: Champion, 2004.

Carroll, Berenice. "Christine de Pizan and the Origins of Peace Theory." In *Women Writers and the Early Modern British Political Tradition,* ed. Hilda L. Smith, 22–39. Cambridge: Cambridge University Press, 1998.

———. "On the Causes of War and the Quest for Peace: Christine de Pizan and Early Peace Theory." In *Au champ des écritures: IIIe colloque international sur Christine de Pizan,* ed. Eric Hicks, Diego Gonzalez, and Philippe Simon, 337–58. Paris: Champion, 2000.

Carroll, Stuart. *Blood and Violence in Early Modern France.* Oxford: Oxford University Press, 2006.

Cartellieri, Otto. *The Court of Burgundy.* 1929. Reprint, London: Routledge and Kegan Paul, 1972.

Cayley, Emma. "Collaborative Communities: The Manuscript Context of Alain Chartier's *Belle Dame sans mercy.*" *Medium Aevum* 71 (2002): 226–331.

———. *Debate and Dialogue: Alain Chartier in His Cultural Context.* Oxford: Oxford University Press, 2006.

Cazelles, Raymond. "Une exigence de l'opinion depuis saint Louis: La réformation du royaume." *Annuaire-Bulletin de la Société de l'Histoire de France*, 1962–63, 91–99.

———. *Société politique, noblesse et couronne sous Jean Le Bon et Charles V.* Geneva: Droz, 1982.

———. *La société politique et la crise de la royauté sous Philippe de Valois.* Paris: D'Argences, 1958.

Chattaway, Carol M. *The Order of the Golden Tree: The Gift-Giving Objectives of Duke Philip the Bold of Burgundy.* Turnhout: Brepols, 2006.

Chaumé, Maurice. "Une prophétie relative à Charles VI." *Revue du Moyen Âge Latin* 3 (1947): 27–42.

Cockshaw, Pierre. "Mentions d'auteurs, de copistes, d'enlumineurs et de libraires dans le comptes généraux de l'état Bourguignon (1384–1419)." *Scriptorium* 23 (1969): 122–44.

Collard, Franck. *Le crime de poison au Moyen Âge.* Paris: Presses Universitaires de France, 2003.

Collas, Emile. *Valentine de Milan, Duchesse d'Orléans.* Paris: Plon, 1911.

Contamine, Philippe, Olivier Guyotjeannin, and Règine Le Jan, eds. *Le Moyen Âge: Le roi, l'église, les grands, le peuple, 481–1514.* Paris: Editions du Seuil, 2002.

Coville, Alfred. "Un ami de Nicolas de Clamanges, Jacques de Nouvion (1372?–1411)." *Biblio-thèque de l'École des Chartes* 96 (1935): 63–99.

———. *Les cabochiens et l'ordonnance de 1413.* Paris: Hachette, 1888.

———. *Gontier et Pierre Col et l'humanisme en France au temps de Charles VI.* Geneva: Droz, 1934.

———. *Jean Petit: La question du tyrannicide au commencement du XVe siècle.* Paris: Picard, 1932.

———. "Recherches sur Jean Courtecuisse et ses oeuvres oratoires." *Bibliothèque de l'École des Chartes* 65 (1904): 469–529.

Creighton, Mandell. *A History of the Papacy from the Great Schism to the Sack of Rome, Part I.* London: Longman, Green, 1882.

Cropp, Glynnis. "Philosophy, the Liberal Arts, and Theology in *Le Livre de la mutacion de Fortune* and *Le Livre de l'advision Cristine.*" In *Healing the Body Politic: Christine de Pizan's Political Thought,* ed. Karen Green and Constant J. Mews, 139–60. Turnhout: Brepols, 2005.

Dale, Sharon. "Contra damnationis filios: The Visconti in Fourteenth-Century Papal Diplo-macy." *Journal of Medieval History* 33 (2007): 1–32.

D'Arcens, Louise. "*Petit estat vesval*: Christine de Pizan's Grieving Body Politic." In *Healing the Body Politic: Christine de Pizan's Political Thought,* ed. Karen Green and Constant J. Mews, 201–26. Turnhout: Brepols, 2005.

Delachenal, Roland. *Histoire de Charles V.* 5 vols. Paris: Picard, 1909–31.

Delany, Sheila. "History, Politics, and Christine Studies: A Polemical Reply." In *Politics, Gen-der, and Genre: The Political Thought of Christine de Pizan,* ed. Margaret Brabant, 193–206. Boulder: Westview Press, 1992.

———. "'Mothers to Think Back Through': Who Are They? The Ambiguous Example of Christine de Pizan." In Delany, *Medieval Literary Politics: Shapes of Ideology,* 88–103. Manchester: Manchester University Press, 1990.

Delisle, Léopold. "Notice sur les sept psaumes allégoriques de Christine de Pizan." *Notices et Extraits des Manuscrits de la Bibliothèque Nationale et Autres Bibliothèques* 35 (1897): 551–59.

———. *Recherches sur la librairie de Charles V.* 2 vols. Paris: Champion, 1907.

Delogu, Daisy. *Theorizing the Ideal Sovereign: The Rise of the French Vernacular Royal Biography.* Toronto: University of Toronto Press, 2008.

Demurger, Alain. *Temps de crises, temps d'espoirs (XIVe–XVe siècle).* Paris: Éditions du Seuil, 1990.

Dequeker-Fergon, Jean-Michel. "L'histoire au service des pouvoirs." *Médiévales* 10 (1986): 51–68.

Desjardins, Mireille. "Les savoirs des notaires et secrétaires du roi et la géographie de la France d'après le manuel d'Odart Morchesne et un index de chancellerie." In *Écrit et pouvoir dans les chancelleries médiévales: Espace français, espace anglais,* ed. Kouky Fianu and DeLloyd J. Guth, 87–97. Louvain-la-Neuve: Collège Cardinal Mercier, 1997.

Desmond, Marilynn, ed. *Christine de Pizan and the Categories of Difference.* Minneapolis: University of Minnesota Press, 1998.

Desmond, Marilynn, and Pamela Sheingorn. *Myth, Montage, and Visuality in Late Medieval Manuscript Culture.* Ann Arbor: University of Michigan Press, 2006.

Dodu, Gaston. "Les idées de Charles V en matière de gouvernement." *Revue des Questions Historiques* 14 (1929): 5–46.

Dudash, Susan J. "Christine de Pizan and the 'Menu Peuple.'" *Speculum* 78 (2003): 788–831.

Dulac, Liliane, and Christine Reno. "Traduction et adaptation dans *l'Advision-Cristine* de Christine de Pizan." In *Traduction et adaptation en France: Actes du colloque organisé par l'Université de Nancy II, 23–25 mars 1995,* ed. Charles Brucker, 121–31. Paris: Champion, 1997.

Dulac, Liliane, and E. Jeffrey Richards. "Affective and Cognitive Contemplation in Christine de Pizan's *Heures de la Contemplacion sur la Passion de Nostre Seigneur Jhesucrist.*" *Médiévales* 53 (2012): 56–71.

Elliott, Elizabeth. *Remembering Boethius: Writing Aristocratic Identity in Late Medieval French and English Literature.* Surrey, UK: Ashgate, 2012.

Famiglietti, R. C. "The French Monarchy Crisis, 1392–1415, and the Political Role of the Dauphin, Louis of France, Duke of Guyenne." PhD diss., City University of New York, 1982.

———. *Royal Intrigue: Crisis at the Court of Charles VI, 1392–1420.* New York: AMS Press, 1986.

Faure, Juliette. *Le marais.* Paris: L'Harmattan, 1997.

Fenster, Thelma. "'Perdre son Latin': Christine de Pizan and Vernacular Humanism." In *Christine de Pizan and the Categories of Difference,* ed. Marilynn Desmond, 91–107. Minneapolis: University of Minnesota Press, 1998.

Fletcher, C. D. "Crisis and *Luxuria* in England and France, ca. 1340–1422." In *The Court as a Stage: England and the Low Countries in the Later Middle Ages,* ed. Steven Gunn and Antheun Janse, 28–38. Woodbridge, UK: Boydell Press, 2006.

Ford, C. J. "Piracy or Policy: The Crisis in the Channel, 1400–1403." *Transactions of the Royal Historical Society,* 1979, 63–78.

Forhan, Kate Langdon. *The Political Theory of Christine de Pizan.* Burlington, Vt.: Ashgate, 2002.

Fresne de Beaucourt, Gaston Louis Emmanuel du. *Histoire de Charles VII.* 6 vols. Paris: Librairie de la Société Bibliographique, A. Picard, 1881–91.

Furr, Grover C. "The Quarrel of the *Roman de la Rose* and Fourteenth-Century Humanism." PhD diss., Princeton University, 1979.

Gauvard, Claude. "Christine de Pisan a-t-elle eu une pensée politique?" *Revue Historique* 250 (1973): 417–30.

———. "Christine de Pizan et ses contemporains: L'engagement politique des écrivains dans le royaume de France aux XIVᵉ et XVᵉ siècles." In *Une femme de lettres au Moyen Âge: Études autour de Christine de Pizan,* ed. Liliane Dulac and Bernard Ribémont, 105–28. Orleans: Paradigme, 1995.

———. *"De grace especial": Crime, état et société en France à la fin du Moyen Âge.* Paris: Publications de la Sorbonne, 1991.

Geremek, Bronislaw. *The Margins of Society in Late Medieval Paris.* Trans. Jean Birrell. Cambridge: Cambridge University Press, 1987.

Gibbons, Rachel C. "The Active Queenship of Isabeau of Bavaria, 1392–1417." PhD diss., University of Reading, 1997.

Giesey, Ralph E. "The Juristic Basis of the Dynastic Right to the French Throne." *Transactions of the American Philosophical Society* 51, no. 5 (1961): 1–47.

Girault, Pierre-Gilles. "Portraits et images du prince vers 1400: L'exemple de Louis d'Orléans." In *La création artistique en France autour de 1400: Actes du colloque international École du Louvre–Musée des beaux-arts de Dijon–Université de Bourgogne,* ed. Elisabeth Taburet-Delahaye, 151–65. Paris: École du Louvre, 2006.

Given-Wilson, Chris. "'The Quarrels of Old Women': Henry IV, Louis of Orléans, and Anglo-French Chivalric Challenges of the Early Fifteenth Century." In *The Reign of Henry IV: Rebellion and Survival, 1403–1413,* ed. Gwilym Dodd and Douglas Biggs, 28–47. Woodbridge, UK: Boydell and Brewer, 2008.

Gonzalez, Elizabeth. *Un prince en son hôtel: Les serviteurs des ducs d'Orléans au XVe siècle.* Paris: Publications de la Sorbonne, 2004.

Grandeau, Yann. "L'itinéraire d'Isabeau de Bavière." *Bulletin Philologique et Historique*, 1964, 569–670.

Green, Karen. "Christine de Pizan: Isolated Individual or Member of a Feminine Community of Learning?" In *Communities of Learning: Networks and the Shaping of Intellectual Identity in Europe, 1100–1500,* ed. Constant J. Mews and J. N. Crossley, 229–50. Turnhout: Brepols, 2011.

———. "Was Christine de Pizan at Poissy 1418–1429?" *Medium Aevum* 83 (2014): 28–40.

Green, Karen, and Constant J. Mews, eds. *Healing the Body Politic: Christine de Pizan's Political Thought.* Turnhout: Brepols, 2005.

Gross, Charles. "The Political Influence of the University of Paris in the Middle Ages." *American Historical Review* 6, no. 3 (1901): 440–45.

Guenée, Bernard. *Between Church and State: The Lives of Four French Prelates in the Late Middle Ages.* Trans. Arthur Goldhammer. Chicago: University of Chicago Press, 1991.

———. *La folie de Charles VI, roi bien-aimé.* Paris: Perrin, 2004.

———. "Les *Grandes chroniques de France,* le roman aux roys (1274–1518)." In *Les lieux de mémoire: II, La Nation,* ed. Pierre Nora, 3 vols., 1:189–214. Paris: Gallimard, 1984–86.

———. *Un meurtre, une société: L'assassinat du duc d'Orléans, 23 novembre 1407.* Paris: Gallimard, 1992.

———. "Le roi, ses parents et son royaume en France au XIVe siècle." *Bulletino dell'Istituto Storico Italiano per il Medio Evo e Archivio Muratoriano* 94 (1988): 439–70.

Guizot, François. *L'histoire de France depuis les temps les plus reculés jusqu'en 1789 racontée à mes petits-enfants.* Vol. 2. Paris: Hachette, 1875.

Guyot-Bachy, Isabelle, and Jean-Marie Moeglin. "Comment ont été continuées les *Grandes chroniques de France* dans la première moitié du XIVe siècle." *Bibliothèque de l'École des Chartes* 63 (2005): 385–433.

Halsall, Guy. "Violence and Society in the Early Medieval West: An Introductory Survey." In *Violence and Society in the Early Medieval West,* ed. Guy Halsall, 1–45. Woodbridge, UK: Boydell and Brewer, 1998.

Heckmann, Marie-Luise. *Stellvertreter, Mit- und Ersatzherrscher: Regenten, Generalstatthalter, Kurfürsten und Reichsvikare in Regnum und Imperium vom 13. bis zum frühen 15. Jahrhundert.* 2 vols. Warendorf: Fahlbusch, 2002.

Hedeman, Anne D. *The Royal Image: Illustrations of the Grandes Chroniques de France, 1274–1422.* Berkeley: University of California Press, 1991.

Henneman, John Bell. "The Military Class and the French Monarchy in the Late Middle Ages." *American Historical Review* 83, no. 4 (1978): 946–65.

————. *Olivier de Clisson and Political Society Under Charles V and Charles VI.* Philadelphia: University of Pennsylvania Press, 1996.

————. "Who Were the Marmousets?" *Medieval Prosopography* 5 (1984): 19–63.

Hicks, Eric. "Excerpts and Originality: Authorial Purpose in the *Fais et Bonnes Meurs*." In *Christine de Pizan 2000: Studies on Christine de Pizan in Honour of Angus J. Kennedy,* ed. John Campbell and Nadia Margolis, 221–250. Amsterdam: Rodopi, 2000.

Hicks, Eric, Diego Gonzalez, and Philippe Simon, eds. *Au champ des écritures: IIIᵉ colloque international sur Christine de Pizan.* Paris: Champion, 2000.

Hindman, Sandra. *Christine de Pizan's "Epistre Othéa": Painting and Politics at the Court of Charles VI.* Toronto: Pontifical Institute of Mediaeval Studies, 1986.

Hobbins, Daniel. "The Schoolman as Public Intellectual: Jean Gerson and the Late Medieval Tract." *American Historical Review* 108, no. 5 (2003): 1308–37.

Holderness, Julia Sims. "Christine, Boèce et saint Augustin: La consolation de la mémoire." In *Desireuse de plus avant enquerre: Actes du VIe Colloque international sur Christine de Pizan,* ed. Liliane Dulac, Anne Paupert, Christine Reno, and Bernard Ribémont, 279–89. Paris: Champion, 2008.

————. "Fiction and Truth in Ballad 15 of the *Cent Balades*." In *Contexts and Continuities: Proceedings of the IVth International Colloquium on Christine de Pizan,* ed. Angus J. Kennedy, Rosalind Brown-Grant, James C. Laidlaw, and Catherine M. Müller, 421–41. Glasgow: University of Glasgow Press, 2002.

Holmyard, Eric John. *Alchemy.* New York: Dover Publications, 1990.

Hutchison, Emily J. "Partisan Identity in the French Civil War, 1405–1418: Reconsidering the Evidence on Livery Badges." *Journal of Medieval History* 33 (2007): 250–74.

————. "Winning Hearts and Minds in Early Fifteenth-Century France: Burgundian Propaganda in Perspective." *French Historical Studies* 35 (2012): 3–30.

Hyams, Paul R. "Was There Really Such a Thing as Feud in the High Middle Ages?" In *Vengeance in the Middle Ages: Emotion, Religion, and Feud,* ed. Susanna A. Throop and Paul R. Hyams, 151–76. Surrey, UK: Ashgate, 2010.

Jameson, Fredric. *The Political Unconscious: Narrative as a Socially Symbolic Act.* Ithaca: Cornell University Press, 1981.

Jarry, Eugène. *La vie politique de Louis de France, duc d'Orléans, 1372–1407.* Paris: Picard, 1889.

————. "La 'voie de fait' et l'alliance franco-milanaise." *Bibliothèque de l'École des Chartes* 53 (1892): 213–53, 505–70.

Johnson, James T. *Ideology, Reason, and the Limitation of War: Religious and Secular Concepts, 1200–1740.* Princeton: Princeton University Press, 1975.

————. *Just War Tradition and the Restraint of War: A Moral and Historical Inquiry.* Princeton: Princeton University Press, 1981.

Jones, Chris. *Eclipse of Empire? Perceptions of the Western Empire and Its Rulers in Late-Medieval France.* Turnhout: Brepols, 2007.

————. "Understanding Political Conceptions in the Later Middle Ages: The French Imperial Candidatures and the Idea of the Nation-State." *Viator* 42 (2011): 83–114.

Kalyvas, Stathis N. *The Logic of Violence in Civil War.* Cambridge: Cambridge University Press, 2006.

Kaminsky, Howard. "The Noble Feud in the Later Middle Ages." *Past and Present* 177 (2002): 55–83.

————. "The Politics of France's Subtraction of Obedience from Pope Benedict XIII, 27 July, 1398." *Proceedings of the American Philosophical Society* 115 (1971): 366–97.

Kay, Sarah. "Touching Singularity: Consolation, Philosophy, and Poetry in the French *Dit*." In *The Erotics of Consolation: Desire and Distance in the Late Middle Ages,* ed. Catherine E. Léglu and Stephen J. Milner, 21–38. New York: Palgrave Macmillan, 2008.

Keen, Maurice. *The Laws of War in the Late Middle Ages.* London: Routledge, 1965.

Kelly, Douglas. *Christine de Pizan's Changing Opinion: A Quest for Certainty in the Midst of Chaos.* Cambridge: D. S. Brewer, 2007.

Kelly, Henry Ansgar. *Chaucer and the Cult of Saint Valentine.* Leiden: Brill, 1986.

Kennedy, Angus J., Rosalind Brown-Grant, James C. Laidlaw, and Catherine M. Müller, eds. *Contexts and Continuities: Proceedings of the IVth International Colloquium on Christine de Pizan.* Glasgow: University of Glasgow Press, 2002.

Kipling, Gordon. *Enter the King: Theatre, Liturgy, and Ritual in the Medieval Civic Triumph.* Oxford: Clarendon Press, 1998.

Kovacs, Eva. *L'âge d'or de l'orfèvrerie Parisienne au temps des princes de Valois.* Dijon: Éditions Faton, 2004.

Krappe, Alexander Haggerty. "The Legend of Buridan and the Tour de Nesle." *Modern Language Review* 23, no. 2 (1928): 216–22.

Krueger, Roberta. "Christine's Anxious Lessons: Gender, Morality, and Social Order from the *Enseignemens* to the *Avision.*" In *Christine de Pizan and the Categories of Difference,* ed. Marilynn Desmond, 16–40. Minneapolis: University of Minnesota Press, 1998.

Krynen, Jacques. *L'empire du roi: Idées et croyances en France, XIIIᵉ–XVᵉ siècle.* Paris: Gallimard, 1993.

———. *Idéal du prince et pouvoir royal en France à la fin du Moyen Âge (1380–1440): Étude de la littérature du temps.* Paris: Picard, 1981.

Laennec, Christine. "Prophétie, interprétation et écriture dans *L'Avision-Christine.*" In *Une femme de lettres au Moyen Âge: Études autour de Christine de Pizan,* ed. Liliane Dulac and Bernard Ribémont, 131–38. Orleans: Paradigme, 1995.

Laidlaw, James. "The *Cent balades:* Marriage of Content and Form." In *Christine de Pizan and Medieval French Lyric,* ed. E. Jeffrey Richards, 53–82. Gainesville: University Press of Florida, 1998.

———. "Christine de Pizan: A Publisher's Progress." *Modern Language Review* 82, no. 1 (1987): 35–75.

———. "Christine de Pizan, the Earl of Salisbury, and Henry IV." *French Studies* 36 (1982): 129–43.

———. "Christine de Pizan: The Making of the Queen's Manuscript (London, British Library, Harley 4431)." In *Patrons, Authors, and Workshops: Books and Book Production in Paris Around 1400,* ed. Gottfried Croenen and Peter Ainsworth, 297–310. Louvain: Peeters, 2006.

Le Blanc, Yvonne. *Va Lettre Va: The French Verse Epistle (1400–1550).* Birmingham, Ala.: Summa Publications, 1995.

Léglu, Catherine E., and Stephen J. Milner, eds. *The Erotics of Consolation: Desire and Distance in the Late Middle Ages.* New York: Palgrave Macmillan, 2008.

Leguai, André. "Les revoltes rurales dans le royaume de France du milieu du XIVᵉᵐᵉ siècle à la fin du XVᵉᵐᵉ siècle." *Le Moyen Âge* 88 (1982): 49–76.

———. "Les troubles urbains dans le nord de la France à la fin du XIIIᵉ et au début du XIVᵉ siècle." *Revue d'Histoire Économique et Sociale* 54 (1976): 281–303.

Lehoux, Françoise. *Jean de France, Duc de Berri: Sa vie; Son action politique (1340–1416).* 4 vols. Paris: Picard, 1966.

Le Ninan, Claire. "L'idée de croisade dans deux œuvres de Christine de Pizan." *Cahiers de Recherches Médiévales et Humanistes* 8 (2001): 251–61.

———. *Le sage roi et la clergesse: L'écriture du politique dans l'œuvre de Christine de Pizan.* Paris: Champion, 2013.

Leri, Jean-Marc, and Andrée Jacob. *Vie et histoire du IVe arrondissement.* Paris: Éditions Hervas, 1988.

Leveleux-Teixeira, Corinne. "Du crime atroce à la qualification impossible: Les débats doctrinaux autour de l'assassinat du duc d'Orléans (1408–1418)." In *Violences souveraines au Moyen Âge: Travaux d'une école historique,* ed. François Foronda, Christine Barralis, and Bénédicte Sère, 261–70. Paris: Presses Universitaires de France, 2010.

Lot, Ferdinand, and Robert Fawtier. *Histoire des institutions françaises au Moyen Âge.* Paris: Presses Universitaires de France, 1957.

Major, John Russell. *Representative Institutions in Renaissance France, 1421–1559.* Madison: University of Wisconsin Press, 1960.

Margolis, Nadia. "The Fortunes of a Text: *Autres Balades,* no. 42." In *Christine de Pizan 2000: Studies on Christine de Pizan in Honour of Angus J. Kennedy,* ed. John Campbell and Nadia Margolis, 251–62. Amsterdam: Rodopi, 2000.

———. *Introduction to Christine de Pizan.* Gainesville: University Press of Florida, 2011.

Martin, Henri. *L'histoire de France populaire depuis les temps les plus reculés jusqu'à nos jours.* Vol. 1. Paris: Furne, 1867.

McGrady, Deborah. "De 'l'onneur et louenge des femmes': Les dédicaces épistolaires du *Débat sur le Roman de la Rose* et la réinvention d'un débat littéraire en éloge de femmes." *Études Françaises* 47 (2011): 11–27.

———. "Reading for Authority: Portraits of Christine de Pizan and Her Readers." In *Author, Reader, Book: Medieval Authorship in Theory and Practice,* ed. Stephen Partridge and Erik Kwakkel, 154–77. Toronto: University of Toronto Press, 2012.

McGuire, Brian Patrick. *A Companion to Jean Gerson.* Leiden: Brill, 2009.

———. *Jean Gerson and the Last Medieval Reformation.* University Park: Pennsylvania State University Press, 2005.

Mehl, Jean-Michel. "Le roi de l'échiquier: Approche du mythe royal à la fin du Moyen-Âge." *Revue d'Histoire et de Philosophie Religieuse* 58 (1978): 145–61.

Meyjes, Guillaume Henri Marie Posthumus. *Jean Gerson, Apostle of Unity: His Church Politics and Ecclesiology.* Leiden: Brill, 1999.

Michelet, Jules. *L'histoire de France.* Vol. 5. Paris: Hachette, 1833.

Minois, George. *La Guerre de Cent Ans: Naissance de deux nations.* Paris: Perrin, 2008.

Mirot, Léon. "Autour de la paix d'Arras, 1414–1415." *Bibliothèque de l'École des Chartes* 75 (1914): 253–327.

———. "L'enlèvement du dauphin et le premier conflit entre Jean sans Peur et Louis d'Orléans (1405)." *Revue des Questions Historiques* 95 (1914): 329–55; 96 (1914): 47–88, 369–419.

———. "La formation et le démembrement de l'Hôtel St Pol." *La Cité: Bulletin de la Société Historique et Archéologique du IVe Arrondissement,* October 1916, 269–319.

———. *Les insurrections urbaines au début du règne de Charles VI (1380–1383), leurs causes, leurs conséquences.* Paris: Fontemoing, 1905.

Miskimin, Harry A. "The Last Act of Charles V: The Background of the Revolts of 1382." *Speculum* 38 (1963): 433–42.

Mollat du Jourdin, Michel. *La Guerre de Cent Ans vue par ceux qui l'ont vécue.* Paris: Éditions du Seuil, 1993.

Monfrin, Jacques. "Humanisme et traductions au Moyen Âge." *Journal des Savants* 3 (1963): 161–90.

Morall, John. *Gerson and the Great Schism.* Manchester: Manchester University Press, 1960.

Mortimer, Ian. *The Fears of Henry IV: The Life of England's Self-Made King.* London: Jonathan Cape, 2007.

Müller, Heribert. *Frankreich, Burgund und das Reich im späten Mittelalter.* Tübingen: Mohr Siebeck, 2011.

Nederman, Cary J. "The Expanding Body Politic: Christine de Pizan and Medieval Political Economy." In *Au champ des écritures: IIIᵉ colloque international sur Christine de Pizan,* ed. Eric Hicks, Diego Gonzalez, and Philippe Simon, 383–97. Paris: Champion, 2000.

———. "The Expanding Body Politic: The Diversification of Organic Metaphors in Nicole Oresme and Christine de Pizan." In *Healing the Body Politic: Christine de Pizan's Political Thought,* ed. Karen Green and Constant J. Mews, 19–33. Turnhout: Brepols, 2005.

Netterstrøm, Jeppe Büchert, and Bjørn Poulsen, eds. *Feud in Medieval and Early Modern Europe.* Aarhus: Aarhus University Press, 2007.

Newman, William R., and Anthony Grafton. "Introduction: The Problematic Status of Astrology and Alchemy in Pre-Modern Europe." In *Secrets of Nature: Astrology and Alchemy in Early Modern Europe,* ed. William R. Newman and Anthony Grafton, 22–23. Cambridge: MIT Press, 2001.

Nichols, Stephen G. Review of *A New History of Medieval French Literature,* by Jacqueline Cerquiglini-Toulet. *H-France Review* 12 (October 2012). http://www.h-france.net/vol12reviews/vol12no138nichols.pdf.

Norbye, Marigold Anne. "Genealogies and Dynastic Awareness in the Hundred Years War: The Evidence of *A tous nobles qui aiment beaux faits et bonnes histoires.*" *Journal of Medieval History* 33 (2007): 297–319.

Nordberg, Michael. *Les ducs et la royauté: Étude sur la rivalité des ducs d'Orléans et de Bourgogne, 1392–1407.* Uppsala: Svenska Bokförlaget, 1964.

———. "Les sources Bourguignonnes des accusations portées contre la mémoire de Louis d'Orléans." *Annales de Bourgognes* 31 (1959): 81–98.

Novák, Veronika. "La source du savoir: Publication officielle et communication informelle à Paris au début du XVᵉ siècle." In *Information et société en Occident à la fin du Moyen Âge,* ed. Claire Boudreau, Kouky Fianu, Claude Gauvard, and Michel Hébert, 151–63. Paris: Publications de la Sorbonne, 2004.

Nuttall, Jenny. *The Creation of Lancastrian Kingship: Literature, Language, and Politics in Late Medieval England.* Cambridge: Cambridge University Press, 2007.

Offenstadt, Nicolas. "Les crieurs publics à la fin du Moyen-Âge." In *Information et société en Occident à la fin du Moyen Âge,* ed. Claire Boudreau, Kouky Fianu, Claude Gauvard, and Michel Hébert, 203–17. Paris: Publications de la Sorbonne, 2004.

Ornato, Ezio. *Jean Muret et ses amis Nicolas de Clamanges et Jean de Montreuil.* Geneva: Droz, 1969.

Ostoia, Vera K. "Two Riddles of the Queen of Sheba." *Metropolitan Museum Journal* 6 (1972): 73–103.

Otterbein, Kenneth L. *The Anthropology of War.* Long Grove, Ill.: Waveland Press, 2009.

Ouy, Gilbert. "Humanisme et propagande politique en France au début du XVᵉᵐᵉ siècle: Ambrogio Migli et les ambitions impériales de Louis d'Orléans." In *Culture et politique en France à l'époque de l'humanisme et de la Renaissance,* ed. Franco Simone, 13–42. Turin: Accademia delle Scienze, 1974.

———. "Paris, l'un des principaux foyers de l'humanisme en Europe au début du XVᵉ siècle." *Bulletin de la Société de l'Histoire de Paris et de l'Ile-de-France,* 1967–68, 71–98.

Ouy, Gilbert, and Christine Reno. "Où mène *Le chemin de long estude?* Christine de Pizan, Ambrogio Migli et les ambitions impériales de Louis d'Orléans (a propos du ms. BNF fr 1436)." In *Christine de Pizan 2000: Studies on Christine de Pizan in Honour of Angus J. Kennedy,* ed. John Campbell and Nadia Margolis, 177–196. Amsterdam: Rodopi, 2000.

Ouy, Gilbert, Christine Reno, Inès Villela-Petit, Olivier Delsaux, and Tania van Hemelryck. *Album Christine de Pizan.* Turnhout: Brepols, 2012.

Palmer, J. J. N. *England, France, and Christendom.* London: Routledge and Kegan Paul, 1972.

Paravicini, Werner. "Paris, capitale des ducs de Bourgogne?" In *Paris, capitale des ducs de Bourgogne,* ed. Werner Paravicini and Bertrand Schnerb, 471–77. Ostfildern: Jan Thorbecke Verlag, 2007.

Petit, Ernest. *Itinéraires de Philippe Le Hardi et de Jean sans Peur, ducs de Bourgogne (1363–1419) d'après les comptes de dépenses de leur hôtel.* Paris: L'Imprimerie Nationale, 1888.

Phillpotts, Christopher. "The Fate of the Truce of Paris, 1396–1415." *Journal of Medieval History* 24 (1998): 61–80.

Piaget, Arthur. "La cour amoureuse dite de Charles VI." *Romania* 20 (1891): 417–54.

———. "Un manuscrit de la cour amoureuse de Charles VI." *Romania* 31 (1902): 597–603.

Picherit, Jean Louis. "Le *Livre de la prod'hommie de l'homme* et le *Livre de prudence* de Christine de Pizan: Chronologie, structure et composition." *Le Moyen Âge* 91, nos. 3–4 (1985): 381–413.

Pinet, Marie-Josèphe. *Christine de Pisan, 1364–1430: Étude bibliographique et littéraire.* Paris: Champion, 1927.

Pleybert, Frédéric, ed. *Paris et Charles V.* Paris: Action Artistique de la Ville de Paris, 2001.

Poirion, Daniel. *Le poète et le prince: L'évolution du lyrisme courtois de Guillaume de Machaut à Charles d'Orléans.* Grenoble: Presses Universitaires de France, 1965.

Pollack-Lagushenko, Timur R. "The Armagnac Faction: New Patterns of Political Violence in Late Medieval France." PhD diss., Johns Hopkins University, 2004.

Potin, Yann. "Le coup d'état 'révélé': Régence et trésors du roi (septembre–novembre 1380)." In *Coups d'état à la fin du Moyen-Âge? Aux fondements du pouvoir politique en Europe occidentale, colloque international, 25–27 novembre 2002,* ed. François Foronda, Jean-Philippe Genet, and José Manuel Nieto Soria, 181–213. Madrid: Casa de Velasquez, 2005.

Potter, John Milton. "The Development and Significance of the Salic Law of the French." *English Historical Review* 52 (1937): 235–53.

Quillet, Jeannine. *Charles V le roi lettré: Essai sur la pensée politique d'un règne.* Paris: Perrin, 1984.

Radding, Charles M. "The Estates of Normandy and the Revolts in the Towns at the Beginning of the Reign of Charles VI." *Speculum* 47 (1972): 79–90.

Reeves, Marjorie. *The Influence of Prophecy in the Later Middle Ages: A Study in Joachimism.* Oxford: Clarendon Press, 1969.

Reid, Dylan. "Patrons of Poetry: Rouen's Confraternity of the Immaculate Conception of Our Lady." In *The Reach of the Republic of Letters: Literary and Learned Societies in Late Medieval and Early Modern Europe,* ed. Arjan van Dixhoorn and Susie Speakman Sutch, 33–77. Leiden: Brill, 2008.

———. "Piety, Poetry, and Politics: Rouen's Confraternity of the Immaculate Conception and the French Wars of Religion." In *Early Modern Confraternities in Europe and the Americas,* ed. Christopher F. Black and Pamela Gravestock, 151–70. Aldershot, UK: Ashgate, 2006.

Reno, Christine. "Christine de Pizan: 'At Best a Contradictory Figure'?" In *Politics, Gender, and Genre: The Political Thought of Christine de Pizan,* ed. Margaret Brabant, 171–92. Boulder: Westview Press, 1992.

———. "Le *Livre de prudence/Livre de la prod'hommie de l'homme*: Nouvelles perspectives." In *Une femme de lettres au Moyen Âge: Études autour de Christine de Pizan,* ed. Liliane Dulac and Bernard Ribémont, 25–37. Orleans: Paradigme, 1995.

Rey, Maurice. *Le domaine du roi et les finances extraordinaires sous Charles VI (1388–1413).* Paris: SEVPEN, 1965.

———. *Les finances royales sous Charles VI: Les causes du déficit, 1388–1413.* Paris: SEVPEN, 1956.

Ricci, Pier Giorgio. "La cronologia dell'ultimo 'certamen' petrarchesco." *Studi Petrarcheschi* 4 (1951): 47–59.

Richards, E. Jeffrey. "Christine de Pizan and Jean Gerson: An Intellectual Friendship." In *Christine de Pizan 2000: Studies on Christine de Pizan in Honour of Angus J. Kennedy,* ed. John Campbell and Nadia Margolis, 197–208. Amsterdam: Rodopi, 2000.

———. "Jean Gerson's Writings to His Sisters and Christine de Pizan's *Livre des trois vertus:* An Intellectual Dialogue Culminating in Friendship." In *Virtue Ethics for Women: 1250–1500,* ed. Karen Green and Constant J. Mews, 81–98. Dordrecht: Springer, 2011.

———. "Poems of Water Without Salt and Ballades Without Feeling, or Reintroducing History into the Text: Prose and Verse in the Works of Christine de Pizan." In *Christine de Pizan and Medieval French Lyric,* ed. E. Jeffrey Richards, 206–30. Gainesville: University Press of Florida, 1998.

———. "Political Thought as Improvisation: Female Regency and Mariology in Late Medieval French Thought." In *Virtue, Liberty, and Toleration: Political Ideas of European Women, 1400–1800,* ed. Jacqueline Broad and Karen Green, 1–22. Berlin: Springer, 2007.

Rickard, Marcia R. "The Iconography of the Virgin Portal at Amiens." *Gesta* 22 (1983): 147–57.

Roux, Suzanne. *Christine de Pizan: Femme de tête, dame de cœur.* Paris: Payot, 2006.

Russell, Frederick H. *The Just War in the Middle Ages.* Cambridge: Cambridge University Press, 1975.

Salet, François. "Mécénat royal et princier au Moyen Âge." *Comptes-Rendus des Séances de l'Académie des Inscriptions et Belles-Lettres* 129 (1985): 620–29.

Scanlon, Larry. "The King's Two Voices: Narrative and Power in Hoccleve's *Regiment of Princes.*" In *Literary Practice and Social Change in Britain, 1380–1530,* ed. Lee Patterson, 216–47. Berkeley: University of California Press, 1990.

———. *Narrative, Authority, and Power: The Medieval Exemplum and the Chaucerian Tradition.* Cambridge: Cambridge University Press, 1994.

Schnerb, Bertrand. *Les Armagnacs et les Bourguignons: La maudite guerre.* Paris: Perrin, 1988.

———. *Jean sans Peur: Le prince meurtrier.* Paris: Payot, 2005.

Schultz, Christopher Ronald. "The Artistic and Literary Patronage of Louis of Orléans and His Wife, Valentine Visconti, 1399–1408." PhD diss., Emory University, 1977.

Semple, Benjamin. "The Critique of Knowledge as Power: The Limits of Philosophy and Theology in Christine de Pizan." In *Christine de Pizan and the Categories of Difference,* ed. Marilynn Desmond, 108–27. Minneapolis: University of Minnesota Press, 1998.

Sherman, Claire Richter. *The Portraits of Charles V of France (1338–1380).* New York: New York University Press, 1969.

———. "Representations of Charles V of France (1338–1380) as a Wise Ruler." *Medievalia et Humanistica,* new ser., 2 (1971): 83–96.

Sizer, Michael. "The Calamity of Violence: Reading the Paris Massacres of 1418." *Proceedings of the Western Society for French History* 35 (2007): 19–39.

———. "Making Revolution Medieval: Revolt and Political Culture in Fifteenth-Century Paris." PhD diss., University of Minnesota, 2007.

Smail, Daniel Lord. *The Consumption of Justice: Emotions, Publicity, and Legal Culture in Marseille, 1263–1423.* Ithaca: Cornell University Press, 2003.

———. "Faction and Feud in Fourteenth-Century Marseille." In *Feud in Medieval and Early Modern Europe,* ed. Jeppe Büchert Netterstrøm and Bjørn Poulsen, 113–32. Aarhus: Aarhus University Press, 2007.

Small, Graeme. "The Centre, the Periphery, and the Problem of Power Distribution in Late Medieval France: Tournai, 1384–1477." In *War, Government, and Power in Later Medieval France,* ed. C. T. Allmand, 145–74. Liverpool: Liverpool University Press, 2000.

———. *Late Medieval France.* Basingstoke, UK: Palgrave Macmillan, 2009.

Solente, Suzanne. "Date de deux ouvrages de Christine de Pisan." *Bibliothèque de l'École des Chartes* 94 (1933): 422.

———. Review of *Les sept psaumes allégorisés de Christine de Pisan,* ed. Ruth Ringland Rains. *Le Moyen Âge* 73 (1967): 171–73.

Spiegel, Gabrielle. *The Chronicle Tradition of Saint-Denis: A Survey.* Brookline, Mass.: Classical Folia Editions, 1978.

———. *The Past as Text: The Theory and Practice of Medieval Historiography.* Baltimore: Johns Hopkins University Press, 1997.

Stafford, Pauline. *Queens, Concubines, and Dowagers: The King's Wife in the Early Middle Ages.* Athens: University of Georgia Press, 1983.

Straub, Theodor. "Die Grundung des Pariser Minnehofs von 1400." *Zeitschrift für Romanische Philologie* 77 (1961): 1–14.

Sumption, Jonathan. *Trial by Fire.* Vol. 2 of *The Hundred Years War.* 3 vols. London: Faber and Faber, 1999.

Swift, Helen J. *Gender, Writing, and Performance: Men Defending Women in Late Medieval France, 1440–1538.* Oxford: Clarendon Press, 2008.

Tarnowski, Andrea. "Perspectives on the *Advision.*" In *Christine de Pizan 2000: Studies on Christine de Pizan in Honour of Angus J. Kennedy,* ed. John Campbell and Nadia Margolis, 105–14. Amsterdam: Rodopi, 2000.

Taylor, Craig, ed. *Debating the Hundred Years War: Pour ce que plusieurs (la loy Salicque) and a Declaration of the Trew and Dewe Title of Henry VIII.* Cambridge: Cambridge University Press, 2007.

———. "The Salic Law, French Queenship, and the Defence of Women in the Late Middle Ages." *French Historical Studies* 29 (2006): 543–64.

———. "The Salic Law and the Valois Succession to the French Crown." *French History* 15 (2001): 358–77.

Taylor, Jane H. M. "Courtly Gatherings and Poetic Games: 'Coterie' Anthologies in the Late Middle Ages in France." In *Book and Text in France, 1400–1600: Poetry on the Page,* ed. Adrian Armstrong and Malcolm Quainton, 13–30. Aldershot, UK: Ashgate, 2007.

———. *The Making of Poetry: Late-Medieval French Poetic Anthologies.* Turnhout: Brepols, 2007.

Thibault, Marcel. *Isabeau de Bavière: Reine de France; La Jeunesse (1370–1405).* Paris: Perrin et Cie, 1903.

Thomas, André. "Jean Castel." *Romania* 21 (1892): 271–74.

Thomassy, Raimond. *Essai sur les écrits politiques de Christine de Pisan suivi d'une notice littéraire et de pièces inédites.* Paris: Debécourt, 1838.

Thonon, Sandrine. "Les métiers sur l'échiquier: Leurs représentations littéraire et figurée dans les traductions françaises de l'œuvre de Jacques de Cessoles." In *Le verbe, l'image et les représentations de la société urbaine au Moyen Âge,* ed. Marc Boone, Elodie Lecuppre-Desjardin, and Jean-Pierre Sosson, 207–19. Antwerp: Garant, 2002.

Thorndike, Lynn. *A History of Magic and Experimental Science.* 8 vols. New York: Macmillan, 1923–58.

Tournier, Laurent. "Jeans sans Peur et l'Université de Paris." In *Paris, capitale des ducs de Bourgogne,* ed. Werner Paravicini and Bertrand Schnerb, 299–318. Ostfildern: Jan Thorbecke Verlag, 2007.

Tuck, Anthony. "Richard II and the Hundred Years' War." In *Politics and Crisis in Fourteenth-Century England,* ed. Wendy R. Childs and John Taylor, 117–31. Gloucester, UK: Alan Sutton, 1990.

Tuilier, André. *Histoire de l'Université de Paris et de la Sorbonne.* 2 vols. Paris: Nouvelle Librairie de France, 1994.

Valois, Noël. *La France et le grand schisme d'Occident.* 4 vols. Paris: Picard, 1896–1902.

van Hemelryck, Tania. "Christine de Pizan et la paix: La rhétorique et les mots pour le dire." In *Au champ des écritures: IIIᵉ colloque international sur Christine de Pizan,* ed. Eric Hicks, Diego Gonzalez, and Philippe Simon, 663–89. Paris: Champion, 2000.

Vaughan, Richard. *John the Fearless: The Growth of Burgundian Power.* Woodbridge, UK: Boydell Press, 2002.

———. *Philip the Bold: The Formation of the Burgundian State.* Woodbridge, UK: Boydell Press, 2002.

Viennot, Eliane. *La France, les femmes et le pouvoir: L'invention de la loi salique (V^e–XVIe siècle).* Paris: Perrin, 2006.

Viollet, Paul. "Comment les femmes ont été exclues en France de la succession à la Couronne." *Mémoires de l'Académie des Inscriptions* 34, no. 2 (1893): 125–78.

Walters, Lori. "Boethius and the Triple Ending of the *Cent Balades.*" *French Studies* 50 (1996): 129–37.

———. "The Figure of the *Seulette* in the Works of Christine de Pizan and Jean Gerson." In *Desireuse de plus avant enquerre: Actes du VIe Colloque international sur Christine de Pizan,* ed. Liliane Dulac, Anne Paupert, Christine Reno, and Bernard Ribémont, 119–39. Paris: Champion, 2008.

Wandruzka, Nikolai. "Familial Traditions of the *de Piçano* at Bologna." In *Contexts and Continuities: Proceedings of the IVth International Colloquium on Christine de Pizan,* ed. Angus J. Kennedy, Rosalind Brown-Grant, James C. Laidlaw, and Catherine M. Müller, 889–906. Glasgow: University of Glasgow Press, 2002.

Watson, Paul F. "The Queen of Sheba in Christian Tradition." In *Solomon and Sheba,* ed. James B. Pritchard, 115–45. London: Phaidon Press, 1974.

Wheeler, Everett L. "Christine de Pizan's *Livre des fais d'armes et de chevalerie:* Gender and the Prefaces." *Nottingham Medieval Studies* 46 (2002): 119–61.

Wilkins, Ernest H. *Petrarch's Later Years.* Cambridge: Medieval Academy of America, 1959.

Willard, Charity Cannon. "Christine de Pizan: From Poet to Political Commentator." In *Politics, Gender, and Genre: The Political Thought of Christine de Pizan,* ed. Margaret Brabant, 17–32. Boulder: Westview Press, 1992.

———. *Christine de Pizan: Her Life and Works.* New York: Persea Books, 1984.

———. Christine de Pizan's Allegorized Psalms." In *Une femme de lettres au Moyen Âge: Études autour de Christine de Pizan,* ed. Liliane Dulac and Bernard Ribémont, 317–324. Orleans: Paradigme, 1995.

———. "The Manuscripts of Jean Petit's Justification: Some Burgundian Propaganda Methods of the Early Fifteenth Century." *Studi Francesi* 3 (1969): 271–80.

Zeller, Gaston. "Les rois de France candidats à l'empire: Essai sur l'idéologie impériale en France." *Revue Historique* 173 (1934): 273–311, 497–533.

Index